£2.95

A

D0717340

A guide to the castles of England and Wales

By the same author

Neolithic cultures of North Africa
History from the earth
Hillforts of the Iron Age in England and Wales
Prehistoric Britain and Ireland
Castles and Fortifications of Britain and Ireland
Hadrian's Wall
Great Medieval Castles of Britain

A guide to the

Castles of England and Wales

James Forde-Johnston MA FSA

Constable London

First published in Great Britain 1981
by Constable and Company Limited
10 Orange Street London WC2H 7EG
Copyright © 1981 by James Forde-Johnston
ISBN 0 09 463730 X
Set in Times New Roman 10 pt by
Inforum Ltd, Portsmouth
Printed in Great Britain by
Ebenezer Baylis & Son Ltd
The Trinity Press, Worcester and London

Contents

Contents

Illustrations

Introduction

The Norman Conquest of 1066 provides a convenient starting point for any work dealing with medieval castles, for it was then that such structures were first introduced into the British Isles. Although the Saxons had their defences, these were very different from the stone and timber castles which the Normans built in such large numbers throughout England and Wales. In the centuries before the Conquest the greatest threat to life and property in these islands was the fierce raiding by the Danes, and to counter this threat Alfred the Great (AD 849–99) and his successors built a series of *burhs* or fortified towns to act as strongpoints and places of refuge in times of peril. The surviving remains indicate that the defences of these enclosures consisted principally of an earthern rampart with an outer ditch, and excavation has shown that the rampart was surmounted either by a timber palisade or a stone wall. Two of the best surviving examples, Wareham in Dorset and Wallingford in Oxfordshire, are rectangular in plan, but others are of more irregular shape. Apart from *burhs* (the origin of the word borough), the only other defence-works were the surviving town walls of Roman Britain, by then some 600 years old, but still capable, however patched up, of providing protection when danger threatened from some external source.

In the century or so before the Conquest, the Normans had developed in their homeland of Normandy two main types of castle, one timber-built and one stone-built; and both types were built here in growing numbers in the years following 1066. In a newly conquered territory there was an immediate need for a network of fortifications to secure what had been won, and this need was met by timber-built castles which could be erected in a matter of months, if not weeks, as compared with the years it might take to build a stone castle. Stone castles followed more slowly, and were always fewer in number, although it is the stone castles which have survived. There are now no visible remains of timber-built castles. What do survive are the earthworks which supported them, and these indicate that there were originally some 3,000 castles of this type (not all of them necessarily in use at the same time), built in the century and a half after the Conquest. This compares with 500–600 stone castles (most of which have at least some surviving visible remnant), built between 1066 and the end of the medieval period, c. 1485.

The castles built by the Normans were an integral part of the feudal system which they introduced here at the same time. The system was widespread in Europe and was, in its simplest terms, a method of running a country where there was no centralized administrative, judicial or military organization. Instead, these functions were farmed out to loyal followers who received a fee (Latin *feodum*, hence feudal) in the form of land, in return for their services to the king. All land belonged to the king, who retained part of it for his own use. On it he built his own castles (royal castles), with a constable in charge on his behalf. At any one time in the medieval period there were between 50 and 100 royal castles, less than the total number of baronial castles, but far more than the castles owned by any one baron. The remaining land was parcelled out in greater or lesser quantity among his followers or barons, i.e. men who held land granted by the king. Some holdings were very large, the size of a modern county, while others were much more modest, perhaps an estate of a few thousand acres or so. On this land the baron would build one or more castles, according to his wealth, his needs, or the requirements of the king, from which he would perform those administrative, financial, judicial and military duties required of him in return for his 'fee'.

The men who held land directly from the king were tenants-in-chief. They in turn subdivided their land, keeping so much for their own use and apportioning the rest among their own followers (sub-tenants), in return for whatever services they needed for themselves and their estates, or were required to provide for the king. At the lowest level of the system were the peasantry who held small plots of land on which they supported themselves and their families, and in return for which they worked so many days on the lord's land. In effect, the feudal system used land as currency, purchasing with this fee all the administrative, financial, legal and military services which, in another age, would be provided by a central government. When more centralized government did come (in 1485 with the Tudor kings) the feudal system was finally dispensed with.

Castles were an essential part of feudal life. The network of royal castles enabled the king to keep a watchful eye on his barons, always ready to shrug off his authority and behave like independent princes. The baronial castles (perhaps as many as 500, although again not all necessarily in use together) were the secure local bases from which the authority placed in the barons' hands by the king could be exercised. Without such a base a baron could not carry out the military functions assigned to him; he could not offer to his tenants the protection which they expected of him; he could not dispense justice without leaving himself open to pressure or reprisal; he could not safely take charge of goods, revenues etc., placed in his hands; he could not, finally, secure himself and his family from aggressive and ambitious fellow barons. The accumulation of too much power in one pair of baronial hands was an ever-present threat to medieval kings.

This last point makes it clear that, whatever else it was, the medieval castle was also a home. However large military considerations loomed, the medieval castle was never an entirely military establishment. It was the baron's home, built necessarily in a military framework, but always having a well-defined (if not at first particularly strong) domestic aspect. As the medieval period progressed the balance changed, with greater emphasis on comfort, convenience and privacy, but it was a change of emphasis rather than anything more fundamental. Castles were always domestic to some degree, less so in the earlier periods, more so in the later periods. It was only in later, post-medieval periods that the purely military establishment was introduced into the fortification scene.

TIMBER–BUILT CASTLES

Timber-built castles involve both timber structures and earthworks, and as pointed out earlier, it is the latter which have survived. Although there are variations, most of these earthworks are in what is generally described as motte-and-bailey arrangement. The motte is a circular mound of earth with a flat top and sloping sides,

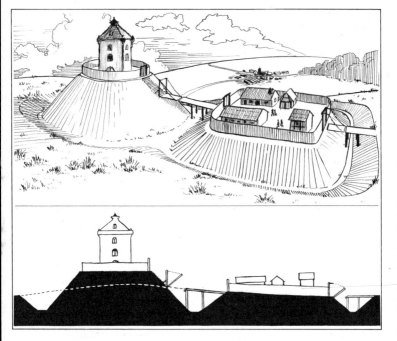

surrounded by a ditch, from which some, if not all, of the material
for its construction was derived. In some cases a convenient natural
hillock or promontory, suitably scarped, was used, and in other
cases there was a combination of natural and man-made features.
On one side of the motte was a bailey, a space enclosed by a bank
and a ditch, the latter linked to the ditch around the motte. In some
cases there was more than one bailey, and, in a few cases, no bailey
at all, the motte and its surrounding ditch standing alone. These
earthworks varied considerably in size. The circular top of the motte
could be c. 30–100 ft in diameter and the motte itself could be
15–50 ft high. In some cases the baileys were similar in ground area
to the motte; in other cases they were very much larger, enclosing
perhaps several acres of ground.

These earthworks formed, as it were, the base on which the
timber castle was built. The central feature was usually a wooden
tower, probably three storeys high, standing in the middle of the
circular area which formed the top of the motte. Little is known
about dimensions since so few have been excavated, but post-holes
of one uncovered at Abinger (Surrey) indicated a tower about 12ft
square, and this must surely be at the lower end of the size range. It
seems not unreasonable to suggest that some such towers were up to
30 ft square, and possibly more, especially on those mottes with
summits up to 100 ft in diameter. For the same reasons as given
above, little is known about their original appearance (apart from
those shown on the Bayeux Tapestry), but it would be difficult to
believe that at least some of them were not embellished with carved
decoration and, in view of the prevailing climatic conditions in the
British Isles, that all of them were not painted, in however
utilitarian a fashion. It is not unlikely that the more elaborate
towers were richly carved and brightly painted. The building
involved may not always have been a tower. In some cases a
single-storey hall (i.e. an ordinary house of the period) may have
occupied the summit, and on the larger mottes there may well have
been more than one building.

Surrounding the top of the motte and whatever structures it
supported was a timber fence or palisade, perhaps 10 or 12 ft high,
with a sentry walk on the inside. Presumably the top of this palisade
was crenellated, i.e. it had alternating high and low sections. In the
case of larger mottes, the palisade may have been additionally
strengthened by wooden towers or turrets. Whether or not there
were towers or turrets, there would probably have been some
additional precaution at the entrance which provided access to this
upper part of the castle. The entrance was reached by steps up the
sloping sides of the motte, at the foot of which there was a bridge
with a lifting section (a drawbridge) across the surrounding ditch.

The bridge led from the bailey, the associated lower enclosure.
The bailey too was surrounded by a ditch (linked to the motte
ditch), the earth from which was thrown inwards to form a bank or
rampart perhaps 10 ft high and 25–30 ft wide. Along the crest of
this bank was a timber palisade with a sentry walk, probably very

similar to the one surrounding the top of the motte, and, like that, in some cases embellished with towers or turrets. Access to the bailey was via a bridge (with a lifting section) across the ditch, almost certainly on the side away from the motte. The bailey contained various buildings: stables, barn, chapel, kitchen, retainers' quarters, and possibly a hall for use by the lord of the manor in times of peace, or simply for daytime use, leaving the tower on the motte as a safe retreat in time of danger, or at night, or both.

Such was the Norman timber motte-and-bailey castle, as far as we can visualize it on existing evidence. There were certainly considerable variations in size, and almost certainly variations in richness and elaboration. Painting and carving must have played a considerable part in the castles of the richer barons. Increasing prosperity and a larger following must have produced a need for additional baileys, and sites with two, three, and four baileys are known. Eventually the same prosperity, and the vulnerability of wood to decay, led to the rebuilding of some timber castles in stone, and these will be dealt with in the section on shell-keeps. Most timber castles, however, simply fell into decay, having been abandoned eventually for more comfortable and more commodious forms of accommodation, principally the moated manor house.

STONE CASTLES

The remaining castles to be considered here, both Norman and later, are all stone-built. They include the most enduring of all medieval military structures, the great rectangular stone keeps first introduced into the British Isles in the years following 1066; these continued to be built until around 1200. Alongside them were the so-called shell-keeps, which were, in a sense, the stone versions of the timber motte-and-bailey castles. The rectangular keeps were followed first by polygonal keeps and then by round keeps in the years between c. 1170 and c. 1270. Alongside the round keeps, however, from c. 1200 on, were castles without keeps, consisting of an enclosing curtain wall with regularly spaced wall-towers and a gatehouse, which became, in effect, the replacement for the keep. These keepless castles culminated in the Edwardian period (after Edward I, 1272–1307), one of the greatest periods of medieval castle building either here or in Europe as a whole. Among the greatest achievements of the Edwardian period were the concentric castles, brilliantly exemplified at Harlech, Beaumaris and the Tower of London. The final, post-Edwardian period (1307–1485), is marked mainly by what can be termed courtyard castles (such as Bodiam and Herstmonceux), and by various kinds of tower-houses (such as Nunney and Tattershall). All of these types will be considered in more detail in the following sections.

CASTLES WITH RECTANGULAR KEEPS

The outstanding hallmark of Norman military architecture was the keep, a great rectangular stone tower with a solid base and very thick walls. Most such towers were between 50 and 100 ft square and up to 120 ft high, with walls up to 20 ft thick, at least in the lower storeys. In the upper storeys additional rooms and passages were often contrived in the thickness of the walls, a practice particularly well exemplified at Dover Castle (p 48). Most keeps were of three or four storeys, with the entrance at second-storey level via a forebuilding, a structure housing a staircase built against one wall of the keep. The lowest storey, accessible only from the floor above, was usually given over to storage, an important function in a building designed to stand a siege. Communication between the floors was by means of one or more spiral staircases in the angle turrets, although not infrequently, to confuse an attacker who had penetrated the keep, no one staircase was continuous from top to bottom, making it necessary to cross a room to another flight in order to continue upwards. The second storey (the entrance level) usually formed the hall, the main living area for the inhabitants of the keep (the lord and his family, his officials and servants), while the top storey (or storeys) usually provided more private quarters for the immediate family, recalling the statement above that the castle was also, and always, a home for the lord of the manor.

Because of their immense weight, most stone keeps were built on level ground; there are some which stand on mottes, although these are probably either solid natural features (rather than man-made mounds), or else the keep extends down through the motte to solid

ground. Most keeps have a splayed-out plinth of solid stone
designed to prevent undermining, one of the standard siege
techniques of the medieval period. Above the plinth was the
basement (lowest storey) which was thus above external ground
level. For security reasons it was lit only by very narrow slits high in
the wall. The walls of the keep rose well above the (wooden) roof of
the top storey to prevent attack by fire, and carried a sentry walk
behind a crenellated breastwork. At the four corners the walls rose
higher still to form angle turrets, providing shelter for the sentries
inside and elevated look-out points outside. Although the original
arrangements have often been destroyed by later building, such
stone keeps stood within plain-walled baileys so that the
arrangement can be described as keep-and-bailey, parallel to the
motte-and-bailey arrangement of the timber castles. In a very real
sense the wooden tower on its earth motte was an economical
version of the stone tower on its plinth, and it was very much
quicker to construct.

Most rectangular keeps were built in the twelfth century, the
years 1066–1100 being occupied with consolidating the Norman
grip on the country, mainly with the aid of timber-built castles.
However, some stone castles were begun soon after the Conquest
and these include most notably the Tower of London, the nucleus of
which, the White Tower, is probably the finest and best preserved
stone keep in the British Isles (p 42). The even larger keep at
Colchester (p 123), very much on the same plan as the Tower, was
begun in the same period but was never, in fact, completed. The
general run of rectangular keeps belong to the years 1100–1180 and
include such prime examples as Rochester (p 55), Portchester
(p 85), Hedingham (p 125), Norwich (p 133), Castle Rising
(p 131), Kenilworth (p 156), Scarborough (p 304), Richmond
(p 300), Carlisle (p 322), Newcastle (p 345), Norham (p 339) and
Bamburgh (p 334), and many lesser examples in all areas.

One of the greatest rectangular keeps not so far mentioned is
Dover which was one of the last of the type to be built, in the years
1170–1180, by Henry II (1154–1189). Details of the keep will be

Scarborough Castle: example of a rectangular keep

given in the appropriate section (p 48), but a number of features of the castle as a whole are worth noticing here because of the bearing they have on later developments. As usual the keep stood within a walled bailey, and it is the nature of these outer defences which is so interesting. First of all the bailey wall was strengthened by a series of regularly spaced rectangular towers. Wall-towers had, of course, been used before, but never in this regular fashion and never in such quantity (ten towers). In addition, there were four similar towers forming two twin-towered gatehouses, and this again was the first appearance of a type of entrance which was to become a very important part of castle architecture in the following centuries. Each entrance was, moreover, additionally strengthened by a barbican (an outer entrance), one of which is preserved, and this again was the first appearance of a feature which was to become a regular part of the military repertoire.

All of these features were associated with the enclosing wall of the bailey immediately around the keep. Henry II also began, but never completed, the wall of a second bailey which was almost certainly intended to surround completely the inner bailey and keep, thus forming a concentric arrangement just about a century ahead of the great concentric castles of the Edwardian period. The royal castle of Dover was an important turning point in castle architecture. Although it was one of the last of the great rectangular keeps, it looked not back to earlier keeps but forward to the developments of the thirteenth century. The second bailey wall started by Henry II was completed by his son John (1199–1216), and it is noticeable that John's wall-towers were round rather than rectangular; this marks another significant change taking place around the turn of the century (1200), and this change will be pursued under the heading of polygonal and circular keeps after the next section.

CASTLES WITH SHELL-KEEPS

Of all the stone-built castles those with shell-keeps bear the closest resemblance to timber motte-and-bailey castles. Most, but not all, of them stand on mottes, and there seems little doubt that some of them, at least, were replacements of earlier timber structures on the

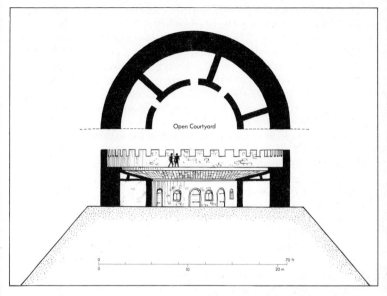

Open Courtyard

0   70 ft
0   10   20 m

same site. The term shell-keep is rather a misleading one because
the structures involved are not keeps in the same sense as the
rectangular, polygonal, and round keeps which are single, compact
buildings crowned by a roof. A shell-keep is essentially a curtain
wall with the space enclosed open to the sky. If there are roofed
structures they are built against the inner face of the curtain, leaving
an open courtyard in the centre, or else they are simply placed
haphazardly in the available space; there is no single roof covering
the whole structure. Unfortunately there is no convenient and
generally acceptable alternative to 'shell-keep', so that the term will
be retained here, with the reservations mentioned above.

Shell-keeps then are circular, oval, or polygonal curtain walls,
80–120 ft in diameter (and occasionally larger), situated in most
cases on top of what need to be fairly large mottes. If they are
replacements of earlier timber structures, as seems likely in many
cases, then the rebuilding in stone seems to have been confined to

the larger wooden castles. In a few cases there is no motte, the shell wall simply surrounding the area isolated by the digging of the enclosed ditch. Internal buildings, up to two storeys high, were usually placed against the inner face of the curtain wall, leaving an open courtyard in the centre. There was a sentry walk along the top of the curtain wall with a protective, crenellated breastwork. Towers, where they existed at all, were later additions, and entrances were fairly simple, consisting of a deep porch or, in some cases, a small rectangular tower.

Shell-keeps seem to have been built from the earliest days of the Conquest and are thus broadly contemporary with rectangular keeps. Perhaps the best known example is Windsor Castle where there was already a shell-keep before the time of Henry II (1154–1189), who built a second shell inside the first, which now forms the surrounding terrace. The first mention of a castle at Windsor is 1067 and the castle then built may have been of timber, later replaced by the first stone shell wall; it may, on the other hand, have been of stone from the beginning. The same may be true in particular areas, such as the south-west, where stone rather than timber has always been the traditional building material. In other areas, however, the shell-keep seems to have been a replacement for an earlier timber castle. In fact, what it replaces is the timber palisade around the top of the motte, described earlier. The timber tower, or whatever else was on the motte, was not however replaced in the same way. In the new stone structure accommodation was again contained in buildings against the enclosing wall, leaving an open courtyard in the centre.

Apart from Windsor, there are examples of shell-keeps at Carisbrooke (p 88), Arundel (p 72), Restormel (p 99), Launceston (p 97), Totnes (p 113), Tamworth (p 181), Cardiff (p 215), Berkeley (p 147) and Durham (p 314).

CASTLES WITH POLYGONAL AND ROUND KEEPS
In the second half of the twelfth century new styles of fortification began to appear in western Europe. Many of these were derived from the more advanced techniques of the Byzantine and Arab world, and were brought back by the returning Crusaders. No doubt

the new features noted earlier at Dover Castles were a result, at least in part, of this process. The main structure at Dover however, the keep, was still in the old rectangular style. By this time (c. 1180) rectangular keeps had been in use for over a century in the British Isles, and longer elsewhere, and one or two drawbacks to the type had been perceived. Because they could be tackled from two sides the angles were vulnerable to undermining; it was difficult for defenders to see what was going on below, and even more difficult to do anything about it. It was also difficult for a sentry to keep a close watch; while he was patrolling one side of the keep sentry walk he was completely blind on the other three. The answer to these shortcomings were keeps which were circular in plan, together with a few polygonal keeps which were in a sense intermediate between the old and the new styles. One of the strengths of the circular plan was that attackers trying to undermine the structure had to work from the front; there were no corners around which they could hide from the defenders above. By the same token the sentry on the rampart walk had a much more extensive view of the ground below; there was still a blind area, but this was far less absolute than the three blind sides of the rectangular keep.

One of the earliest and best preserved of circular keeps is Conisbrough (p 285), built c. 1180, i.e., at about the same time as the rectangular keep at Dover. The Conisbrough keep stands within an oval bailey, and this was the traditional arrangement of keep-and-bailey castles mentioned earlier. By the end of the period, however, c. 1270, the plan was rather different. The keep now formed part of a much more regularly planned castle and acted as one of the series of angle towers, often separated from the remainder of the structure by its own ditch, as at Caldicot (p 221) and Flint (p 250). The move towards more regular rectangular plans was shared by the castles without keeps (below), but before dealing with those, one or two other aspects of the change of style need to be noted.

The change from the rectangular to the circular plan was not confined to keeps; it affected wall-towers also. The direction was already indicated at Dover. Henry II's castle had first of all regularly spaced rectangular towers, and this in itself was an

innovation. Hard on its heels came the change to circular towers, witnessed by King John's work on the same castle only a decade or two later, so that within a very short period two important changes had taken place. Similarly the rectangular twin-towered gatehouses of Dover were followed shortly, at other sites, by circular twin-towered gatehouses. These changes, and the moves towards more regular rectangular plans meant that around the turn of the century (c. 1200) castles began to look very different from those of the preceding period. Skenfrith (p 230), for example, built c. 1200, is a very different castle from Conisbrough built only ten or twenty years earlier. At Skenfrith, the circular keep stands in the middle of a trapeze-shaped enclosure with four circular angle towers and a twin-towered gatehouse, the latter badly ruined. A noticeable feature of the plan is the degree to which the angle towers project to command the adjacent stretches of curtain wall. No less than three-quarters of their circumference stands beyond the walls.

Apart from Conisbrough, Caldicot, Flint and Skenfrith, there are well-preserved examples of circular keeps at Pembroke (p 208), Dynevor (p 191), Bronllys (p 234), Longtown (p 152), and Barnard Castle (p 325). There are also some D-shaped keeps which can be regarded as an intermediate type. Two examples can be mentioned: Helmsley (p 288), and Ewloe (p 248).

CASTLES WITHOUT KEEPS
Although the great rectangular keeps dominated the first century or so of castle architecture, there had always been a few castles without keeps. In some cases the defensive apparatus was confined to an enclosing curtain wall, with only a hall (i.e. a normal domestic house) within. Wall-towers, where they existed at all, were rectangular and haphazardly placed. Around the turn of the century again (c. 1200) castles began to appear in larger numbers without keeps, parallel to those castles in which the keep was now circular. The keep, whether rectangular or round, had always been conceived of as the main defence, with the bailey wall as an outer obstacle. The new concept carried the main line of defence forward

Pembroke Castle: example of a circular keep

Manorbier Castle, seen from the south-west: a keepless castle

to the bailey wall, which, strengthened by the regular wall-towers
and a twin-towered gatehouse, became the main obstacle to be
overcome by an attacker. The result was that in many castles the
keep was dispensed with. The accommodation which it had
provided could now be supplied by the wall-towers, two or three
storeys high, and by the gatehouse, which increasingly became the
replacement for the keep, until eventually the concept of the
keep-gatehouse developed in the second half of the century
(1250–1300). The early keepless castles tended to be rather
irregular in plan, although at sites such as Beeston (p 167) and
Cilgerran (p 199) this is a result of the promontory positions they
occupy. At other early sites the plan was often polygonal, with
(round) towers at the angles and one side occupied by a
double-towered gatehouse. Increasingly, however, there was a
move towards more regular, rectangular plans, with the emphasis

on four boldly projecting angle towers. The same trends are observable in those castles with circular keeps being built around the same time. These more regularly planned castles form the prelude to the great castle building period during the reign of Edward I. In spite of their existing keeps both Richmond (p 300) and Chepstow (p 222) were originally built without keeps, quite early in the Norman period. Other keepless castles include Manorbier (p 206), Grosmont (p 224), Eynsford (p 41) and Framlingham (p 134).

THE CASTLES OF EDWARD I

The thirty-five-year reign of Edward I (1272–1307) marked an unprecedented period of castle-building in England and Wales, most particularly in North Wales, the source of most of Edward's political troubles. All the royal castles were built by, or at least with the advice of, Master James of St George, an outstanding military engineer from Savoy in France who spent most of his professional life in Edward I's service. The castles built during these years are the culmination of the medieval castle in Europe. Although there were many splendid castles still to be built in later centuries, in military terms the peak was reached in the late thirteenth century in the work of James of St George and his Master, Edward I.

The native Welsh princes, based in north-west Wales, had never fully accepted English rule and from time to time they rose in revolt, causing havoc along the English border. Edward resolved to settle the problem once and for all by building a network of powerful castles in and around North Wales to stifle trouble at its source. One of the principles underlying the siting of the major castles was that they could be supplied by sea: Flint, Rhuddlan, Conway, Caernarvon, Beaumaris, Criccieth and Aberystwyth are all accessible to sea-borne supplies. There was thus no need to rely on vulnerable land transport through potentially hostile territory. Edward fought two campaigns against the Welsh, in 1277 and again in 1282–3. Each campaign stimulated the building of a group of castles which will, however, be treated here as a single group.

Edward I built nine new, or virtually new, castles in North Wales: Flint, Rhuddlan, Aberystwyth, Ruthin, Caergwrle, Conway, Caernarvon, Harlech and Beaumaris. Little remains of

Aberystwyth, and Caergwrle and Ruthin are only partially
preserved, but the rest have substantial upstanding remains,
including one of the finest survivals of the medieval period,
Caernarvon Castle, an outstanding piece of architecture by any
standards. In addition to these new castles, Edward also re-used
some existing Welsh castles. There were about a dozen such castles,
although only seven have surviving visible remains: Criccieth,
Dolwyddelan, Castell y Bere, Dolbadarn, Dinas Bran, Ewloe, and
Dolforwyn. Of these Edward made use of three, Criccieth,
Dolwyddelan, and Castell y Bere. Nor was this the end of Edward's
castle-building activities. He also had built four 'lordship' castles,
i.e. castles built by barons in return for a grant of land, and very
much part of the overall strategic plan. The four were Denbigh,
Hawarden, Holt, and Chirk. There are fairly extensive remains of
two of these, which will be described in the appropriate section.
Holt is now difficult to interpret and can be viewed from the outside
only. The remains of Hawarden consist mainly of the circular keep
on the motte.

In summary, Edward I built (or had built) sixteen castles in North
Wales, in the years between 1272 and 1307. In fact, some were still
being built in 1330, and one or two were never actually completed,
but this does not lessen the scale of the original undertaking. Nor
does it take account of Edward's castle-building activities in other
areas (below). Of the sixteen North Wales castles three (Conway,
Caernarvon, and Denbigh) are still accompanied by extensive
remains of town walls, with their own systems of wall-towers and
gatehouses. Gatehouses, too, had by this time assumed a very
important place in castle architecture and there are impressive
examples at Denbigh, Caernarvon, Harlech, and Beaumaris, where
there are, in fact, two gatehouses. The last two castles are of the
concentric type and these will be considered in the following
section.

CONCENTRIC CASTLES
The principle of the concentric castle was referred to earlier in
discussing Dover (above, p 19). This was a very early version of the
type, and the arrangement was not used again until the second half

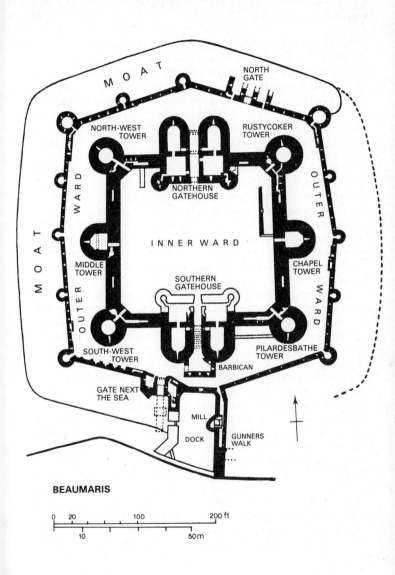

MOAT

NORTH GATE

NORTH-WEST TOWER

RUSTYCOKER TOWER

NORTHERN GATEHOUSE

OUTER WARD

MOAT

INNER WARD

MIDDLE TOWER

CHAPEL TOWER

SOUTHERN GATEHOUSE

OUTER WARD

OUTER WARD

SOUTH-WEST TOWER

PILARDESBATHE TOWER

BARBICAN

GATE NEXT THE SEA

MILL

DOCK

GUNNERS WALK

BEAUMARIS

0   20   100   200 ft

10   50m

of the thirteenth century, when half a dozen such castles were
involved. Unlike Dover, all of them followed a regular, mostly
rectangular, plan. They consist of two basic parts: a high inner
curtain wall, complete with wall-towers and gatehouses, forming a
castle in itself, and closely surrounded by a second and lower curtain
wall, also equipped with towers and gatehouses. The arrangement
was such that anyone attacking the outer curtain could be dealt with
from both walls at the same time, and even if the outer wall was
captured, the attackers were then in a very vulnerable position
immediately below the high inner curtain wall. A concentric castle
was, in effect, two castles, one inside the other, and each one had to
be captured separately. James of St George built four concentric
castles in North Wales: Rhuddlan, Aberystwyth, Harlech, and
Beaumaris. As stated earlier, little remains of Aberystwyth,
although it appears to have resembled Rhuddlan fairly closely.
Harlech and Beaumaris are splendidly preserved and the latter is
generally recognized as the culmination of the concentric castle.
Outside North Wales, Caerphilly (p 211) and the Tower of London
(p 42) also exemplify the concentric principle, and lead on to two
other topics: the remaining castles of the Edwardian period, both
royal and baronial; and water defences, used on a much more
ambitious scale in the second half of the thirteenth century.

OTHER EDWARDIAN CASTLES
Edward I's castle-building activities were by no means confined to
North Wales, nor was castle-building in general confined to royal
undertakings. Baronial castles were being built at the same time in
what may be termed the Edwardian style, i.e. the style of the period
in and around Edward's reign (1272–1307). Apart from the North
Wales castles, one of Edward's major undertakings was the Tower
of London, originally built by William the Conqueror and added to
by many other hands. Details of Edward's (and earlier) work will be
given in the appropriate section (p 42), but in broad terms Edward's
rebuilding gave the castle more or less its present shape, changing it
from a basically keep-and-bailey castle into a formidable concentric
structure. Elsewhere, Edward rebuilt Leeds Castle in Kent (p 53),
with its elaborate water defences, and did substantial work at

Rockingham (p 156), St Briavel's (p 148) and Corfe (p 82). In the later part of his reign he also carried out considerable fortification works in Scotland, although these are outside the scope of the present guide.

Alongside these royal undertakings there was also a considerable amount of building activity by the barons, the greatest of whom built castles as powerful and impressive as anything the king could build. Caerphilly (p 211), a concentric castle with elaborate water defences, is an outstanding example, and so are Goodrich (p 148) and Kidwelly (p 201). Other baronial castles include Carew, Carreg Cennen (p 196), Powys (p 243), and Skipton (p 307).

WATER DEFENCES
One of the features of thirteenth-century castle-building was the increasing use of water as an obstacle to the attacker. The use of wet ditches was not in itself new, although the majority of castles probably had dry ditches, whatever period they belonged to. During the thirteenth century, however, there was a much more positive approach, involving some fairly large-scale engineering works. A fairly simple example of water utilization at the beginning of the century (c. 1200) is provided by Skenfrith, built beside the River Monnow. The river acts as a moat on one side and simply flows into the excavated ditches on the three remaining sides. There was a similar arrangement at the Tower of London in the time of Henry III (1216–1272), before Edward I's rebuilding and the reorganization of the water defences.

At a number of castles, however, built or rebuilt during the thirteenth century, much more positive steps were taken to ensure that there was a surrounding body of protective water. The main technique, where local circumstances were suitable, was to dam a stream or river in order to build up an artificial lake around the castle. Quite clearly this was possible only when the castle was situated in a valley or hollow small enough to act as a basin when closed off by a dam. However, these conditions obtained at Kenilworth (p 156), Leeds Castle (p 53) and Caerphilly (p 211). Kenilworth is now dry, but both Leeds Castle and Caerphilly are still surrounded by wide stretches of water. At Caerphilly the dam,

1,000 ft long, is a formidable part of the castle's defences and is a considerable fortification in its own right. At the Tower of London a different solution was adopted: Edward I built a wharf along the Thames to separate the castle's water defences, now greatly enlarged, from direct dependence on the river. Water also forms a considerable part of the defences of Bodiam (p 63), where the moat is so wide as to form a rectangular artificial lake (c. 500 by 350 ft). Details of all of these water defences will be given in the individual castle entries.

THE POST-EDWARDIAN PERIOD (1307–1485)

The reign of Edward I marked the peak of medieval castle-building. During the 180 years which followed, until the end of the medieval period as a whole, fewer and fewer castles were built. In fact, the near-feverish activity of the Edwardian period was followed, almost inevitably, by a pause which lasted until around 1360. Even then, there was no resumption on the same scale as before, and by about 1400 building, with a few notable exceptions, had slowed almost to a stop. In addition to such new castles as were built there was also a certain amount of rebuilding and extending of existing castles which helps to fill out the picture. The castles of this late medieval period (1307–1485) can be divided into three groups: miscellaneous new castles and additions to existing ones; courtyard castles; and tower-houses.

The first entirely new castle of the post-Edwardian period was Dunstanburgh on the Northumberland coast (p 337), built between 1313 and 1316. Apart from one or two courtyard castles and tower-houses there was not much to follow this until about 1360 when Hadleigh (p 124) was built on the Essex coast as part of the defences of the Thames estuary. There was a renewal of castle-building during the next forty years, when many of the courtyard castles and tower-houses of the late period were actually built. Around the turn of the century (1400) Tutbury (p 183) was so heavily rebuilt as to constitute a new castle, and shortly afterwards (1432) Caister Castle, Norfolk (p 129) was begun for Sir John Fastolf, the man on whom Shakespeare's Falstaff was based. In addition to these new or virtually new castles, there was considerable work done at a number of existing castles, including Alnwick (p 330), Tynemouth (p 314), Carlisle (p 322), Lancaster (p 314), Warwick (p 159) and Ludlow (p 178). In many cases the new works consisted of a powerful gatehouse, not infrequently accompanied by a barbican.

COURTYARD CASTLES
One of the standard types of the post-Edwardian period is the courtyard castle which is almost certainly a development of the rectangular Edwardian castle. In its fully developed form it consists of four ranges of building enclosing a rectangular courtyard. Externally it retains some, if not all, of the military appearance of earlier castles. Internally it is rather more domestic, with a good deal of emphasis on comfort and convenience in the ranges of two- and three-storey buildings which surround the courtyard. The most famous examples of the type are Bodiam (p 63), Herstmonceux (p 65) and Bolton (p 280), and these illustrate a regional difference, with a preference for circular towers in the south and rectangular ones in the north. Most courtyard castles were built between c. 1350 and 1450 and include the following (not all of them fully preserved), in addition to those mentioned above: Farleigh Hungerford (p 117), Donnington (p 77), and Kirby Muxloe (p 173).

The south front of Bodiam Castle: a courtyard castle

TOWER–HOUSES

A tower-house is not strictly a castle, certainly not in the same sense as the great royal and baronial castles considered thus far. It is, in fact, more in the nature of a fortified manor house, but a manor house up-ended in tower form, with the various rooms stacked vertically rather than grouped horizontally. There are large numbers of tower-houses in Scotland and Ireland, and in the Border counties of Cumbria and Northumberland (where they are known as pele towers), built in the years between 1300 and 1600. They all display a fairly high degree of uniformity in plan and elevation. In addition to these, however, there are about ten sites scattered throughout the rest of England and Wales which, although coming under the general heading of tower-houses, display a great deal of variety in both plan and elevation. These were built between about 1300 and 1475. Not all of them conform strictly to the definition of a tower-house (i.e. a self-contained unit), but they are all in tower form, and variations from the basic principle will be noted as they arise in the separate entries. Most English and Welsh tower-houses are additions to existing castles. In the Border regions and in Scotland and Ireland, on the other hand, tower-houses tend to stand alone with only a simple surrounding wall enclosing a yard. Because of their sheer numbers, pele towers of Cumbria and Northumberland will not be dealt with in this guide, and they are not strictly castles anyway. Those towers and tower-houses which will be dealt with include Knaresborough (p 280), Marten's Tower in Chepstow Castle (p 222), Dudley (p 185), Nunney (p 118), Warkworth (p 343), Old Wardour (p 77), Tattershall (p 127), Raglan (p 226), and Ashby de la Zouch (p 173).

This concludes a brief survey of castle-building during the years 1066–c. 1485. Although there is a great deal of variation, with no two castles exactly alike, the broad pattern of castle development is relatively simple, with only half a dozen or so basic types or themes. First of all there are castles with rectangular keeps in the years 1066 to about 1180 (p 19). Alongside these are castles with shell-keeps

Warkworth Castle: example of a tower-house

(which are not keeps in the same sense as the rectangular keeps, as explained earlier, (p 22), and a few castles without keeps (p 27). Rectangular keeps are followed by (a few) polygonal keeps and by the more numerous circular keeps in the years 1180–1280 (p 24). From about 1200 onwards the few early keepless castles are added to by many new castles defended by curtain walls and round towers, these becoming the style in castles of all types (p 27).

Increasingly, plans became more regular until by c. 1250 the rectangular plan with boldly projecting angle towers had emerged. In the same castles the double-towered gatehouse had become a regular feature. The Edwardian period (the reign of Edward I, 1272–1307) saw the culmination of castle-building, most spectacularly in North Wales (p 29). The use of curtain wall and tower reached its greatest expression, and culminated in the concentric castle, which is basically two castles, one inside the other (p 30). In the same castles the double-towered gatehouse developed further into the gatehouse-keep, a self-contained unit like the original keep had been. In the post-Edwardian period the two main types were the courtyard castle (p 35), and the tower-house (p 37). Apart from these, which were relatively few in number, the existing stock of castles served most needs, being added to and refurbished from time to time – processes which explain the almost infinite variety of castle architecture, a variety which is one of its greatest appeals.

1 The South-East

The south-east region embraces Greater London, Kent, Surrey, East Sussex and West Sussex. Within this area there are visible remains of nearly 40 castles, including some of the most famous and best preserved examples in the British Isles: Dover, Leeds, Arundel, Bodiam, Herstmonceux and, above all, the Tower of London. Of the 40 or so surviving castles, more than three-quarters are in the counties of Kent and East Sussex, reflecting the strategic importance of this part of the south-east, facing as it does the short sea crossing from the Continent.

All types of castle are represented in the area, from the beginning of Norman times (1066) to the end of the medieval period (1485). The early period is particularly well represented with ten rectangular keeps (The Tower of London, Dover, Rochester, Canterbury, West Malling, Guildford, Knepp, Pevensey, Aldingbourne, and Sutton Valence), while there is an octagonal keep at Chilham. There are shell-keeps at Lewes, Arundel, Guildford, Farnham and Tonbridge. Leeds and Allington as they exist now are primarily of the Edwardian (1272–1307) and later periods, while there are important Edwardian additions to the Tower, Tonbridge and Leybournc. The later courtyard castles include two famous examples, Bodiam and Herstmonceux, as well as Westenhanger, Scotney and Cooling castles.

Of the 40 or so sites which exist in the south-east, the following thirteen will be dealt with in detail in the entries below: the Tower of London, Allington, Dover, Leeds, Rochester, Saltwood, Tonbridge, Farnham, Bodiam, Herstmonceux, Leeds, Pevensey and Arundel. At the time of writing, all of these are open to the public, at times and on days which vary from castle to castle. To avoid disappointment and inconvenience, opening hours should be checked where possible before planning a visit. The remaining sites (map p 40) are listed below: many of them are likewise open to the public, or at least are freely accessible.

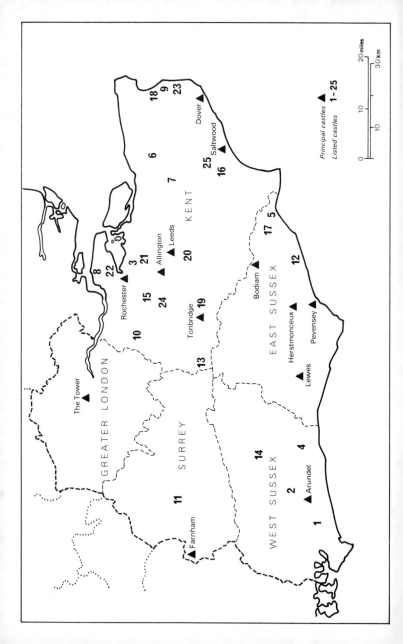

1. Aldingbourne (West Sussex): remains of a square keep and curtain wall.
2. Amberley (West Sussex): built in 1377, of the Bodiam type.
3. Binbury (Kent): remains of a curtain wall and tower.
4. Bramber (West Sussex): fine motte, portions of curtain wall and tower.
5. Camber (East Sussex): one of Henry VIII's artillery forts.
6. Canterbury (Kent): remains of a rectangular keep.
7. Chilham (Kent): small octagonal keep and remains of surrounding wall.
8. Cooling (Kent): fine gatehouse on roadside, rest in private gardens, but visible from road.
9. Deal (Kent): magnificent example of Henry VIII artillery fort.
10. Eynsford (Kent): remains of hall inside plain-walled bailey.
11. Guildford (Surrey): rectangular keep built on side of motte.
12. Hastings (East Sussex): much lost through erosion, but surviving earthworks and stone structure.
13. Hever (Kent): a fortified manor house rather than a true castle.
14. Knepp (West Sussex): fragment of rectangular keep on motte.
15. Leybourne (Kent): chief visible remnant a fine double-towered gatehouse.
16. Lympne (Kent): fortified manor house, fourteenth-century.
17. Rye (East Sussex): Ypres Tower, built c. 1250.
18. Sandown (Kent): Henry VIII artillery castle, now largely destroyed.
19. Scotney (Kent): one tower of a Bodiam-style castle.
20. Sutton Valence (Kent): remains of a square keep.
21. Thurnham (Kent): remains of curtain wall around bailey.
22. Upnor (Kent): artillery castle built in the reign of Elizabeth I.
23. Walmer (Kent): Henry VIII artillery castle.
24. West Malling (Kent): a well preserved rectangular stone keep.
25. Westenhanger (Kent): a Bodiam-type castle, licensed 1343.

The Tower of London (TQ 336805)

Although it was once thought that the White Tower (the keep) of London's castle was built immediately after the Conquest, excavation has shown that it was not begun until about ten years later. For the first decade or so there was a much simpler castle, two sides of which, the south and east, were formed by the south-east angle of the still surviving Roman town wall of London. On the two remaining sides, north and west, William built an earth-and-timber defence, consisting of a bank and ditch, surmounted by a stout timber palisade. This had the advantage of speed, and speed in taking control was important in a newly conquered city. This relatively simple but effective castle seems to have served for about ten years and it was only c. 1077–8 that work was begun on the great stone tower which still forms the centre-piece of the castle, and gives its name to the whole structure, the Tower of London. The new stone tower was built within the existing defences which formed a bailey, although all traces of this early enclosure have now gone, swept away in later reconstructions.

William's keep, the White Tower, is rectangular in plan, c. 120 by 96 ft, not counting the circular north-east angle turret, nor the semi-circular projection of the chapel at the south-east angle. The walls are between 12 and 14 ft thick, and the whole structure stands on a high plinth or base of solid stone. The main walls rise to a height of 90 ft with the four angle turrets (three square, one round) rising another 25 or 30 ft higher. As originally built the keep had three storeys (a fourth was inserted later, below): basement, entrance level, and main floor. Access was at second storey level by means of a forebuilding (above, p 19), now gone. The basement was reached, from above, by a spiral staircase in the north-east angle turret, and this, and other turret staircases, gave access to the upper floor and the battlements.

The plan of the keep is virtually the same on all three floors and is dictated by the presence of a large chapel and by a cross-wall, a common feature in large keeps, designed to reduce the span for flooring purposes. Each floor is divided into three parts, a large

The Tower of London, from the River Thames

room to the west of the cross-wall, with a smaller room to the east, together with the chapel, its crypt and its sub-crypt, according to storey. The basement rooms were probably used for storage, particularly of food, large quantities of which would have been required in the event of a prolonged siege. The middle storey probably housed the garrison and servants while the top floor formed the royal apartments. These consisted of the Great Hall (96 by 40 ft), the principal room of the keep; the Great Chamber (65 by 28 ft), a more private apartment for the king and his immediate entourage; and the chapel with its semi-circular east end projecting beyond the main keep wall. Although only solid main walls now remain it has to be remembered that these very large rooms were probably subdivided into smaller and more convenient units by means of lighter timber walls and screens, so that the original layout was probably rather more complex than now appears. The top storey of the keep was of much greater height than the others and had a surrounding gallery 16 ft above floor level in the thickness of the walls. This was lit by its own row of windows (the top row externally). At a later stage an additional (fourth) storey was created by inserting a floor at gallery level, but this was not part of the original plan.

Thus as completed c. 1097, the castle consisted of a keep (the White Tower), and a bailey, although precise details of the bailey wall are lacking because it has long since disappeared in later rebuilding. Apart from the size and magnificence of its keep, however, the castle was little or no different from other castles of the Norman period, and seems to have remained in this state for about a century, until the reign of Richard I (the Lionheart, 1189–1199), when it was enlarged and strengthened. The bailey was extended to the west and was now defended by a stone wall. In addition, a number of wall-towers were added, only two of which can now be identified, the Bell Tower and Wardrobe Tower. These changes brought the castle up to date but did not fundamentally alter its basic plan which was still that of a keep-and-bailey castle.

The castle was further added to during the long reign of Henry III (1216–1272). One of the main changes was the extension of the castle eastwards, beyond the line of the Roman wall which had since the beginning marked the eastern side of the bailey. Within this new enlarged bailey they built an inner bailey (now gone) between the keep and the south curtain wall. The main curtain wall was equipped with circular angle towers, D-shaped interval towers and (almost certainly) a double-towered gatehouse, all in keeping with current fortification practice in the mid-thirteenth century. Thus by the end of Henry's reign the castle consisted of the White Tower (the keep), a small rectangular inner bailey, and a large outer bailey strengthened with angle and interval towers and a double-towered gatehouse. The castle was protected on three sides by a wet moat and on the fourth, south side by the Thames. Henry's curtain wall forms the basis of the present inner curtain wall which surrounds the keep.

This was the structure which Edward I inherited on his accession in 1272, which he then proceeded to transform into the great concentric castle which is still basically the shape as we see it today. One of the first moves was the filling in of the existing moat, and its transformation into an outer bailey, surrounded by a curtain wall more or less where the outer edge of the moat had been. This made the castle concentric, at least on three sides; on the fourth side, towards the Thames, additional work was required (below). Beyond the new outer curtain wall a new and much wider and deeper moat was dug, between 75 and 125 ft wide, fed from the waters of the Thames.

In Henry III's time the Thames had acted as a moat on the fourth side, running immediately below the southern curtain wall. This, however, made it difficult for Edward to provide a concentric arrangement on this side. His solution was to take in more land from the river by building a wharf along the river frontage. On the land thus gained he built an outer curtain wall, completing the concentric arrangement, with a moat between it and the wharf to the south, continuous with the moat on the three remaining sides. As part of the same scheme he also built a water-gate, now known as Traitor's Gate. Opposite a passage through the wharf from the Thames was a box-like projection of the new outer curtain wall. This enclosed a section of the moat and provided an entrance, which could be closed by gates, at the inner end of the passage mentioned above. The most elaborate entrance, however, was that from the landward side, at the south-west corner of the castle.

In Henry III's time the main entrance had been on the west side, in the position now occupied by Beauchamp Tower, completed in 1281 when Edward's new entrance came into use. The greatly enlarged moat with which Edward surrounded his concentric castle included a D-shaped extension (now gone) at the south-west angle in which the various sections of the long-drawn-out entrance were situated. The main feature of the whole entrance arrangement was a barbican in the form of a D-shaped island, following the shape of the moat extension in which it stood. Access to the island from the outer edge of the moat was via a drawbridge; there was another drawbridge between the island and the second (double-towered)

gate which was itself completely surrounded by water. From it a
long bridge led to a third drawbridge in front of the third (also
double-towered) gate, situated at the south-west angle of the outer
curtain wall. From this point on progress was (as it still is) between
the inner and outer curtain walls as far as the fourth gate, in the
south, inner curtain wall, flanked by the massive circular Wakefield
Tower. This gave access to the Middle Bailey from which another
double-towered gate (now gone) led into the Inner Bailey (also
gone). The north side of the Inner Bailey was formed by the south
wall of the keep and against this wall was the forebuilding (also
gone), through which access was gained to the keep itself.

Although there have been many changes and additions to the
Tower in the succeeding 600 years, the castle has retained the
fundamental concentric shape given to it by Edward I's major
reconstruction in the late thirteenth century. The keep (the White
Tower), the earliest building of the whole complex, still dominates
all else and is a worthy monument to William the Conqueror's
castle-building activities.

KENT

Allington Castle (TQ 752579)

Allington Castle, as it exists today, is the work of Stephen of
Penchester who bought the manor house which then existed on the
site in 1279, and obtained a licence to crenellate in 1281. However,
the castle, on the west bank of the River Medway just outside
Maidstone, had a history going back to the eleventh century, and
Stephen's new castle was, in fact, the third on the site. The first
castle was built by William, Earl Warenne, later Earl of Surrey, late
in the eleventh century, and was of the motte-and-bailey type,
probably with a timber superstructure, although there are early
Norman remains in the stone wall around the bailey. Perhaps even
the first castle was stone-built, or, if timber-built, was quickly
replaced by stone. The remains of the motte survive to the south of
the existing castle, which stands within the original bailey. In the
following century, during the civil war known as the Anarchy

(1135–1154), this was replaced by a stone castle, the remains of which have been uncovered by excavation. The plan is incomplete but presumably the structure was some sort of stone tower or keep, standing within the original bailey enclosed by a stone wall. In the reign of Henry II (1154–1189) there is a record of payments incurred in the dismantling of this castle, presumably because it was unlicensed, in the years 1174–5. The castle was then replaced by a manor house with a walled courtyard, probably enclosing much of the original bailey. This was the establishment bought by Stephen of Penchester in 1279, which he then proceeded to transform into the elaborate castle which still exists today.

The new castle conforms inevitably to the Edwardian plan (p 29), in this case modified by the manor house, which was incorporated in the new scheme, and apparently by remains of the earlier castle, parts of which were presumably still standing. The manor house and its north wing were raised in height and given battlements; the house was also extended to the south, and this provided the west wing of the new castle, with a tower (Solomon's Tower) at the south-west angle. From the gatehouse the north range was built, and then the east range, with another tower at the north-east angle. The south range was complicated by the remains of the earlier castle and the south-east angle has no tower, and indeed does not form an angle, simply curving round the corner as a buttressed, curtain wall. There are two other towers along the east curtain wall, another on the south and another (the Bath-House Tower) on the west side just north of Solomon's Tower, which has a smaller tower attached to its east side. Thus externally the castle conforms for the most part to the Edwardian formula: a rectangular plan, with angle towers, interval towers and a gatehouse. Such variations as there were from this formula were made necessary by the pre-existing structures on the site.

Internally, it was probably Penchester who built the Great Hall on the east side of the castle, with kitchen and buttery to the south and a handsome suite of rooms to the north. There were also ranges of buildings on the three remaining sides, although those to the south were later removed. However, Penchester died in 1299 with the work still not complete. His son-in-law, Sir Henry Cobham,

succeeded him and it was, in fact, he who gave the gatehouse its
present appearance. When Sir Henry died in 1316, the castle was
practically complete as it stands today, except for additions and
alterations of the Tudor period (1485–1603). In the reign of Henry
VII (1485–1509), the current owner, Sir Henry Wyatt, put in new
windows and doors and rebuilt the kitchens. He also cleared away
the south wing and built a cross-wing, sub-dividing the courtyard,
with a long gallery above and domestic offices below, possibly the
earliest long gallery erected in England.

Allington enjoyed its greatest renown in the Tudor period. The
castle was visited by Henry VII, Henry VIII, Anne Boleyn,
Katherine Parr, Cardinal Wolsey and possibly Holbein.
Unfortunately one of the later Wyatts, Sir Thomas Wyatt the
younger, was rash enough to lead the abortive Kentish revolt and
was executed in 1554 by Queen Mary (1553–1558). The estate
came to the Crown and the castle was used as a prison for local
rebels. By the early seventeenth century it was in a bad state of
repair and part of it was restored by a John Best. In 1760, it became
a farmhouse and by the early part of this century was in ruins.
Fortunately at this stage (1905) it was bought by Sir Martin
Conway, under whom began the restoration which has brought the
castle to its present excellent state.

Dover Castle (TR 326417)
Dover Castle, the 'Key of England' has a long history going back
before the Roman period into prehistoric times. The main
earthworks beyond the outer curtain wall, which are still such a
prominent feature of the castle, are almost certainly those of an
Iron Age hill-fort built in the last few centuries before the Roman
Conquest of AD 43. Within this enclosure the Romans built a
lighthouse (*pharos*), probably in the first century AD, which still
survives alongside the church of St Mary-in-Castro (i.e. St Mary's in
the Castle). Later again, but still before the Conquest of 1066, there
are references to a castle at Dover, and this was almost certainly an
Anglo-Saxon *burh* (p 13), re-using the Iron Age ramparts. Within
this existing fortification Duke William built the first castle on the
site, a timber motte-and-bailey structure, probably on the site of the

Dover Castle – one of the most impressive of medieval fortresses

present keep and its surrounding curtain wall.

Whatever its form, and wherever located, Duke William's castle seems to have served its purpose without fundamental change for about a century, until the time of Henry II (1154–1189), and it was he who began the present splendid castle, around 1170. The centre-piece is the great square keep which still dominates the whole complex. This is virtually a cube in shape (98 by 96 by 95 ft high), with unusually thick walls (17–21 ft), and this may explain the large number of subsidiary rooms contrived in the thickness of the walls in the upper levels, in addition to the principal rooms. The floor arrangements are similar to those of the White Tower (basement, middle floor, main floor with gallery above). In the case of Dover, however, entry is at main floor (i.e. top storey) level rather than middle storey as at the Tower. Access to the keep is via an elaborate forebuilding along part of the south-eastern side and the whole of the north-eastern side. The main internal space is subdivided by a cross-wall providing four principal rooms (each c. 50 by 20 ft.) on the two main floors apart from the basement, but there are another dozen or so smaller rooms (15 by 10 ft or thereabouts) contrived in the thickness of the walls. Altogether the Dover keep must have provided a great deal of accommodation in a compact space, including two chapels, one above the other, in the south-east angle of the forebuilding.

Splendid as the keep was, and still is, it was by no means the limit of Henry's endeavours at Dover. The keep was, in fact, the centre-piece of what was, for its period, a very elaborate castle, much of which was completed in Henry's lifetime. The works surrounding the keep consisted of the inner curtain wall, ten wall-towers, two double-towered gatehouses, and two barbicans. Apart from the south barbican these features survive in the existing castle. Their significance has been commented on already (p 22). Dover was an important milestone, marking the end of one phase of castle development and the beginning of another.

Henry's work was continued by King John (1199–1216) who completed the outer curtain around the northern part of the castle, including wall-towers which were now D-shaped, following current fashion, rather than rectangular. John also built the original main gate of the castle at its northern apex, although it did not survive as such for very long. In 1216 the castle was besieged by Prince Louis of France and was defended on behalf of the King by Hubert de Burgh. The French succeeded in undermining the northern gateway and caused its eastern tower to collapse. Under Henry III (1216–1272), who succeeded John in the same year, a great deal of additional money was spent on Dover Castle. The outer curtain wall was extended southwards to the cliff-head on both east and west sides (if this, or some part of it, had not been done already), but the major work of Henry's reign was the impressive new entrance on the west side, the Constable's Gate, which is still the main entrance for visitors; this replaced the undermined northern entrance which was now blocked up.

The Constable's Gate was built between 1221 and 1227, and, in spite of some later additions and alterations, most of its medieval structure is still preserved. In particular its towers, unlike so many other towers both at Dover and elsewhere, have not been reduced in height, possibly because it has always been, as it still is, the official residence of the Constable or Deputy-Constable of the Castle. The main external additions are the rooms, carried on arches, built between the forward porch tower and the flanking towers on either side, which were added probably in the eighteenth century. Otherwise, apart from the windows, the external elevation survives largely as it was built in the thirteenth century.

The nucleus of the new entrance was one of John's D-shaped towers, built when he completed the northern outer curtain between 1199 and 1216. This was pierced to provide an entrance passage, and a wide porch was added in front. This consisted of two D-shaped towers, back to back, with the outer entrance passage between them, forming in effect a single, elongated tower with rounded ends, at right angles to the main axis. The main D-shaped tower was flanked by additional round-fronted towers, a smaller one to the south and a larger, more elaborate double tower to the north, all linked to form a single structure providing a great deal of accommodation for the castle's garrison. This included the Constable's residence, a suite of rooms on the first floor above the entrance passage, consisting of the Constable's Hall, with an entrance lobby to the south, and a more private room, the Constable's Chamber, opening from it to the north. Opening off it to the west was the room above the porch, and since this forms part of the suite and is not accessible in any other way, it may have been the accommodation for some of the Constable's officers or officials. Of the remaining rooms, the first floor of the south tower probably acted as a guardroom to the Constable's suite, while there were twin guardrooms at ground-floor level at the inner end of the entrance passage. The remaining rooms (ground and first floor of the north tower, ground floor of the south tower), all three equipped with latrines, must have provided barrack accommodation for the garrison of what was, in effect, a miniature fortress in itself. The Constable's Gate provided three tiers of firing positions for defenders: fifteen at ground-floor level, thirteen at first-floor level, and any number of positions on the ramparts above.

Significant visible remains are: Peverell's Tower (which is, in fact, a double-towered gatehouse), built in the time of John and Henry III (1199–1272); the circular St John's Tower, built in the ditch after the undermining of the north entrance; and the twin-towered Fitzwilliam Gate, built c. 1227 on the north-eastern side, which led to a covered passage across the ditch and through the bank on the other side, enabling defenders to issue forth and take their attackers in the rear.

Dover Castle was substantially complete by about 1250 and survived in its medieval state for about 500 years. In the mid-eighteenth century much of the medieval fabric was radically altered or completely destroyed in bringing the castle up to date, and in particular, in providing for artillery. Nevertheless, Dover Castle remains one of the most impressive and elaborate of all medieval fortresses, either in the British Isles or in Europe as a whole.

Entry through the Constable's Gate on the north-west side leads into the Middle Bailey. Immediately in front is a steep grassy slope (probably the original motte of William the Conqueror), surmounted by the well-preserved polygonal curtain wall and rectangular towers of Henry II's Inner Bailey. This is the best view of the wall, since the Inner Bailey is lined on the inside with much later buildings. On the far right from the Constable's Gate is Peverell's Tower, a double-towered gatehouse which leads into the Outer Bailey. From Peverell's Tower the outer curtain wall and its towers can be followed to the south. From the curtain wall can be seen the great outer ditch, which is probably the ditch of the original hill-fort. From either Peverell's Tower or the Constable's Gate visitors can move around the south side of the Inner Bailey and either proceed straight ahead to the Roman lighthouse and the church of St Mary-in-Castro, or turn sharp left and enter the Inner Bailey by the double-towered South Gate; the original barbican in front of this has now gone but it must have closely resembled the one in front of the North Gate. Before entering the keep it is worth walking through the bailey and out by the double-towered North Gate and the surviving barbican in front of it. From here visitors can reach the outer curtain on the north-side and from the top of the earth rampart behind it can see the outer earthworks again. Looking back there is a view which embraces the north barbican, the Inner Bailey Wall and the keep. Returning to the Inner Bailey visitors can examine the keep in the light of the description given earlier.

Leeds Castle (TQ 837533)

In its water setting, Leeds Castle is one of the most picturesque of all English castles. It occupies two (originally three) islands in an artificial lake formed by damming the River Len, probably during the thirteenth century, in much the same way as the water defences of Kenilworth (p 156) and Caerphilly (p 211) were formed. There are references to a Castle of Slede (the origin of the name Leeds) in 1139, although nothing of this survives above ground. An early curtain wall with square towers traced on the main island probably belongs to the latter part of the same century. The visible remains, however, are of the thirteenth century or later.

If the original twelfth-century castle was indeed earlier than the water defences, then presumably it was of the motte- and/or keep-and-bailey type, occupying two knolls which later became the two outermost islands when the valley in which they were situated was flooded. The third island formed a barbican in front of the main entrance and was approached by three causeways ending in drawbridges. From the barbican a stone bridge, originally including a drawbridge, leads to the gatehouse on the main island, the oval bailey (c. 500 by 250 ft). This is surrounded by a curtain wall with semi-circular towers, both now drastically cut down but quite clearly of the thirteenth century and almost certainly contemporary with the creation of the water defences, which may be of the time of Edward I (1272–1307). The square gatehouse, with the Constable's quarters on the first floor and stables and barrack accommodation on either side, may be somewhat earlier, perhaps c. 1230, in the time of Henry III (1216–1272). The house at the far end of the bailey is nineteenth-century (built 1822), but the building on the right (Maiden's Tower) was built as a self-contained house by Henry VIII (1509–1547), traditionally for the Queen's Maids of Honour, although the same tradition has it that Henry had the keys.

From the main island or bailey a magnificent two-tier bridge leads
to the Gloriette or keep, the walls of which rise sheer from the
water. The keep, spade-like in plan, has an internal courtyard so
that it must be classed as a shell-keep. The lower part is certainly of
Edward I's time and the whole shell may be Edwardian, the upper
parts having been drastically altered by Henry VIII. The interior of
the Gloriette was burned down in 1665, and reconstructed, and
much altered, in 1822, when the house mentioned above was built.

Rochester Castle (TQ 742686)
Not much remains of Rochester Castle apart from the keep, but that
keep is one of the most impressive of its type, still standing 125 ft
high to the top of the angle turrets. There was an early castle on the
site (c. 1087–9), probably consisting of a simple stone curtain-wall
enclosure. The keep, however, belongs to the following century and
was built c. 1130 by the Archbishop of Canterbury, great
churchmen at this time having as much need of castles as great
barons. Rochester (c. 70 ft square) is of four storeys and has an
elaborate forebuilding with a chapel above. Entry was originally at
first-floor level with a spiral staircase giving access to the basement
below. The space within the main walls of the keep (c. 12 ft thick) is
c. 40 by 40 ft, and this was subdivided by a cross-wall on all four
floors. The cross-wall housed a well-pipe from which water could be
drawn as required at each level. The Great Hall was at second-floor
level, and there the cross-wall is pierced by a columned arcade so
that the whole floor formed a single room. Because of its great
height it was served by two rows of windows (the second and third
from the top, externally). The upper row opened on to a gallery
which was built in the thickness of the wall some 14 ft above the
floor level of the hall. Above the hall was a fourth storey with mural
galleries between the window openings, and above the fourth storey
are the battlements with crenellated parapet and angle turrets. Of
the latter, three are square and one circular. However, all four were
originally square. The castle was besieged by King John in 1215 and
his sappers brought down the south angle by undermining. When it

Leeds Castle: the two-tier bridge to the keep

Rochester Castle: the interior of the keep

was repaired, under Henry III, it was rebuilt in the then current circular style, which was appearing in all castles of this period.

Access is now at ground level, but at the time of writing (1980) work is in progress to restore the original means of entry at first-floor level via the forebuilding. All floors and the roof have now gone but the keep can be examined at every level via the spiral staircase in the east angle turret. The impression of a basement below the level of the modern platform at ground-floor level is misleading. This was dug out only in the nineteenth century. As built, the lowest of the four storeys in the keep was at ground level. The chapel (in the forebuilding) can be seen, but not entered, at second-floor level, and the gallery above this floor, in the thickness of the wall, is also accessible. At the top of the keep the rampart walk gives a fine view of the adjacent Rochester Cathedral. Apart from the keep, the main features of the castle are the east curtain wall with two rectangular towers, a stretch of the west curtain, and the remains of the north-west bastion. Most, if not all, of these structures represent building, or rebuilding, in the period 1367–83, after the castle had been neglected for a century or so following the damage it sustained in 1264 during the Barons' War between Henry III and a faction led by Simon de Montfort.

Saltwood Castle (TR 161359)

For about 300 years, from the time of King John (1199–1216) until that of Henry VIII (1509–1547), Saltwood Castle was one of the palaces (albeit fortified) of the Archbishops of Canterbury. The original castle was probably built by Henry of Essex around 1160. Surrounded by a wide moat, it consisted of an oval curtain wall (c. 325 by 225 ft) with three square internal towers, one of which formed a gatehouse, and two small projecting turrets. Presumably there was a hall and other domestic buildings, but the surviving internal structures are all of a later date. The original south curtain wall appears to have been demolished c. 1175. It was rebuilt, with two square towers, on a straight rather than the original curving line, c. 1240. This seems to have been part of a large programme of work about this time. A hall and associated domestic offices were built against the new wall, and a new outer bailey wall with circular towers (but rectangular outer gatehouse) was added on the east side of the main bailey. Around the turn of the century (1300) a new (solar) wing was added to the western end of the hall block, and about 25 years later a chapel was added beyond the kitchen to the east. Towards the end of the century Archbishop Courtney (1381–1396) built a new hall to the north-west of the existing domestic complex. He also built a new twin-towered gatehouse on to the front of the old rectangular inner gateway of the original castle. This has now been restored to form an imposing residence.

Tonbridge Castle (TQ 589466)

There was a castle here as early as 1088, since there are records that it was held by Bishop Odo and his allies against William Rufus (William II, 1087–1100). The castle is of the motte-and-bailey type;

there are, in fact, two baileys, one to the north and one to the
south-east, although the stone remains are confined to the latter and
the motte, now laid out as a pleasant public park. The motte is
surmounted by the somewhat battered remains of an oval
shell-keep (c. 80 by 70 ft), probably built in the eleventh century; if
this is so, then presumably the castle did not have a preceding
timber phase but was stone-built from the beginning. The existing
curtain wall of the bailey (c. 9 ft thick), with substantial buttresses
along the south face towards the river, was built around 1180,
replacing an earlier and thinner wall. It is noticeable that the bailey
walls did not end at the motte ditch, but ran across it and up the
sides of the motte to abut the walls of the keep. The principal
surviving feature of Tonbridge, however, is the great gatehouse,
added c. 1300, on the north side of the bailey, close to the motte

The gatehouse at Tonbridge Castle, seen from inside

ditch. It is a typical example of the Edwardian double-towered type, four storeys high plus a basement below ground level. The entrance passage between the towers had a formidable array of defences. Apart from the drawbridge in front, there were successively a row of machicolations, a portcullis, a second row of machicolations, and a double-leaved door. These defended the passage from outside attack. The passage was also defended from attack from the bailey by a row of machicolations, a portcullis and a double-leaved door at its inner end. The entrances to the guard-chambers on either side were also defended by portcullises. From the guard chamber rose the only stairs to the upper floors. There were also portcullises defending the doors on to the rampart walk on either side. The gatehouse could thus be completely isolated from the rest of the castle and was, in effect, a keep. Its third storey formed a handsome great hall (c. 50 by 30 ft) with a fine fireplace and traceried windows on the courtyard side.

SURREY

Farnham Castle (SU 837473)
Farnham began as a castle with a square keep and ended as one with a shell-keep. This interesting, and unusual, development is bound up with the history of the mid-twelfth century. The original Farnham Castle was built in 1140 by Henry de Blois, Bishop of Winchester and brother of King Stephen (1135–54). The castle then consisted of a square stone keep, c. 50 by 50 ft, standing on top of a motte, the summit of which was about 90 ft in diameter. Attached to the south side of the motte was a small triangular courtyard or inner bailey, and these two features were surrounded by the earth bank and ditch on which the existing (later) outer curtain wall stands, probably replacing an earlier timber palisade contemporary with the square keep. Shortly after his accession in 1154, Henry II seized all the de Blois castles, along with many others, and ordered them to be dismantled. During the Anarchy (civil war 1135–54), a great many castles had been erected, too many for Henry's liking, and there was a considerable outlay of money on

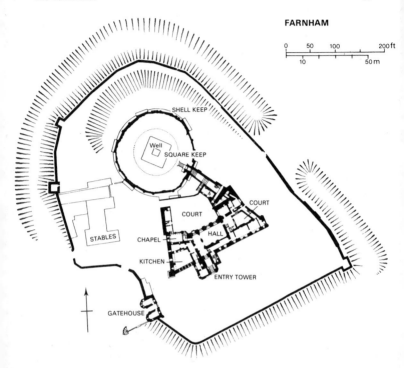

FARNHAM

dismantling baronial castles at the same time as new royal castles were being built.

How long the castle remained in its dismantled state is not precisely known, since there is little or no documentary evidence relating to its reconstruction. However, this seems to have taken place in the late twelfth and early thirteenth centuries, i.e. in the reign of King John (1199–1216). By this time the de Blois family seem to have regained possession of the castle, and the reconstruction may have been the work of the original Henry de Blois (at the end of his life) or of his successors. However, the date of the rebuilding is less interesting than the method adopted.

Instead of simply rebuilding the keep on its original foundations, an entirely new and radically different scheme was adopted. The bottom edge of the motte was cut back and a high circular wall, completely embracing it, was built to a height of about 40 ft, i.e. somewhat higher than the summit of the motte. The sloping space between the wall and the motte summit was then filled up, forming a level interior space. The result was a shell keep, around rather than on a motte, with its interior ground surface some 30 ft. above external ground level. The wall is reinforced with regularly-spaced buttresses and has four shallow turrets and a gatehouse. Only a short section of the exterior of the keep is accessible, but this includes the West Turret and a number of buttresses to the left of the site-custodian's office.

Most of the shell-keep is surrounded by private gardens and has to be examined from the inside. Beyond the custodian's office a modern flight of steps leads into one side of the original stone staircase built against the east wall of the triangular inner bailey. This leads through the gatehouse, one of the best preserved parts of the shell-keep, and into the interior of the keep. The remains of the square keep are now covered by a modern concrete platform, but the space beneath is accessible. Excavation has uncovered the foundations of the square keep which go down to original ground level, i.e. 30 ft beneath the motte top. In the centre of the foundations is a well-shaft which goes well below original ground surface. This secured a safe water-supply for the original square keep and for the later shell-keep, the well remaining in use after the early keep was pulled down.

The buildings of the inner, triangular bailey are not accessible to visitors, but they are substantially structures of the early thirteenth century, although somewhat altered and adapted in later periods. They contained a hall, a kitchen, a chapel and many other rooms, and quite clearly Farnham was conceived not only as a castle but also as a very comfortable country residence. Because the space between the shell wall and the outer curtain wall (again probably of the early thirteenth century) is now private gardens, the outer defences can best be examined from the main road to the west of the castle and from the playing-fields to the north, where both the

original ditch (c. 1140) and the later stone curtain (c. 1300) can be clearly seen. The double-towered gatehouse on the south-west side (close to the visitors' entrance) is now covered with a modern cement rendering, but is essentially the original gatehouse of the thirteenth century.

EAST SUSSEX

Bodiam Castle (TQ 785257)
As at Leeds Castle (Kent), the water defences at Bodiam help to make it one of the most picturesque castles in Britain. It was built by Sir Edward Dallingrigge who was granted a licence to build in 1385, and is a fine example of the courtyard castles of late medieval times. Unlike many earlier castles, Bodiam is all of one period, and although many of the interior buildings are in ruins, the exterior is substantially complete as built and was never subsequently altered. The castle is rectangular in plan (c. 150 by 140 ft) with four boldly projecting circular angle towers, three mid-wall rectangular towers (the one on the south forming a postern gate), and a double-towered gatehouse with rectangular towers on the north, all of them still standing virtually to their original height. The internal arrangements show a clear division between the family accommodation and the accommodation for the mercenary soldiers made necessary by the troublesome times in which the castle was built. The family section included three of the four angle towers and both entrances, so that in the event of disaffection by the mercenaries, never entirely reliable, the lord still retained effective control of most of the castle. The mercenaries' quarters were contained between two blank walls, one on the north side of the lord's kitchen and one on the west side of the main entrance.

The moat around Bodiam is virtually an artificial lake, c. 500 by 350 ft, fed from the nearby River Rother. Approach to the main entrance involved crossing from the west bank to the octagonal island, then turning right to a barbican, beyond which was the

Guildford Castle: the keep

Bodiam Castle: the main gatehouse seen from the courtyard

entrance proper, with three drawbridges *en route*. Approach to the postern gate was more direct, but still embraced two drawbridges, one at each end of the original wooden bridge across the moat. Entry to the castle is now from the north bank, across the octagonal island and the barbican, and in through the main, double-towered gatehouse. This leads into the courtyard, the surrounding walls of which are mostly fairly low, although both high and low portions contain some fine windows. The internal layout of the castle is fairly clear. In the far corner on the right from the entrance is the Lord's kitchen, notable for its two huge fireplaces, with a well in the adjacent south-east tower. The L-shaped range between the kitchen and the gatehouse forms the retainers' quarters, with its own hall and separate kitchen. To the left of the kitchen, in the south range, are the buttery and pantry, and beyond these, the Great Hall.

Beyond this, and now in the east range, are more private rooms, the Great Chamber, the solar, and the chapel. The half of the north range to the east of the gatehouse was probably used for storage, while the upper floors probably provided additional accommodation for members of the household.

The gatehouse is accessible, as is the adjacent section of rampart walk and part of the north-west tower. The staircase in the gatehouse leads up to the second-floor rooms above the portcullis room over the entrance passage. The second-floor room has a fireplace and rooms on either side, and was clearly designed as living accommodation. The rampart walk leads along to the north-west tower and a room with three windows, a fireplace and a garderobe (latrine). The rooms below now have no floors. The north-east and south-east angle towers, and the square interval tower between, are all roofed but have no internal floors; the main details of the four storeys involved in each case can be seen from their accessible ground floors. The postern gate in the middle of the south range still has the vaulted roof to its entrance passage, with double doors beyond leading to the porch-like projection which can be seen standing in front of it when viewed from the exterior across the wide moat. Originally there would have been a drawbridge in front of this, with a long wooden bridge leading to it.

Herstmonceux Castle (TQ 646104)
Herstmonceux is a large, impressive, and well-preserved (indeed still occupied) courtyard castle. It is brick-built, this latter being perhaps its most unusual feature in a context where stone had reigned supreme for so long. The castle was built in 1441 by Sir Roger Fiennes, some 50 years after Bodiam, but on a much larger scale, measuring over 200 ft square. There are four tall octagonal towers at the angles, three semi-octagonal towers on each of the east, west and north sides, and two semi-octagonal towers and a double-towered gatehouse on the south front. The gatehouse towers are semi-octagonal below, semi-circular above, with two tiers of battlements, one rising inside the other. There was a wide enclosing moat as at Bodiam, now partly refilled. Externally the castle still stands much as it was built more than 500 years ago.

Internally the story is very different, the existing buildings dating only from the early part of this century. After some 300 years of use the castle was abandoned, and about 30 years later (1774) much of the interior was stripped out to build the neighbouring Herstmonceux Place. Restoration work began in 1911, although the new internal buildings bore no relation to the original structures. Fortunately, however, there are surviving plans of the interior as it was originally built and subsequently added to. In addition to the four ranges of buildings usual in most courtyard castles, Herstmonceux possessed a fifth range, subdividing the interior into two oblong courtyards, north and south. This additional range contained the Great Hall and its associated offices. At a later date the interior was further subdivided by two smaller additional ranges of buildings, producing four courtyards in all. The interior of the castle is not accessible, except in part for exhibitions, but, as already indicated, the whole interior is modern. The original parts of Herstmonceux are the curtain wall and towers, and these can be viewed from the outside. The castle is now occupied by offices of the Royal Observatory.

Lewes Castle (TQ 415101)

Many castles have two or more baileys, but very few have two mottes. Lewes is one such and Lincoln (p 125) is another. At Lewes the mottes are at opposite ends, east and west, of an oval bailey. Both originally supported shell-keeps although little or nothing remains of the eastern one. In the absence of any evidence to the contrary, it must be assumed that both were in use together, and probably from an early date, 1080 or thereabouts. The western shell, c. 110 by 100 ft overall, is oval in plan, and much of its southern half survives. In the middle of the thirteenth century two fine semi-octagonal towers were added to its southern and western sides. Apart from the western shell, the main survivals are some portions of the curving south curtain wall of the bailey, with the remains of a square tower and a square gatehouse belonging to the original castle. Early in the fourteenth century a fine

Herstmonceux Castle: the gatehouse

double-towered barbican was built in front of the original Norman gatehouse, and this is the outstanding surviving feature of the site. On the motte the remains of the shell wall stand to a height of about five or six feet, but the best surviving feature here is one of the two semi-octagonal towers, three storeys high, which is accessible to its battlements and from which there is a panoramic view of the castle and of the town of Lewes.

Pevensey Castle (TQ 644048)
Pevensey has a long history, going back not only to the first days of the Norman Conquest but also to Roman times, for the medieval castle is built within an oval eight-acre Roman fort (called Anderida) of the third century AD, one of the forts of the Saxon Shore. Much of the Roman curtain wall (c. 12 ft thick and 25 ft high) survives, together with about ten of its D-shaped bastions, and forms the outer bailey of the castle. It was at Pevensey that William the Conqueror landed in 1066, and he made good use of the large space offered by the Roman walls to house his troops. In the south-east corner, in the position later occupied by the stone castle, he built an inner enclosure defended by an earth bank and ditch surmounted by a timber palisade. Late in the eleventh century or early in the twelfth, a rectangular stone keep of unusual type was added to the inner bailey. Its eastern side was formed by a section of the Roman wall which included a solid D-shaped bastion, and to complement this another five even larger D-shaped bastions were added, two more on the east, one on the north and two on the west. About a century later, in the first half of the thirteenth century, the defences of the inner bailey were rebuilt and now form the most substantial part of the surviving remains. A stone curtain wall was built on the northern and western sides, together with three projecting D-shaped towers and a double-towered gatehouse. The walls were set well back from the ditch, leaving a wide space or berm (c. 40 ft wide), and a number of postern gates led on to this area, allowing defenders to issue forth suddenly and take attackers by surprise. The three D-shaped towers were of three storeys each,

The gatehouse and barbican, Lewes Castle

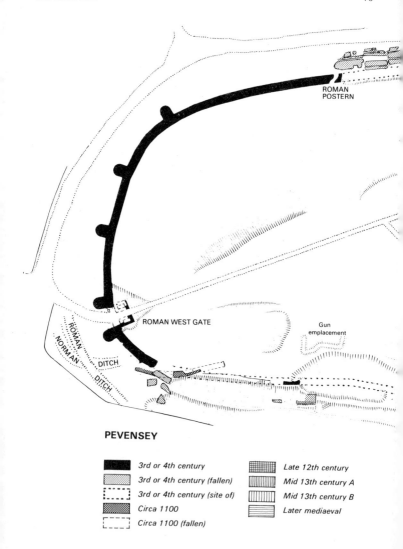

ROMAN
POSTERN

ROMAN WEST GATE

Gun
emplacement

ROMAN

NORMAN

DITCH

DITCH

PEVENSEY

■ 3rd or 4th century	▥ Late 12th century
▨ 3rd or 4th century (fallen)	▥ Mid 13th century A
⸬ 3rd or 4th century (site of)	▥ Mid 13th century B
▨ Circa 1100	▤ Later mediaeval
▯ Circa 1100 (fallen)	

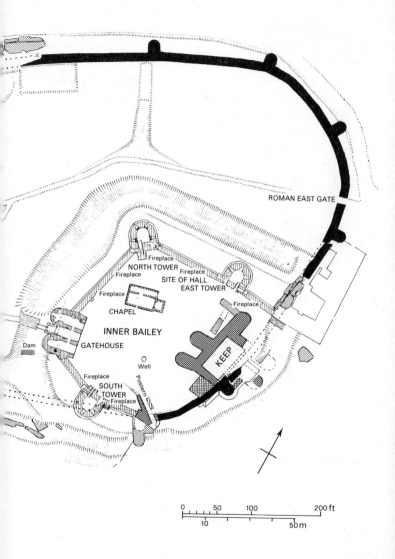

ROMAN EAST GATE

Fireplace
NORTH TOWER
Fireplace   Fireplace
                   SITE OF HALL
                   EAST TOWER
Fireplace
                              Fireplace
CHAPEL

INNER BAILEY

Dam
        GATEHOUSE   KEEP

        O Well

        Fireplace
Postern
        SOUTH
        TOWER
             Fireplace

0   50   100   200 ft
    10
                        50 m

Pevensey Castle

one below ground level, one at courtyard level and one above, the latter reached only from the rampart walks. The upper rooms had fireplaces and must have formed private rooms for senior members of the military establishment. The present brick linings and wooden floors of the towers were inserted in the last war, when Pevensey was garrisoned against attack across the south coast.

WEST SUSSEX

Arundel Castle (TQ 018073)

The general plan of Arundel closely resembles that of Windsor: a great central motte with two large baileys, one on each side. The motte is surmounted by a well preserved shell-keep, from which two walls run down the slope to north and south, linking on to the west

Arundel Castle: the shell-keep

curtain walls of the north and south baileys. On the east side the
north and south bailey walls are continuous, by-passing the motte
just beyond its surrounding ditch. The main internal buildings of the
original castle appear to have been in the south bailey.
Unfortunately, this part was severely damaged and left in ruins after
a siege by Parliamentary forces in 1644 during the Civil War. Two
subsequent rebuilding programmes (1791–1815 and 1890–1903)
mean that virtually everything visible in the southern part of the
castle is modern, although there are some medieval remains
beneath later buildings. However, it is a different story in the
central and northern parts of the castle where the remains are
among the best preserved of any medieval castle. The motte
supporting the shell-keep is of impressive size, c. 250 ft in diameter
at the base and 70 ft high. On it is a very well preserved oval
shell-keep (c. 80 by 70 ft. overall) with walls 9 ft thick. Internally

there is evidence of two-storey buildings against the inner face of the wall, with a central courtyard open to the sky. Externally there are flat pilaster buttresses, between one of which and a later tower is the original richly decorated entrance, blocked up in the thirteenth century. At this time a new entrance was contrived in the adjacent tower or forebuilding, in conjunction with the flight of steps up the motte alongside the wall mentioned earlier. Alongside this tower is another, smaller tower covering a well, the lower parts of which at least appear to have been built at the same time as the keep (c. 1130). Apart from the shell-keep and its associated structures, the other principal, and outstanding, medieval remnant is the main entrance to the castle as a whole, situated just south of the motte. The original Norman entrance is a great square tower on the inner side of the curtain wall, and this still forms the innermost part of the entrance arrangements. The most prominent and most striking feature, however, is the barbican or outer entrance added in the mid-thirteenth century, with two great square towers rising from the bottom of the wide ditch. At about the same time a new entrance (much restored) to the north bailey was added (St Bevis's Tower). The north bailey wall still stands, surrounding the so-called Tilt Yard, and although much restored its lower parts are certainly original Norman work.

Arundel is a large and imposing castle, not only in respect of its medieval remains but also of its nineteenth-century pseudo-medieval reconstruction which is a magnificent example of Victorian baronial architecture. Most of the tour of the castle is concerned with this portion of the castle, which is well worth seeing in its own right.

2 The South

The South region consists of the counties of Berkshire, Hampshire, the Isle of Wight, Dorset and Wiltshire. Within this area of central southern England there are remains of about twenty castles, noticeably fewer than in the south-east – probably because the latter, facing a much shorter sea crossing, was more vulnerable to attack from the Continent. Castles in the region include half a dozen or so with rectangular keeps, at Christchurch, Portchester, Old Sarum, Ludgershall, Sherborne, Marshwood and Corfe. There is also an octagonal keep at Odiham; and two shell-keeps, one at Windsor and one at Carisbrooke. Of the later castles, Donnington is of the courtyard type and Wardour combines both courtyard and tower-house characteristics. Even later are the artillery castles, mostly built by Henry VIII: Brownsea, Rufus, Portland, Sandsfoot and Yarmouth. Longford Castle in Wiltshire is, in fact, an Elizabethan house, built in 1573 on a triangular plan with three round angle towers.

Of these southern castles, the following eight will be dealt with in detail in the section which follows: Donnington, Windsor, Corfe, Sherborne, Christchurch, Porchester, Carisbrooke and Old Sarum. The remaining sites are shown on the map (page 76) and are listed below in alphabetical order.

1. Basing (Hampshire): existing remains mostly 1530 and later.
2. Bishop's Waltham (Hampshire): remains of an archbishop's fortified palace.
3. Brownsea (Dorset): Henry VIII artillery fort.
4. Longford (Wiltshire): triangular Elizabethan house with angle towers.
5. Ludgershall (Wiltshire): south face of small rectangular keep.
6. Marshwood (Dorset): motte with stump of a small rectangular keep.
7. Merdon (Hampshire): remains of curtain wall and square gatehouse.
8. Odiham (Hampshire): remains of an octagonal keep.

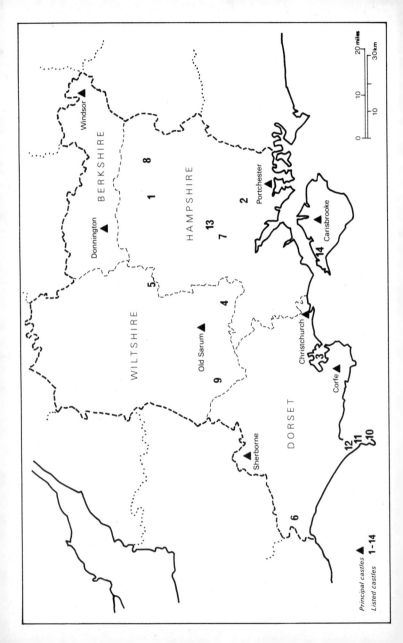

Principal castles ▲
Listed castles 1–14

9. Old Wardour (Wiltshire): well preserved tower-house.
10. Portland (Dorset): Henry VIII artillery fort.
11. Rufus, Portland (Dorset): fifteenth-century artillery fort.
12. Sandsfoot (Dorset): Henry VIII artillery fort.
13. Wolvesey, Winchester (Hants): remains of an archbishop's fortified palace.
14. Yarmouth (Isle of Wight): Henry VIII artillery fort.

BERKSHIRE

Donnington Castle (SU 461692)
Donnington is, or was, a courtyard castle of the Bodiam type, and the licence for it was, in fact, granted in the same year as Bodiam's, 1385. The castle was built by Sir Richard Abberbury but unfortunately, apart from the gatehouse, only the lower walls of the castle are preserved. The foundations show that it was rectangular in plan on three sides and semi-octagonal on the fourth (west) side, with small round towers at the four angles and two rectangular interval towers on the north and south sides. In the middle of the east front is the surviving, and impressive, gatehouse. It consists of a rectangular three-storey block projecting forward from the curtain wall, with tall four-storey circular towers at its two outer angles, with the entrance passage between them. A spiral staircase in the south tower provided access to the battlements. There are remains of a barbican-like structure in front of the gatehouse which indicate that, whatever else it was, Donnington was built with a serious military function in mind. The gatehouse interior is not accessible, but the plan and main features of the whole castle can be followed from external ground examination. Within the curtain walls are remains of some of the interior buildings.

Windsor Castle (SU 970770)
With a structural history covering some 800 years, Windsor is undoubtedly one of the most complex castles in the British Isles, and is, therefore, correspondingly difficult to deal with within the compass of a guide-book. The castle has been rebuilt, refurbished,

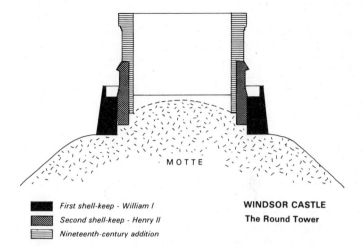

First shell-keep - William I
Second shell-keep - Henry II
Nineteenth-century addition

MOTTE

WINDSOR CASTLE
The Round Tower

and added to on many occasions, with the result that the remains of earlier periods are often fragmentary or are masked (if not completely destroyed) by later work. Fortunately, the history and structure of the castle's central feature, the great Round Tower on the motte, are fairly clear. The first references to a castle at Windsor occur in 1067 when the land on which it was to be built was acquired. The castle then built by William the Conqueror was of the motte-and-bailey type, with the motte formed by scarping the sides of a natural mound or knoll of chalk. The large bailey to the east is now occupied by the later buildings which form the castle's Upper Ward. On the motte William built a stone shell-keep some 120 ft in diameter with walls c. 10 ft thick. The bailey (c. 400 ft square) was probably surrounded by a plain curtain wall.

This castle, completed c. 1075, remained in use (doubtless with the addition of many internal timber buildings), for about a century, until the reign of Henry II (1154–1189), who rebuilt the castle on much more imposing lines. Inside the existing shell Henry built a new shell-keep, leaving the earlier structures as the terrace which

Donnington Castle: the gatehouse

still surrounds the Round Tower. The later consists of two main
parts: the lower half, below the horizontal moulding, is Henry's
shell; the upper half is a nineteenth-century addition, made during
the great rebuilding which took place under George IV (1820–30).
Henry also did a great deal of work not only in the existing east
bailey (the Upper Ward) but also in the new bailey (Lower Ward)
which he added on the west. In the Upper Ward he rebuilt the
curtain wall and added regularly spaced rectangular towers on very
much the same lines as at Dover Castle (p 48). Although heavily
rebuilt in later centuries, the plan and foundations of some of these
towers survive in the existing towers on the south and east sides of
the Upper Ward. In the Lower Ward the surviving structures reflect
work of a slightly later period, and there is even less visible
indication of Henry II's work. By the end of Henry's reign (1189)
the castle had reached its present very considerable extent, some
1500 ft from east to west and around 450 ft from north to south, a
very large castle by any standards, and more particularly for one of
the twelfth century. Although the rest of the castle was of stone, the
western end of the Lower Ward at this time appears to have
consisted of a timber palisade surmounting an earth bank and ditch.

The next major work on the castle was undertaken by Henry's
grandson, Henry III (1216–1272), taking up where his grandfather
had left off, which was the west end of the Lower Ward. He
replaced the timber palisade with a stone curtain wall and added the
circular towers which had become the fashion around the turn of the
century (1200). The three round towers which still form the western
end of the Lower Ward, together with the curtain wall between and
on either side of them, are his work, as are the other round towers
along the south side of the castle. There was also a double-towered
gatehouse, although this was replaced by the existing gatehouse
about two centuries later. Henry III also did a great deal of work on
the internal buildings of the Lower Ward but most of this has been
destroyed or obscured by later work.

Surprisingly Edward I (1272–1307), a great castle-builder, did
virtually nothing at Windsor, nor did his son, Edward II
(1307–1327). It was, in fact, another century or so after Henry III's
work that his great-grandson, Edward III (1327–77) carried out a

major reconstruction of the castle, most of the work being concentrated on the Upper Ward and the shell-keep. The Upper Ward formed the royal apartments and was lined on three sides by new buildings surrounding an open courtyard. Much of this work is now concealed by later structures, but in the south range the east tower of the George IV gateway and the curtain wall to the east of it as far as the next tower are Edward III's work, as is the south-west angle of the north range within the courtyard. The so-called Norman gate, a double-towered gatehouse just north of the motte, was also rebuilt during Edward's reign (c. 1360). Edward also rebuilt the timber structures within the shell-keep. There are some indications of earlier buildings (almost certainly those of Henry II), but the existing structures within the Round Tower are still substantially those erected by Edward III. At the same time, a new approach to the keep, up the north-east side of the motte, was completed. The Edwardian work of the mid-fourteenth century did much to give the castle its present shape and appearance.

About a century after Edward III's work the next major feature was added to the site: St George's Chapel. Although it forms no part of the castle's military apparatus, it now dominates the Lower Ward and as one of the most magnificent pieces of English Perpendicular architecture it should not be missed by any visitor. The chapel was begun under Edward IV (1461–1483) and was completed in the time of Henry VIII (1509–1547). It is the first building one sees on entering the castle through the Henry VIII gateway, a replacement in Henry's time of an earlier double-towered gateway of Henry III (1216–1272), who first completed the Lower Ward in stone.

Although there is a certain amount of work by Elizabeth I (1558–1603), and Charles II (1660–1685), the next major building work on Windsor was carried out early in the nineteenth century for George IV (1820–1830). His architect was Sir Jeffry Wyatville, whose work affected virtually every part of the castle, but most particularly the keep and the Upper Ward. In order to preserve the dominant position of the keep in the revised scheme Wyatville virtually doubled its height, and the portion above the horizontal moulding mentioned earlier is the nineteenth-century addition (the portion below being Henry II's work). The buildings on the north, east and west sides of the Upper Ward were extensively added to and rebuilt, and a new profile for the castle was achieved. One of the aims was to recreate the Gothic appearance of a medieval castle, and even if the Gothic is quite clearly nineteenth-century, the result, particularly in the distant view, is undoubtedly very successful. As it now stands Windsor is one of the finest monuments in the British Isles, without any regard to its earlier history. When the latter is taken into account, then Windsor takes on a new significance as a record of castle-building and royal accommodation covering more than nine centuries and reaching back to the earliest days of the Norman Conquest.

DORSET

Corfe Castle (SY 958823)

Corfe Castle occupies a splendid position on an isolated hill in the long east-to-west ridge of the Purbeck Hills. Before the castle was built there was a stone hall on the site, the remains of which were later incorporated in the Middle Bailey. The earliest castle, built c. 1100, was of the simplest kind, a plain curtain wall (c. 10–12 ft thick) surrounding the pear-shaped plateau which forms the highest part of the hill (Inner Bailey). It was not until some 30 or 40 years later that the rectangular keep (c. 70 by 60 ft.) was added against the inner face of the south curtain wall, transforming the castle into a more or less standard keep-and-bailey type. The castle remained in this state until the following century when, in the reign of King John (1199–1216), the West or Middle Bailey was built, bringing the old hall within the castle precincts. The new bailey enclosed the western end of the secondary plateau on which the whole castle is situated, and terminated in a large octagonal tower, with two smaller semi-circular towers at the junction of the old and new work. At about the same time the latrine block, still standing some 60 ft high, was built against the south face of the keep. Later in the same century John's son, Henry III (1216–1272) began work on the large Outer Bailey to the south-east of the earlier structures. This

reflected thirteenth-century fashion in its regularly spaced
semi-circular towers and its double-towered gatehouses, the Outer
Gate at the south-east end giving access to the whole castle, and the
Middle Gate controlling movement from the Outer to the Middle
Bailey. Henry III's building programme seems to have been
unfinished at his death, and the Outer Gateway, and probably one
or two other parts, were finished by his son, Edward I (1272–1307).
The present ruinous condition of the castle is due in no small part to
the slighting (i.e. rendering it useless for military purposes) which
took place in 1646 during the Civil War. The northern half of the
keep was destroyed then and gaps were blown in the curtain wall,
causing great chunks of masonry to tumble downhill, leaving some
of the towers tipped forward at a very unmilitary angle.

Sherborne Old Castle (ST 648168)

The old castle at Sherborne (to distinguish it from the later
Sherborne Castle which is an Elizabethan house), was built c. 1120
by Roger, Bishop of Salisbury, and has a number of unusual
features. It consists of a keep, with a group of associated buildings,
standing at the centre of a large walled bailey. The bailey is, for its
period, unusually regular in plan and takes the form of a rectangle
(c. 460 by 360 ft) with the four angles cut off so that it is technically
octagonal, although the four main sides (north, south, east and
west) are very much longer than the four intervening sides. There
were five towers on the circuit (at the east and west angles and on
the north wall), three of which formed entrances (south-west,
north-east and north). The north gate was the most elaborate, with
a drawbridge in front, across the outer ditch, approached by a
vaulted passage through the outer bank beyond the ditch. The
arrangement of the internal buildings was also unusual. The original
keep (c. 60 by 40 ft) was later lengthened by about 15 ft, the new
walls being only half the thickness of the original, which were 9 ft
thick. Attached to the keep on the north and east sides is a
rectangular block of two-storey buildings (c. 130 by 100 ft)
surrounding a small courtyard (c. 60 by 50 ft) which forms a sort of
inner bailey. Although parts are destroyed down to their
foundations, the overall plan is reasonably clear, with a hall in the

north range and other domestic offices (kitchens, servants' quarters, storage, chapel, and private accommodation) in the other ranges. This arrangement of keep and courtyard block is probably to be explained on the ground that Sherborne was an ecclesiastical palace, inevitably at this period fortified (hence the curtain wall and keep), but a bishop's residence nonetheless, and this is why it differs from the run-of-the-mill keep-and-bailey castles of the period.

HAMPSHIRE

Christchurch Castle (SZ 160926)
Christchurch is a motte-and-bailey castle with the remains of a rectangular stone keep on the motte. Excavation has revealed a doorway below the present level of the motte summit, so that presumably the keep originally stood on a lower motte, or no motte at all, the existing motte material being heaped against the lower walls of the tower and blocking a doorway in the process. The principal and most interesting remnant of Christchurch is, however, in the bailey, and it consists of the well preserved remains of the medieval hall (i.e. the main dwelling of the castle), built c. 1160. It is of the usual two-storey form with the upper floor, the principal residential accommodation, lit by fine two-light windows with richly carved chevron decoration above. Between two of the windows was a fireplace, and its well-preserved Norman chimney still stands high above the existing walls. A garderobe (latrine) tower was added at the south-east angle in the thirteenth century.

Portchester Castle (SU 625046)
Portchester Castle stands in the north-west angle of a well-preserved Roman fort of the Saxon Shore, built c. AD 300, which was utilized as the Outer Bailey. The Roman fort is almost square in plan (c. 600 by 600 ft.), with a well preserved stone curtain wall and fourteen surviving D-shaped bastions (out of an original total of twenty). The Roman entrances, on the east and

Sherborne Old Castle – the south-west gate-tower

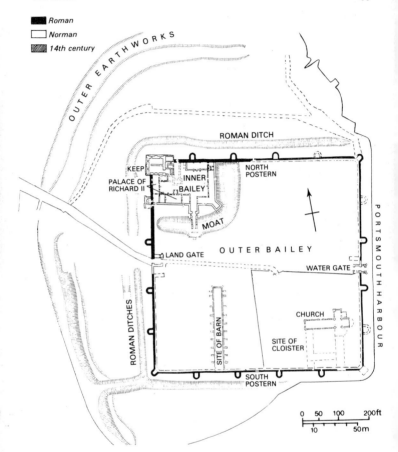

PORTCHESTER

west sides, were destroyed to make way for new Norman entrances
(the Land Gate and the Water Gate), in the form of rectangular
towers with a central, tunnel-shaped, passageway. The main
Norman building work, however, was in the north-west corner of
the Roman fort where an entirely new medieval castle was built c.

Portchester Castle

1120. This was formed by building a new curtain wall on the south
and east and utilizing the existing Roman walls on the north and
west, the resulting enclosure being c. 200 by 135 ft overall. A wide
moat separates the new structure (the Inner Bailey) from the Outer
Bailey formed by the Roman walls. The new curtain wall was plain
except for a rectangular tower at the south-east angle and another in
the south curtain which formed the gatehouse. This was
strengthened on three subsequent occasions (c. 1320, 1385, and
possibly in the seventeenth century) by extending it forwards, more
than doubling its length although at the same time narrowing its
width. The tower at the north-east angle (Assheton's Tower), is a
later addition built by, and ever since named after, a constable of
the castle in the fourteenth century. The courtyard is lined with
stone buildings, mostly of the same period (including much work by
Richard II, 1377–99), although no doubt these replaced earlier
buildings in the same position. The original Norman buildings were
probably of timber.

At the north-west corner of the whole site stands the great

rectangular keep which cuts through the Roman defences, projecting about 12 ft beyond the wall on two sides. The keep is, in fact, of two periods. As first built (c. 1120), it consisted of basement (originally accessible only from the floor above) and a main floor, with a garret or loft in the roof space above. The height of this early keep is indicated by the angle buttresses and (on the north and west faces) the interval buttresses which rise to the top of the original building but which now end a long way below the existing summit. The keep appears to have been increased in height about 1170, some 50 years after it was first built. The garret was converted into a second floor, and a third floor was added on top of that, so that the keep was finally of four storeys including the basement. The existing battlements are of Richard II's time (1377–99). The forebuilding to the east of the keep was built at the same time as the two upper storeys, and contained the chapel and probably accommodation for the chaplain.

ISLE OF WIGHT

Carisbrooke Castle (SZ 488878)

Carisbrooke Castle embraces three fortifications, all of which have visible remains: a late Roman fort (c. AD 300); a medieval castle, built before 1136; and an Elizabethan artillery fort, built between 1587 and 1600. The Roman fort, one of the forts of the Saxon Shore, was nearly square in plan (c. 480 by 450 ft) and much of its outline can be followed in the outer face of its stone wall which is visible in the banks below the medieval walls. It is, in fact, highly probable that the mass of debris formed by the collapse of the Roman walls dictated the line of the later medieval structures. One of the best surviving sections is on the east side at the foot of the motte, where the Roman walling is still up to 5 ft high.

There appears to have been a medieval castle at Carisbrooke as early as 1082, although at this stage it was probably timber-built. The surviving earthworks indicate that it consisted of a motte with two more or less rectangular baileys, east and west, with the motte in the north-east corner of the western one. Early in the following century, and before 1136, the castle was rebuilt in stone, although the rebuilding seems to have been confined to the motte and the west bailey. The motte was surmounted by an oval shell-keep which is still substantially intact, and the west bailey was surrounded by a curtain wall with rectangular towers at the south-east, south-west and (probably) the north-east angles. At the north-east angle the curtain walls ran up the slope of the motte and abutted the shell wall on the west and the south-east. The original Norman angle towers at the south-east and south-west corners were swallowed up in the Elizabethan artillery bastions, but the early remains are still visible. There is now no sign of an angle tower at the north-west corner but it seems unlikely that one did not originally exist there, although it may have been felt that the immediately adjacent gatehouse was close enough to make an angle tower superfluous. The existing gatehouse is of later date (c. 1335), with the upper portions later still (c. 1470), when Anthony Wydville, Lord of the Castle, put his arms above the entrance; presumably the fourteenth-century structure replaced an original gatehouse of the Norman period.

In the Elizabethan period (1558–1603) the whole castle, including the old east bailey, was incorporated in a fortification designed for artillery. It was more or less rectangular in plan with straight curtain walls linking five great angular bastions, four at the angles and an additional one on the west side covering the Elizabethan outer entrance. At the same time the south-east and south-west angle towers of the medieval castle were incorporated in larger stone bastions as mentioned earlier.

WILTSHIRE

Old Sarum Castle (SU 138327)
The site of Old Sarum (i.e. Salisbury) is an ancient one, for the outermost earthwork, within which the later castle stands, was originally an Iron Age hill-fort built in the last few centuries before the Roman conquest. The site (as *Sorbiodunum*) was also important in Roman times, and although few remains have been found, there is clear evidence that four Roman roads converged in the general

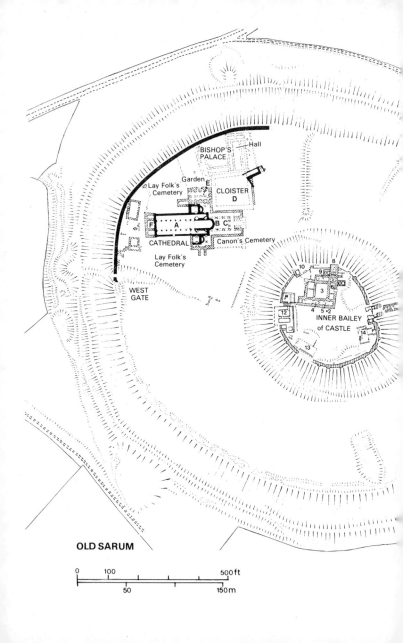

BISHOP'S PALACE

Hall

Garden

Lay Folk's Cemetery

CLOISTER
D

E

F A B C

CATHEDRAL

Canon's Cemetery

Lay Folk's Cemetery

WEST GATE

10   8

9   7

F   3   6

12   4 5 2

INNER BAILEY
of CASTLE

13   14

OLD SARUM

0   100   500 ft

50   150 m

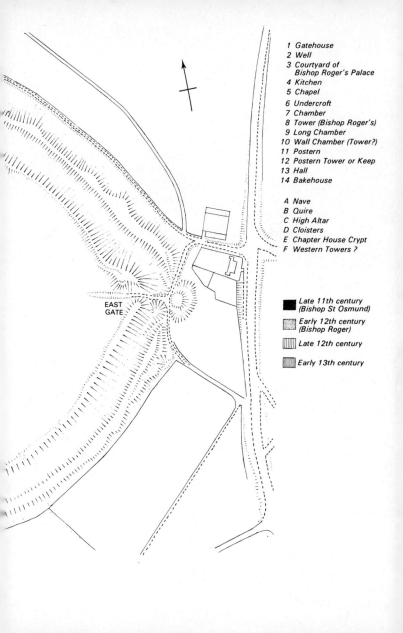

1 Gatehouse
2 Well
3 Courtyard of
   Bishop Roger's Palace
4 Kitchen
5 Chapel
6 Undercroft
7 Chamber
8 Tower (Bishop Roger's)
9 Long Chamber
10 Wall Chamber (Tower?)
11 Postern
12 Postern Tower or Keep
13 Hall
14 Bakehouse

A Nave
B Quire
C High Altar
D Cloisters
E Chapter House Crypt
F Western Towers ?

■ Late 11th century
   (Bishop St Osmund)

▨ Early 12th century
   (Bishop Roger)

▥ Late 12th century

▦ Early 13th century

EAST
GATE

Old Sarum: Bishop Roger's palace

area of the hill. In Saxon times *Searisbyrig* is mentioned both by
Alfred the Great (871–99) and by King Edgar (959–75). After the
Conquest, William disbanded his victorious army at Old Sarum in
1070.

It was thus on a site with a history of well over 1,000 years that a
castle was begun c. 1075. A ring work, c. 300 ft in diameter, was
constructed in the centre of the original earthwork, which thus
became the outer bailey of the castle. At this stage, both inner and
outer rings were probably surmounted by timber palisades. In fact,
only the eastern half of the outer work formed the castle bailey. The
western half was given over to ecclesiastical use, and contained the
original Salisbury Cathedral, the foundations of which have been
cleared for visitors. This went out of use when the existing cathedral
(started in 1220) was built in present-day Salisbury, about a mile
away to the south.

Early in the following century, under Bishop Roger (1107–1139),
the timber work was replaced by stone. A curtain wall was built on
top of the bank around the outer bailey, and another, strengthened
with flat external buttresses, around the inner bailey. The most
interesting aspect of the stone buildings within the inner bailey is

their striking resemblance to those at Sherborne (p 83), another of Bishop Roger's castles. The north-west quarter of the inner bailey is occupied by the remains of a palace or residential block very much on the same lines as the central group of buildings at Sherborne, and of very much the same size: a rectangular courtyard with ranges of buildings on all four sides. At Old Sarum, however, the remains of the keep-like tower (the so-called Postern Tower) are not incorporated in the main block, but stand close by to the south-west, projecting a little beyond the west curtain wall and commanding the postern gate on this side. Apart from the gatehouse on the east side, the other buildings in the inner bailey were a bakehouse and a hall (additional to the one in the courtyard group), probably intended for use by the garrison troops. The northern end of the east range in the courtyard group projected a little through the curtain as a small, strongly built tower, and there was probably another tower on the north-west curtain midway between it and the large Postern Tower, which, as indicated earlier, was probably a keep.

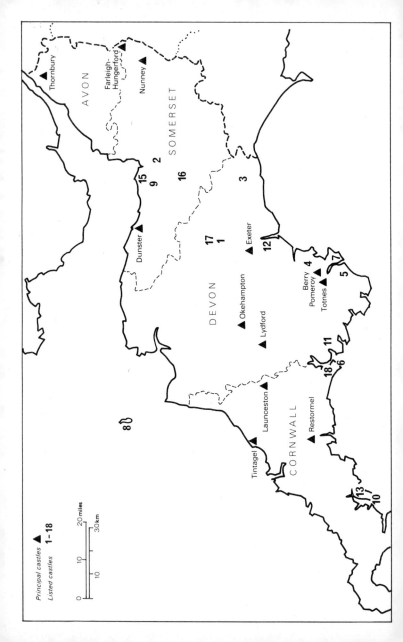

Principal castles ▲
Listed castles 1–18

20 miles
30 km
0   10   10   20

AVON

Thornbury ▲

Farleigh-
Hungerford ▲

Nunney ▲

SOMERSET

2
15   16
9

3

Dunster ▲

17
1
Exeter ▲
12

DEVON

Okehampton ▲
Lydford ▲

Berry 4
Pomeroy ▲
Totnes ▲
5
7

11
6
18

Launceston ▲

8

Tintagel ▲

Restormel ▲

CORNWALL

13
10

3 The South-West

The south-west region embraces the counties of Cornwall, Devon and Somerset. Within this area there are remains of about 30 castles, of which a dozen or so will be dealt with in the main inventory; the remainder will be listed at the end of this introduction. Particularly characteristic of the south-west are the shell-keeps (p 22), of which there are outstanding examples at Restormel, Launceston, Totnes, and Trematon, the latter visible but not accessible to the public. At Launceston the shell wall surrounds a later, circular keep. Because of the predominance of shell-keeps, rectangular keeps are comparatively few in number, the two best surviving examples being Lydford and Okehampton. At Exeter, the main defence is a curtain wall, although the rectangular gate-tower probably acted also as a keep. Curtain walls are also the principal feature at Tintagel, although their irregular plan is the result of exploiting a spectacular coastal promontory site. Thirteenth-century 'Edwardian' castles are represented by Tiverton and Berry Pomeroy, although they are incomplete, parts of both sites being occupied by later buildings. Farleigh Hungerford and Nunney represent the two main fourteenth-century types, courtyard castles and tower-houses respectively. Compton and Powderham, both splendid remains, are fortified manor houses rather than true castles. Five other castles (Dartmouth, Kingswear, Pendennis, St Mawes and Salcombe) built for artillery purposes, belong to the Tudor period (starting 1485) and so fall outside the medieval period. Sites not included in the main inventory are listed below in alphabetical order:

1. Bickleigh (Devon): fine gatehouse, the rest late and fragmentary.
2. Bridgewater (Somerset): built in 1216, but only Water Gate survives (on West Quay).
3. Colcombe (Devon): built in thirteenth century, now mostly in ruins.

4. Compton (Devon): splendid fortified manor house, built in three periods, 1320, 1440 and 1550.

5. Dartmouth (Devon): originally built 1380–90, rebuilt for artillery 1491–1494.

6. Gidleigh (Devon): remains of small rectangular keep.

7. Kingswear (Devon): remains of small rectangular keep.

8. Marisco (Devon): remains of rectangular keep and curtain wall, with outer ditch.

9. Nether Stowey (Somerset): large motte with (excavated) remains of rectangular keep.

10. Pendennis (Cornwall): Henry VIII artillery castle, built 1543.

11. Plympton (Devon): motte-and-bailey, with remains of shell-keep.

12. Powderham (Devon): first built c. 1390, a fortified manor house.

13. St Mawes (Cornwall): Henry VIII artillery castle, built c. 1540.

14. Salcombe (Devon): a round tower, built for artillery.

15. Stogursey (Somerset): remains of shell wall (twelfth century), remains of outer curtain and gatehouse later (late thirteenth/early fourteenth century).

16. Taunton (Somerset): much rebuilt, now houses County Museum.

17. Tiverton (Devon): two angle towers (one round, one rectangular) of thirteenth-century castle, later gatehouse and east range.

18. Trematon (Cornwall): fine shell-keep and other remains, but now part of private house: shell visible from road.

CORNWALL

Launceston Castle (SX 331847)

As a reward for his part in the Conquest, Robert de Mortain, one of William's brothers, received, among other lands, the whole of Cornwall, and chose Launceston as the place to build his castle. The site is distinguished by a very high, steep-sided motte surmounted by an unusual stone structure, a shell-keep with a taller round tower within. There was an extensive bailey to the west and south-west, the curtain wall of which is preserved in places. The original castle, built very soon after the Conquest, was of timber, and was not rebuilt in stone until early in the thirteenth century. A massive oval shell-keep, (c. 85 by 75 ft) with walls 12 ft thick and more than 30 ft high, was then built on top of the motte, and this is still preserved to a considerable height. Access was via a flight of steps (still preserved) up the south side of the motte, originally flanked by the curtain wall of the bailey which ran right up to the shell-keep on this side. At the same time the bailey was walled in stone, still preserved in parts on the south and east sides. Later in the thirteenth century Launceston received the addition which was to give it the unusual profile it bears today. This was probably the work of Richard, Earl of Cornwall, the brother of Henry III (1216–1272). Around 1240 he cleared out whatever buildings there were within the existing shell and built a circular tower, some 35 ft in diameter, at the centre, rising to about twice the height of the shell wall. This structure, of two storeys, was, in effect, a keep with a double shell surrounding its lower room. The narrow space between the shell and the tower was roofed over and provided with a parapet, forming the middle of three fighting platforms. Another was provided at the top of the tower and a third at the foot of the shell wall by means of a wall at the edge of the terrace surrounding it, although virtually nothing of this wall now remains. The visible walling at the upper edge of the motte on the south side is a Victorian reinforcement to prevent erosion of the mound.

Entry to the castle is via either the north or south gates, both leading into the small public park which now occupies the area of the bailey. The South Gate (early thirteenth-century) with flanking

Launceston Castle: the shell-keep and later tower

towers is preserved to first-floor level. In front of it are the parallel
walls of a later barbican. To left and right are remains of the bailey
wall. The fourteenth-century North Gate is on the opposite side of
the bailey. Within the Department of the Environment precinct are
the remains of the east bailey wall, the inner gatehouse, and the
structures surmounting the motte, including the two-storey circular
keep. This is accessible to the top. The staircase rises in the
thickness of the wall. From the gap (originally the doorway) at
first-floor level can be seen the window (opposite) and the fireplace
(right) which served the room at this level. The stairs continue to
rampart-walk level, from which there is a commanding view of the
castle, the town, and the surrounding countryside.

Restormel Castle (SX 104614)

Restormel Castle now consists of a large shell-keep and its surrounding ditch. Virtually all trace of the bailey which originally flanked it to the west has now gone. In spite of its external appearance, the shell-keep does not stand upon a motte. This impression arises from the earth piled against its outer face, prolonging the slope of the ditch. Within the enclosure, however, the shell wall can be seen to stand on the same ground level as the

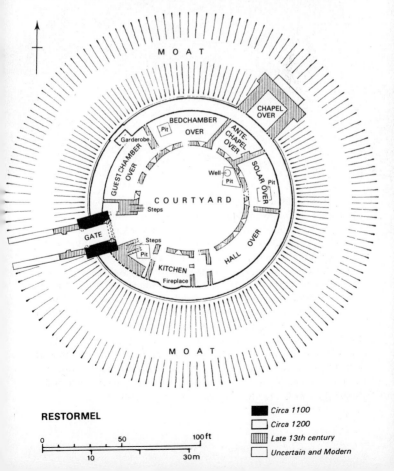

MOAT

CHAPEL OVER

BEDCHAMBER OVER

ANTE-CHAPEL OVER

Garderobe

Pit

GUEST CHAMBER OVER

SOLAR OVER

Well

Pit

Pit

COURTYARD

Steps

GATE

Steps

HALL OVER

Pit

KITCHEN

Fireplace

MOAT

RESTORMEL

| 0 | 50 | 100 ft |

| 10 | 30 m |

■ Circa 1100

□ Circa 1200

▥ Late 13th century

□ Uncertain and Modern

Restormel Castle

general level outside the ditch. There may well have been an earlier
ringwork phase with the bank surmounted by a timber palisade.
When it was decided to rebuild in stone the bank was probably cut
back inside so that the shell wall could stand on solid ground, hence
the appearance of a low motte. The first castle on the site (whether
of earthwork-and-timber or stone) was built by Baldwin Fitz
Turstin, around the year 1100, to command the crossing of the river
Fowey. If it was originally of timber, then it was probably rebuilt in
stone in the first half of the twelfth century.

The shell-keep at Restormel is circular in plan, 125 ft in diameter,
with walls $8\frac{1}{2}$ ft thick, preserved virtually to their original height of
30 ft. There is a small square entrance tower (originally built
c. 1100 and now heavily rebuilt) on the south-west side, and a single
rectangular tower, added late in the thirteenth century, on the
opposite side, projecting beyond the curtain wall and housing the

chapel at first-floor level. The building of this tower was accompanied by an extensive rebuilding of the castle's interior. The range of buildings surrounding the central courtyard (c. 70 ft in diameter) which are such an impressive feature of Restormel, date to this period. They were two storeys high, with the ground floor given over to storage and garrison accommodation, and the upper floor to the greater and lesser halls, the kitchen and the private accommodation of the lord and his family. These buildings completely surround the courtyard except in the entrance area, where there are two flights of steps, to left and right, giving access to the rampart walk where the best view of the interior buildings can be obtained. Judging by fragments of carved stone found on the site, these buildings appear to have been richly decorated. The Black Prince visited Restormel twice after it was rebuilt, and on the second occasion spent Christmas there, in 1362.

Tintagel Castle (SX 050890)
There is inevitably a great deal of legend, mostly Arthurian, connected with Tintagel Castle, and very early dates have been suggested for its construction, long before the Norman Conquest. The earliest part of the existing castle, however, cannot be dated earlier than about the year 1145 when Reginald, Earl of Cornwall and illegitimate son of Henry I (1100–1135), fortified the site for the first time. There are indeed earlier remains around the site on which the castle stands, but they are not military remains. Scattered over the steep slopes of the headland are the remnants of a Celtic monastic settlement, dating from about AD 350–850. It may have been the existence of these structures which led Geoffrey of Monmouth, writing in the mid-twelfth century, to suggest the existence of an earlier castle and a connection with the legendary King Arthur. There is no doubt, however, that the remains of the existing castle are of the twelfth century and later, and can therefore have no possible connection with King Arthur, whether he be a legendary or a historical personage.

Tintagel is very irregular in plan and this irregularity is due almost entirely to the castle's situation on a rugged coastal promontory. The outer part of the promontory is almost, but not quite, cut off

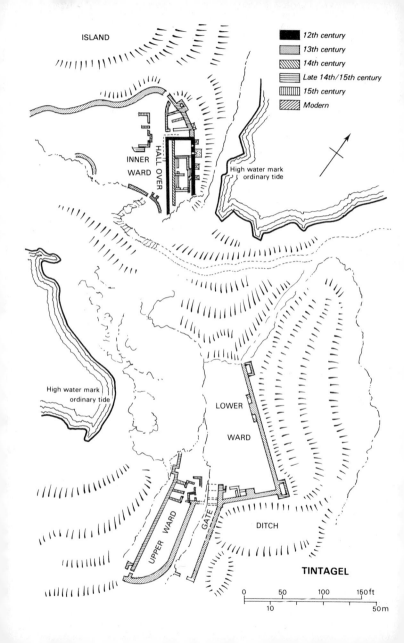

ISLAND

	12th century
	13th century
	14th century
	Late 14th/15th century
	15th century
	Modern

INNER
WARD

HALL OVER

High water mark
ordinary tide

High water mark
ordinary tide

LOWER

WARD

UPPER WARD

GATE

DITCH

TINTAGEL

0   50   100   150 ft

0   10   50 m

from the mainland by a relatively narrow, low-lying isthmus or neck of land. This now separates the two main parts of the castle and is the result of erosion. When the castle was first built, however, the isthmus stood at a much higher level and it was possible to pass directly from the Lower Ward to Inner Ward, two enclosures which are now separated by a deep, 200-ft wide gap. The first castle at Tintagel (built c. 1145) was situated on the isthmus, with the result that not much of it survives. The two principal remnants of this period are the Great Hall in the Inner Ward, and the chapel, which is, in fact, outside the Inner Ward defences, on the summit of the 'island'. However, with the isthmus completely blocked by the castle, the whole of the island could be treated as part of the castle and there may at this time have been no other defences around either hall or chapel.

Apart from the hall and the chapel, most of the existing remains belong to the rebuilding of the castle about a century after its foundation. This was carried out in the years 1235–40 by Henry III's brother, Richard, Earl of Cornwall. The two parts of the new castle (on the mainland and on the 'island') were now linked by a bridge, so presumably the erosion of the isthmus had already begun – unless the gap was deliberately created for defensive purposes. However, if it could be spanned by a bridge, the gap must have been considerably less than it is now. The new arrangement involved a Lower Ward and an Upper Ward on the mainland and an Inner Ward, including the earlier Great Hall, on the 'island'. The castle is approached from the road leading down to the beach from Tintagel village. The final approach to the main gate is along a corridor or passage, c. 100 ft long, formed by the cliff below the Upper Ward on the left, and the remains of a wall on the right, c. 2 ft high. This was originally much higher, probably 10 or 12 ft, and would effectively have constricted any approach to the entrance to a front about 10 ft wide. The remains of the entrance lead into the trapeze-shaped Lower Ward. This has its original walls (c. 1240) on the south and east (now reduced in height), and modern walls on the north and west where erosion has eaten into the enclosure. The lower part of a double flight of steps leading to the rampart walk is preserved against the east curtain wall and there are remains of two rectangular angle towers at the north-east and south-east angles, added in the fourteenth century. From the Lower Ward steps lead up to the Upper Ward which stands on a rocky knoll above and to the west of the entrance corridor mentioned earlier. The thicker, east curtain wall is c. 1240; the thinner, west curtain about a century later.

From the north end of the Lower Ward a modern flight of steps leads down into the deep gap which now divides the two parts of the castle, although this point can also be reached by continuing down the beach road, bypassing the mainland portion of the castle, and turning left into the bottom of the gap. From here another twisting flight of steps leads up to the Inner Ward on the south-eastern side of the 'island'. The wall and entrance at the top of these steps are modern, with the date of 1852 over the doorway. To the right, on entering, are the remains of the hall belonging to the original castle of 1145, still presumably in use in the rebuilt castle of a century later. The outer, east wall of the hall also serves as the curtain wall on this side and is preserved to a height of about 10 ft. It is reinforced with a series of substantial buttresses externally and these are continued round to the north entrance which leads out on to the headland. Beyond the entrance the curtain, rising up a steep slope, is well preserved, although the battlemented upper part is a nineteenth-century restoration. The hall, at first-floor level, was a large one, 36 ft wide and probably, when complete, over 100 ft long. By the early fourteenth century the hall was in ruins, the whole castle having been neglected by its owners for several generations. In 1337 it became the property of the Black Prince, created Duke of Cornwall in that year by his father, Edward III. A new and smaller hall was erected within the ruins of the old one, using the old north and east walls, with new walls on the west and (presumably) the south, where the ends of both halls are missing. The new hall did not apparently last very long, and by the end of the century a third building was erected within the remains of the other two. This was not a hall but a lodging or a small house and contained, among other rooms, a living-room and a bed-chamber, both with fireplaces. This may have been used as the accommodation for important prisoners – one of the uses of Tintagel in the late fourteenth century.

The castle gradually decayed over the next century or two and the linking bridge eventually collapsed, leaving the outer part of the promontory difficult of access. Easier access was re-established in 1852, and the castle was put in DOE (then Ministry of Works) care in 1930 by the Duchy of Cornwall.

DEVON

Berry Pomeroy Castle (SX 838623)
Berry Pomeroy Castle has had only two owners in its long history, dating back to the Conquest in 1066. The de Pomeroys owned it from c. 1066 to 1548, and then sold it to the Seymours who retained possession until recently, when it was placed in the care of the DOE. There are, in fact, two distinct buildings on the site: a medieval castle, the work of the de Pomeroys, and a Tudor mansion, the work of the Seymour family. The existing castle was built around 1300, but cannot be the earliest castle on the site. The first de Pomeroys must have had a castle, and in the early days of

Berry Pomeroy Castle: the gatehouse

the Conquest this would almost certainly have been an earthwork-and-timber structure cutting off the end of the promontory on which the existing buildings stand. The de Pomeroys became a powerful and wealthy family and it seems unlikely that their timber castle was not replaced by a more substantial one of stone, as happened in so many other cases, during the twelfth century. It seems likely, therefore, that there were two earlier castles on the site before the present castle was built, although there is now no trace of these earlier fortifications.

The new castle built by the de Pomeroys around 1300 is inevitably of the Edwardian type, although not all of it is preserved owing to the building of the later mansion. What is preserved is the south curtain and a portion of the west curtain, together with a fine twin-towered gatehouse at the south-west angle, a D-shaped angle tower (St Margaret's Tower) at the south-east angle, and the Western Tower on the surviving portion of the west curtain wall. The walls of the Tudor mansion probably follow the lines of the original castle, so that the plan of the latter was probably rectangular, or at least trapeze-shaped, very much the sort of shape to be expected in an Edwardian castle. There were presumably angle towers similar to St Margaret's Tower at the north-west and north-east angles. The gatehouse towers are semi-hexagonal to the front and the whole structure is preserved virtually to its full height.

In 1548 the de Pomeroys sold the castle to Edward Seymour, Lord Protector of Somerset, and around 1600 his descendants built a fine Tudor mansion in the northern and eastern parts of the existing castle. The main castle gatehouse leads into the courtyard with the best preserved portion of the mansion on the right, and substantial but less complete remains in front, across what would have been the castle's north range. Both castle and house were badly damaged in the Civil War and the whole site was abandoned before the end of the century. Although the roof has gone, the walls of the main part of the house are preserved virtually to their original three-storey height.

Exeter Castle (SX 921929)

Exeter is one of the castles known to have been built within a few years of the Conquest, and was certainly in existence by 1071. It was built in the north angle of the medieval walls which followed the line of the original Roman walls, stones (and possibly original foundations) of which are probably incorporated in it. The castle is roughly rectangular in plan (c. 300 by 300 ft) with the north-west and north-east sides formed by the existing town wall. On the two remaining sides, facing the town, an L-shaped bank and ditch were dug, completing the enclosure. As first built, the bank may have been surmounted by a timber palisade, but by 1138 there was a stone curtain wall on these two sides and this may have existed from the beginning. The curtain walls still stand in places to a considerable height and there are remains of towers at the east and west angles (the latter accessible) where the new walls joined the existing city walls. There are also considerable remains of an interesting gatehouse near the rounded southern angle, facing into the city. This consists of a rectangular tower (c. 24 ft square) projecting in front of the curtain wall, with barbican in front. The ground floor, now blocked, formed the entrance passage and there were originally two rooms above, so that the tower probably acted as a small keep. The first-floor room was lit by two (well preserved) triangular-headed windows and there was another in the room above. These are an Anglo-Saxon type and indicate a persistence of the native tradition, hardly surprising if the tower was built, as seems likely, within a few years of the Conquest. The barbican, most of which is preserved, consists of two walls, linked at the front by a high arch, projecting in front of the gatehouse. From a chamber (not preserved) at the top of the structure missiles could be directed through the machicolations, or apertures in the floor, at the enemy assaulting the entrance.

The interior of the castle is not accessible (except to those on legal business with the courts within), but most of its features can be examined from the outside, from the public park in which the castle and surviving portion of the town wall stand.

Lydford Castle (SX 510848)
Lydford is a motte-and-bailey castle with the motte surmounted by a square stone keep, but this is by no means the earliest fortification

on the site. The first stronghold was an Anglo-Saxon *burh* or fortified town (p 13), erected in the last century or two before the Conquest. Lydford stands on a promontory, and an area of about twenty acres was cut off by a cross-bank and ditch, the remains of which can be seen from the village street by the Nicholls Memorial Hall. Two later fortifications stand within this pre-Conquest earthwork. Some time after 1066 a small area at the end of the promontory (on the other side of the church from the stone castle) was cut off by a well-preserved bank and ditch, no doubt surmounted originally by a timber palisade. Excavation evidence suggests that this was in use for only a short period, probably during the first half of the twelfth century.

The next event was the building of the stone castle, but not the one now visible on the motte. The first stone structure was a square tower (52 by 52 ft) standing on level ground and apparently two storeys (or more) high, since there are no doors at ground level. This seems to have been built in the second half of the twelfth century, presumably replacing the earthwork on the other side of the church. For reasons which cannot now be ascertained, this tower was soon in need of major reconstruction and this took place early in the following century, on somewhat unusual lines. The existing tower was first of all reduced to a single storey. Then a ditch was dug around the site and the earth from it piled against the remaining walls to form a motte of the same height. Finally, the interior of the tower, now below motte level, was filled up to the top so that eventually only the tops of the four walls were visible. On this foundation the existing two-storey tower was built, its walls following the line of the earlier walls. In effect, the Lydford keep is supported by the bottom storey of the earlier tower rather than by the motte. The two towers do not coincide exactly, and the top of the wall of the earlier tower can be seen just above ground level on the south-western side of the later keep. The filling of the earlier tower has now been cleared out, giving the impression of a three-storey tower, but this is misleading. When the existing keep was in use the basement was filled to entrance level and there were

Exeter Castle: the Norman gate-tower

Lydford Castle: the keep

only two storeys above. The motte and keep were accompanied by a
bailey, the substantial earthworks of which survive, running out to
the north-west where the gorge surrounding the promontory
formed the fourth side.

The entrance to the keep is on the north-west side, facing the
bailey. It is subdivided by a cross-wall just to the left of the
entrance, and along the cross-wall is a modern gangway leading to a
modern spiral staircase down to the cleared-out basement, the
lower storey of the original tower. In the thickness of the wall to the
right of the entrance is the original staircase up to the first floor
where the principal apartments were situated. Although all floors
and roof have gone, the interior can be viewed at this level from the
top of the stairs. The larger room on the near side of the cross-wall
(which has a fireplace in it) formed the hall, with more private
quarters in the smaller room beyond. The rooms below probably

provided storage and servant accommodation. Lydford soon lost its military importance and became instead a combined court and prison, with a reputation for somewhat rough justice.

Okehampton Castle (SX 584943)

Okehampton is basically a motte-and-bailey castle, with a fine oval motte surmounted by a double-keep, and a long narrow bailey extending along the ridge to the north-east. Okehampton was one of those castles built within the first 20 years of the Conquest, and at this stage both motte and bailey must have had timber superstructures. This first castle was built by Baldwin Fitz Gilbert, Sheriff of the county of Devon, who had considerable estates in the area. In 1172 the castle ceased to be FitzGilbert property and came into the hands of the de Courtenays who were to hold it for the next 350 years and who were to be responsible for most of the existing stone structures. However, it seems unlikely that the castle remained a timber structure until the de Courtenays acquired it. At some stage, the earlier (western) half of the stone keep on the motte must have replaced whatever timber structures were there originally and this is most likely to have happened during the first half of the twelfth century. At the same time the timber palisade around the bailey might well have been replaced by a stone curtain wall, although not much of the bailey wall survives, either from this period or later. The later, eastern portion of the keep, overlooking the bailey, was not added until the fourteenth century.

The de Courtenay who had first acquired the castle in 1172 had been a local knight, Sir Robert de Courtenay. By the end of the thirteenth century the de Courtenays had considerably enhanced their social position and had become Earls of Devon, and it was the first earl, Hugh (1292–1341) who carried out the major reconstruction of Okehampton which brought it more or less to its present shape. Virtually all the stone buildings in the bailey are the outcome of this reconstruction, and it was probably at or around this time that the eastern extension was added to the keep. Some two centuries later the then Earl of Devon, Henry, was elevated to be Marquis of Exeter (1525), but only thirteen years later he was tried and beheaded for treason (1538). As a result Okehampton

Okehampton Castle

Castle was pulled down and remained in its dismantled state until
the present century. It came into the Ministry of Works' (now
DOE) hands in 1967.

Entry to the castle is via the remains of an outer gate-tower or
barbican. Beyond this are parallel walls leading up the slope of the
ridge to the entrance. These walls are about 100 ft long, 15 ft apart
and originally probably 10 or 12 ft high, and would have constricted
any approach to the main gatehouse, in much the same way as the
wall and parallel cliff at Tintagel (p 101). The main gatehouse leads
into a long, narrow bailey with ranges of buildings on either side,
and virtually all the buildings involved are the result of the
de Courtenay reconstruction mentioned earlier. To the right of the
gatehouse is the hall with a small two-storey section at the far end,
the lower perhaps providing buttery and pantry services, the upper

forming a solar or private withdrawing-room. Beyond the hall, and running up to the foot of the motte, is the kitchen block which, apart from the kitchen itself, included a small yard, a well and probably a bakehouse and a brewhouse as well. To the left of the gatehouse, facing the hall, are the remains of what are termed lodgings. These form a two-storey range with servants' quarters and storage accommodation below and three large rooms above, each equipped with a fireplace and a garderobe or latrine. These would have provided spacious, comfortable, private accommodation for the most important members of the family and household. Beyond the lodgings is the chapel, together with the priest's quarters, and beyond these another smaller kitchen near the foot of the mound again. Thus all domestic services were grouped at one end of the bailey, all the living quarters at the other.

On the motte the original two-storey rectangular keep, on the far (west) side from the bailey, had a two-storey extension added in the fourteenth century, probably during the major reconstruction of the castle. The result was to provide two well-lit first-floor rooms, side by side, each equipped with a fireplace and garderobe. It looks, therefore, in spite of the provision of more comfortable and more convenient accommodation in the bailey, as if the keep remained in use in the fourteenth century, and was indeed added to, although perhaps functioning not so much as a keep but rather as another block of lodgings, similar to those on the south-east side of the bailey.

Totnes Castle (SX 800605)
Totnes is a motte-and-bailey castle surmounted by a very well preserved shell-keep with its rampart walk and crenellations virtually intact. The visible stonework is of early fourteenth-century date, but the original castle goes back to the first days of the Conquest and the history of the site as a whole goes back to Anglo-Saxon times. There was a mint here under King Edgar (959–75), and the medieval town wall (possibly of the thirteenth century) follows the line of the Anglo-Saxon *burh* (a defensive enclosure). After the Conquest, in 1068, Totnes was granted to Judhael, a Breton (rather than a Norman) follower of William, and

Totnes Castle: the shell-keep

it was he who built the first castle, placing the motte just inside the line of the town wall on the north-west and the bailey just beyond. At this stage the motte was surmounted by a wooden tower (c. 20 ft square) on a stone foundation (marked in the grass), the remains of which were discovered by excavation in the 1950s. The site was extensively rebuilt by Reginald de Braose who came into possession of Totnes in 1219. Under his direction the first shell-keep was built on the motte and the bailey was surrounded by a stone curtain wall. By 1273, however, all this work was in ruins, and when the castle eventually came into the hands of the Zouch family (from the Midlands), all the defences had to be rebuilt. The work was completed by 1326 and it is this work which is still visible to-day, in a remarkable state of preservation.

The shell-keep is more or less circular in plan (c. 80 ft in overall diameter), with walls 6½ ft thick and 20 ft high. No trace now remains of any internal buildings which might have once existed. Access to the well preserved ramparts is via two mural staircases, and there is a latrine on the west side. The pear-shaped bailey to the north-west was surrounded by a curtain wall, about a quarter of which, on the west side, is preserved. The remainder follows the original line but is later and thinner. As rebuilt in the early fourteenth century, the ends of the curtain ran up the side of the motte and abutted the shell-keep on the north and west. Originally, however, only the west curtain did this, flanking the flight of steps which provided access to the motte summit. Present-day access is via a curving flight of stone steps which mount the motte from the north-west.

SOMERSET

Dunster Castle (SS 992433)

The earliest castle at Dunster was built within 20 years of the Conquest but, apart from the earthworks, nothing of this early period survives. Much of the existing structure is of the seventeenth to nineteenth centuries, although there are some thirteenth- and fifteenth-century portions. Until its sale just prior to 1950 the castle had had only two owners in its 900 years' history: the de Mohuns, who came over with William the Conqueror, and the Luttrells, who took possession (after purchase) in 1376. The castle is now mainly a castellated house, remodelled by the Victorian architect Anthony Salvin in the years 1868–72, but there are some remains of earlier fortifications. The earliest castle was of the motte-and-bailey type, and the huge motte, a scarped natural hillock, still dominates the site, although it is now surmounted by nothing more menacing than a pleasant garden. Originally there would have been a stout timber palisade around the edge with a timber tower and/or other buildings within. The bailey below, now occupied by the house and remains of the later stone castle, would have been similarly defended. The earliest surviving stone structures are of the thirteenth century, and it seems unlikely that Dunster would have retained its original timber defences for this length of time. There was, presumably, an intervening phase when the timber was replaced by stone, in the twelfth century, as in so many other cases, although no trace of such a replacement now survives. There is no sign of a rectangular keep on the motte, so presumably any rebuilding took the form of replacing the timber palisade with a shell-keep, although it should be emphasized that there is no surviving evidence to support this. However, the motte must have had later defences of some sort, contemporary with the thirteenth-century bailey defences, otherwise it would have formed a very large blind area for the defenders below in the bailey.

The surviving stone structures are concentrated mainly in the entrance area. The castle is entered through an imposing rectangular gatehouse, built in 1420 by Sir Hugh Luttrell, the first

Dunster Castle: the outer gatehouse

Luttrell after the purchase to live in the castle. The coat of arms
over the entrance arches was added by another Sir Hugh Luttrell,
about a century later. This gatehouse was an addition to the existing
thirteenth-century gatehouse and stands at right angles to the
curtain wall. Passing through the archway, the earlier twin-towered
gatehouse is on the right and the space between the two gatehouses
must originally have been enclosed by a curtain wall to prevent the
outer one being by-passed. The inner gatehouse now leads to a
flight of stone steps which lead up to the Green Court. This
arrangement dates to 1765 when the Green Court was formed by
raising the level of the bailey. Originally the inner gatehouse led
directly into the bailey which was surrounded by a curtain wall,
which now acts as a retaining wall to the raised court. To the right of
the gatehouse are the remains of a D-shaped tower. The upper part
of the gatehouse on the courtyard side was remodelled in 1764
when the Green Court was created.

Farleigh Hungerford Castle (ST 801577)
The castle was built by Sir Thomas Hungerford (Speaker of the
House of Commons in 1377), who bought the estate of Farleigh in
1370 and proceeded to build his castle there. In fact, the earliest
building on the site is the Chapel of St Leonard (c. 1350), originally
the parish church, which was incorporated in the castle when the
Outer Court was added early in the fifteenth century. Sir Thomas's
castle was of the Bodiam type, a rectangular courtyard castle (c. 190
by 170 ft) with four circular angle towers and a double-towered
gatehouse. In this case, however, there was a fifth range, containing
the main domestic accommodation, running across the courtyard
from east to west and subdividing it into a small courtyard to the
south and a garden area to the north. The castle was, in effect, a
fortified manor house, and this interpretation is supported by the
comparative thinness of the curtain walls (c. 5 ft). Although the
whole plan is clear, the remains consist mostly of foundations and
low walls. The exceptions are the south-west and south-east towers
which are preserved virtually to their original height.
    This rectangular castle stood as built until about 1425, when Sir
Thomas's son, Sir Walter Hungerford, added the Outer Court

against the south front of the original building. This brought
Farleigh parish church (St Leonard's) within the castle precinct, so
Sir Walter made it his chapel and built the parishioners a new
church (the existing parish church) in its place. The Outer Court,
which more than doubled the size of the castle, was defended by a
polygonal curtain wall with at least two circular angle towers and
two entrances, the one on the south-east in the form of a rectangular
tower. The Hungerford coat of arms above the archway was added
in 1520 by Sir Edward Hungerford. At the same time as the Outer
Court was built, a barbican was added to the front of the inner gate,
so that quite clearly considerations of defence were involved in the
early fifteenth-century additions to the castle.

Nunney Castle (ST 736457)

Nunney Castle is, in fact, a tower-house (above, p 37), built by Sir
John de la Mare in the years following 1373. Sir John was a veteran
of Edward III's French wars, and this no doubt explains why his
castle took the form of a towered keep, a type popular in France at
the time. The tower is still surrounded by a wet moat, 30–40 ft wide,
and it originally stood within a large rectangular bailey (c. 400 ft
square) of earlier date, with a curtain wall on three sides and
Nunney Brook on the fourth.

  The surviving structure consists of a rectangular tower, 80 by 40
ft, with four boldly projecting round towers (c. 30 ft in diameter) at
the four angles. On the shorter sides the wall is reduced to a very
narrow strip between the towers. Internally there were four storeys,
each comprising a large main room and four smaller rooms in the
angle towers. Entry was at ground-floor level, leading into the
kitchen and associated domestic offices. From the right of the
entrance passage a straight staircase in the thickness of the wall led
up to the first floor where the main, central room formed the
common hall. A spiral staircase led up to the Lord's hall on the
second floor, with a solar or more private apartment on the third
floor. On the south side the structure is preserved very nearly to its
full height, although the roof and upper floors have gone. There

Farleigh Hungerford Castle: a circular angle tower

are a number of fine windows and, at the top of the walls, the supports for the continuous machicolated parapet which ran round the whole tower. Within each angle tower is a narrower portion rising one storey higher and originally crowned with a conical roof, as is made clear in a sketch made in 1644 by a Cavalier officer. The finished tower must have looked very French and this no doubt was Sir John's intention, after his years of service in France. Nunney was very much a self-contained, self-sufficient residence in tower form, its independence emphasized by the surrounding moat.

4 East Anglia

The East Anglian region includes the counties of Norfolk, Suffolk, Essex, Lincolnshire, and Cambridgeshire, although remains in the latter county are few and far between. Within this area there are remains of some two dozen castles, of which about half will be dealt with in detail in the main inventory. There are half a dozen castles with rectangular keeps, of which Norwich, Colchester, Castle Rising, and Castle Hedingham are, in their different ways, outstanding examples. There is also a magnificently preserved polygonal keep at Orford and remains of a circular keep, possibly the earliest in Britain, at Buckenham. Shell-keeps are represented by Castle Acre, and by Lincoln and Clare Castles. There are castles without keeps (i.e. relying on curtain walls and towers) at Framlingham, Old Bolingbroke and Hadleigh, and courtyard castles at Baconsthorpe, Gresham and Wingfield. Tattershall is distinguished by its magnificent brick tower, and there is a similar tower at Buckden. The tower at Caister is of unusual type, as is the castle which it accompanies, and both must be attributed to influence from the Rhineland area of Germany. Of the remaining castles, there is only a gatehouse at Mettingham, a long wall with three towers at Claxton, and a pentagonal tower at Dilham. Grimsthorpe is now mainly a Tudor house, but the four angle towers are probably those of a rectangular thirteenth-century Edwardian-type castle. Somerton is of similar date and type.

The castles not included in the main inventory are listed below and shown on the map on p 122.

1. Baconsthorpe (Norfolk): inner and outer gatehouses of late courtyard castle.
2. Buckden Palace (Cambridgeshire): tower-house (1480), closely resembling the one at Tattershall.
3. Buckenham (Norfolk): remains of a circular keep (1145–50), possibly earliest such in England.
4. Bungay (Suffolk): some remains of rectangular keep and twin-towered gatehouses.

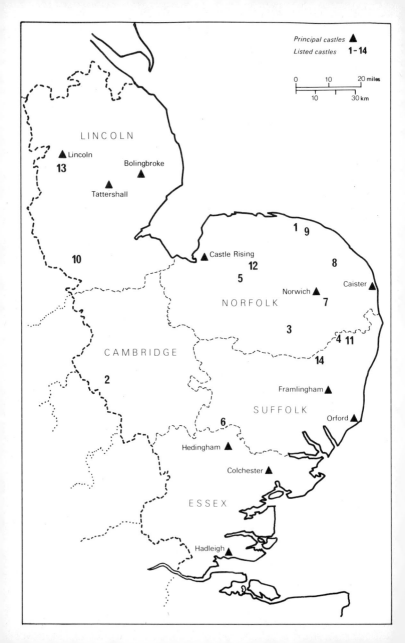

5. Castle Acre (Norfolk): shell-keep (under restoration), remains of walled bailey.
6. Clare (Suffolk): remains of a shell-keep and traces of a bailey wall.
7. Claxton (Norfolk): wall and three towers (brick) of fifteenth-century castle.
8. Dilham (Norfolk): a pentagonal tower and stretch of wall.
9. Gresham (Norfolk): rectangular, fourteenth-century castle, similar to Baconsthorpe.
10. Grimsthorpe (Lincolnshire): now a Tudor house but four angle towers probably of a thirteenth-century castle.
11. Mettingham (Suffolk): a surviving double-towered gatehouse (1342).
12. Mileham (Norfolk): stub of a rectangular keep on top of motte with two baileys.
13. Somerton (Lincolnshire): castle (1281), rectangular with four circular angle towers.
14. Wingfield (Suffolk): gatehouse, with flanking walls and angle towers (1384); house beyond built 1544.

ESSEX

Colchester Castle (TL 998252)

Although in plan it bears a close resemblance to the Tower of London, Colchester was conceived on an even larger scale and was intended to be half as big again. For various reasons it was never finished and the surviving structure consists of the two lower storeys only. It was probably begun in 1071 after the town was burned by the Danes, and appears to have reached its existing extent within William's reign (1066–1087). It was almost certainly intended to have a third storey, as at the Tower, probably with a gallery, so that its planned height should be visualized as being about twice that of the present structure. With a ground plan covering an area c. 170 by 145 ft overall, it would have formed a truly imposing and formidable structure.

The present richly decorated entrance, at ground-floor level in the south wall, is not the original entrance which was in the north wall, at first-floor level. The change was probably made when the plan for a third storey was abandoned and the internal arrangements had to be altered accordingly. The Great Hall now occupied the first floor, on the west side, with the Great Chamber on the east and the chapel, in what was originally planned as the chapel crypt, in the south-east corner, with a large apsidal (semi-circular) projection to the east, as at the Tower of London. As thus planned the Great Hall would have been c. 110 ft long and 55 ft wide, and it seems likely that this was further subdivided by a north-south wall, for which there is some evidence, reducing the span for flooring purposes. It also seems likely that there were smaller rooms at the southern end, west of the chapel. The ground floor, traditionally given over to stores, must now have had to accommodate not only these but also servants, garrison etc., who in other circumstances would have been accommodated on the first floor. Ground and first floor inevitably follow very much the same plan, and the ground floor provides the evidence for the subdivisions suggested above. Externally, the four angle turrets rose above the rest of the two-storey keep, but were reduced to their present height in 1683.

Hadleigh Castle (TQ 811865)

Hadleigh was one of the castles built to strengthen the defences of the Thames estuary towards the end of Edward III's reign (1327–77), when there was a serious threat of French raids and even invasion. The work was begun in 1359, but it was, in fact, a rebuilding of an earlier castle which probably explains its somewhat old-fashioned plan. It consists of a single, polygonal bailey, some 350 ft by 150 ft, with round or half-round towers at the angles. The best preserved parts of the site are the round towers at the north-east and south-east angles which project for three-quarters of their circumference. They are 36 ft in diameter and three storeys in height, with hexagonal interior rooms. On the south-west side of the castle, are the remains of three square towers, probably structures from the earlier castle incorporated in the rebuilding. A landslip has moved the south side of the castle some 40 ft downhill but the main

lines of its layout can still be made out. It seems to have
incorporated the main domestic buildings of the castle.

Hedingham Castle (TL 787359)

Hedingham has a well-preserved, four-storey keep with some fine
windows, and still stands, as far as two of its four angle turrets are
concerned, very nearly to its original height of c. 100 ft. Access is at
first-floor level via a flight of steps along the west wall and a
forebuilding, the lower walls of which are still standing. The upper
walls have gone, but the line of the forebuilding roof can still be
seen in the keep wall above the decorated, round-headed doorway.
This leads into a single rectangular room, c. 37 by 28 ft, within walls
some 12 ft thick. To the left of the doorway, in the north-west angle
turret, a single spiral staircase rises from the basement to the
battlements and is the only means of communication between the
various floors. An arch (now broken) across the middle of the room
provided intermediate support for the storey above. This third
storey housed the Great Hall and has a surrounding gallery in the
thickness of the wall, with its own row of windows, $12\frac{1}{2}$ ft above
floor level. It too was crossed by an arch supporting a fourth storey,
above which are the roof and the battlements.

   The keep stands in the middle of a ringwork and bailey, although,
apart from earthworks, all traces of any outer defences have now
gone. Besides the keep, the ringwork originally contained a hall on
a vaulted basement, a chapel and other buildings. The bailey is now
occupied by a fine Queen Anne house. The keep was built c. 1130
and was well maintained until recent times when a fire damaged
much of the interior (since restored). The exterior was largely
unaffected and the tower is still one of the finest examples of
Norman military architecture.

LINCOLNSHIRE

Lincoln Castle (SK 975718)

Like Lewes (Sussex, p 67) Lincoln Castle has two mottes, one
surmounted by a shell-keep and the other by a rectangular tower.

The first mention of a castle here is as early as 1068, when 166 houses were destroyed to make way for it. Whether the castle then built was of timber or stone is difficult to say, but by the early part of the following century (c. 1115), it was certainly of stone, and a great deal of the stonework is still preserved. Apart from the shell-keep and rectangular tower, there is a complete curtain wall enclosing a sub-rectangular area, c. 500 by 450 ft; two entrances, north-west and east, the latter with later elaborations, and a drum tower at the north-east angle. The curtain wall runs up the sides of the larger motte and abuts the north and south walls of the shell-keep, so that half of it is within the castle and half beyond the curtain wall. The shell-keep is generally oval (actually multangular) in plan (c. 95 by 80 ft), with external pilaster buttresses. Its walls are 8 ft thick and it still stands in places over 20 ft high. The curtain walls also run up the slopes of the smaller motte, at the south-west corner, to abut the rectangular tower (c. 45 by 35 ft) on its summit. This tower, of two storeys, appears to have been built about the same time as the shell-keep (c. 1100). Why two mottes should have been required is difficult to say, unless the castle was intended to house two establishments, each of which required its own final refuge in time of danger.

Old Bolingbroke Castle (TF 349650)

Only the lower walls of Old Bolingbroke Castle remain, but the overall plan is clear. The castle was built by Randulph de Blundeville, Earl of Chester, who also built, around the same time (1220–1230), Beeston Castle (Cheshire, p 167) and Chartley Castle (Staffordshire, p 166). Old Bolingbroke is a curtain-wall-and-tower castle; there is no keep. The plan is an irregular hexagon with projecting D-shaped (in one case semi-octagonal) towers at five of the angles and a double-towered gatehouse at the sixth, linked by curtain walls 13 ft thick. Within the courtyard thus defined (c. 200 by 175 ft) there was a hall against the north-east curtain, and service quarters against the south wall. The future King Henry IV (1399–1413) was born in the castle as Henry Bolingbroke, hence the name of the castle.

Tattershall Castle (TF 211576)

The first castle at Tattershall was built around 1230, but the chief
glory of the site is the great tower, c. 120 ft high, added some 200
years later, and a magnificent example of early English brickwork.
The early castle, of which not much more than foundations remain,
had a polygonal curtain wall with round towers at the angles,
probably very much on the lines of the nearby Bolingbroke Castle
(p 126), which must have been under construction at the same time.
This castle, with only minor changes, remained in use for the next
200 years or so, until the time of Lord Cromwell, High Treasurer of
England, who in the years 1432–45 added the great tower which
now dominates the site. The structure is of the same general shape
as Nunney in Somerset (p 118), a basically rectangular tower with
four boldly projecting angle towers, but the overall effect is rather
different, possibly due to the different building materials used. The
grey stonework of Nunney creates a much sterner impression than
the warm brickwork of Tattershall, which suggests a domestic rather
than a military structure, in spite of its great size and state of
preservation. Internally there is a basement below ground level, and
four storeys above (six in the angle towers). At each floor-level
there is a single large room, with smaller rooms in three of the
towers and a staircase in the fourth, together with a number of
chambers and passages contrived in the thickness of the walls. It is
noticeable that there is no kitchen, buttery, pantry, chapel, etc., and
it is quite clear that Tattershall did not form a self-contained
tower-house in the same way as Nunney or Warkworth. These
services were provided in an adjacent building, now gone, against
which the tower was built. The beam holes for the two-storey link
between the two structures can still be seen above the three
doorways which now open from the courtyard, and such generous
provision of entrances again argues against a military purpose.
These three doorways were, in fact, internal doors originally. The
right-hand door leads into the ground-floor room of the tower
which simply acted as a parlour for the adjacent building. The
middle door leads down to the basement. The left-hand door, in the
angle tower, leads to the spiral staircase which provides access to all
the floors above. The first-floor room was a hall, the second an

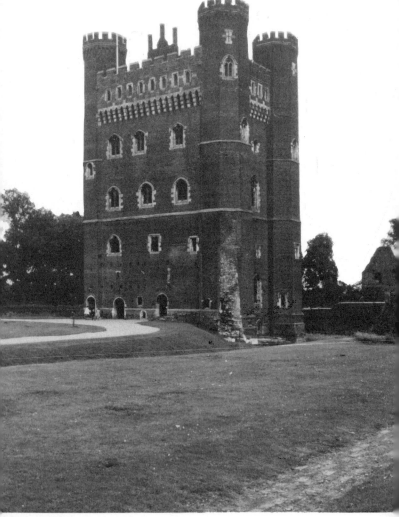

audience chamber, and the third a bed-chamber. This was all spacious domestic accommodation, but it did not constitute a true tower-house. Tattershall tower could never have stood alone, nor was it intended to. It was simply an imposing architectural addition to the existing castle in tower-house form, a splendid showpiece, which indeed it still is today.

NORFOLK

Caister Castle (TG 502120)
Caister Castle has two claims to fame. The first is that it was built by Sir John Fastolf, the original of Shakespeare's Falstaff, and the second that it was built on the lines of a German *Wasserburg* (literally water-castle) of the lower Rhineland area, and as such is virtually unique in this country. Sir John Fastolf was born at Caister in 1378, in a manor house which had been there since the time of Edward I (1272–1307). This was damaged during the Peasants' Revolt of 1381 and its walls may have been utilized to form the eastern forecourt of the later castle. The castle itself was begun in 1432 and was brickbuilt with stone dressings. It was in three sections: main castle, eastern forecourt, and western forecourt, separated by wet moats linked to a moat surrounding the whole structure. The nucleus is a slightly irregular courtyard castle (c. 165 by 145 ft) with eastern and western gatehouses and, at the north-west angle, a slim lofty tower. Beyond the moat (now filled in) on the east side of the courtyard castle is the eastern forecourt (c. 200 by 120 ft), with a curtain wall on three sides (north, east, and south) originally with ranges of internal buildings against them, and round towers at the two angles. The open side of the forecourt faced the castle, and from the middle of this side a bridge with a lifting section led across to the east gatehouse. Access to the forecourt from the exterior was via another bridge on its north side. The western forecourt, now occupied by later buildings, was generally similar, although it provided for access by water rather than land.

Tattershall Castle: the tower-house is a magnificent example of early English brickwork

From it an arched passage gave access to a canal linked to the River Bure, and this seems to have been the means of conveying goods to and from Caister Castle. The plan of the castle, as just outlined, is a most unusual one for England and may represent Sir John's personal taste in military architecture, based on what he had seen and learned abroad during his career. Not the least unusual aspect is the round tower mentioned earlier, some 90 ft high and only 23 ft in diameter, with the attached octagonal stair turret rising to nearly 100 ft. Internally there are five storeys with a single hexagonal room on each floor, four of them equipped with windows and fireplaces, presumably private rooms for members of the family or household. The topmost room had no fireplace and therefore presumably had some other function. The tower, still largely preserved, dominates the remains, as it must once have dominated the original castle, and is accessible to its summit.

Castle Rising (TF 666246)

Castle Rising possesses not only a fine keep but also magnificent earthworks, the latter divided into three sections, east, centre, and west. It was long assumed that the east and west sections belonged to an early, pre-Norman enclosure, cut in two by the Norman ringwork which now occupies the centre of the complex and contains the stone keep. However, recent excavation has confirmed that all three enclosures are Norman: what was built was, in fact, a large oval ringwork, with roughly rectangular baileys to east and west. All the earthworks are large scale, particularly those of the main ringwork where the enclosing bank rises 10 ft above the interior and falls some 30 ft to the bottom of the surrounding ditch. The surviving stonework is confined to the keep (below), the gatehouse, and a short section of curtain wall adjacent to it; there are also remains of an early Norman church already on the site when the castle came to be built. This was evidently the parish church, and a new parish church (the present St Lawrence's) was built to replace it in the village to the north of the castle. The gatehouse is a simple rectangular tower (its upper part gone), with

Caister Castle: the great tower

an entrance passage below and a room above, and was built at the same time as the keep. The surviving portion of curtain wall does not belong to the original castle; it is of late fourteenth-century date but must follow the line of an earlier wall (according to tradition strengthened by three mural towers), also built at the same time as the keep.

The keep itself, with fine decorative detail, particularly in the forebuilding, is unusual in possessing only two main storeys; it is, in consequence, somewhat squat in appearance (c. 50 ft high). It is far less tower-like than most keeps, and is more in the nature of an elaborate first-floor hall (a standard domestic type) than a true keep, although it follows the keep plan and general external appearance. The forebuilding occupies the whole of the east side of the keep, although not to its full height. Its southern portion is a long, enclosed flight of steps rising to first-floor height at the forebuilding proper, a projecting rectangular room immediately in front of the main entrance, acting as a vestibule. The five windows which light this room are original, although they were then unglazed and closed, when necessary, by wooden shutters. From the vestibule a finely decorated doorway led into the Great Hall, but this entrance was blocked by a Tudor fireplace which is still in position. The original vestibule was of only two storeys, but a third storey was added in the early fourteenth century, lit by the topmost row of windows.

Access to the keep itself is now via a small doorway to the right of the blocked entrance, or by a later break through the basement wall at the foot of the forebuilding staircase. Both basement and first floor were divided into two unequal parts by east-west cross-walls in order to reduce the span for flooring purposes. Only at the western end of the north basement (below the kitchens) and the eastern end of the south basement (below the chapel) was there stone vaulting to support the floor above. The main floor was a very compact arrangement of domestic rooms, now open to the sky. The entrance mentioned above led into a corridor which ran up one side of the Great Hall (c. 47 by 23 ft). At the western end were the domestic offices (kitchen and service room). To the south of the cross-wall was the Great Chamber (c. 44 by 16 ft) with a chapel at its eastern

The keep at Castle Rising

end, accessible also from the Great Hall via a vestibule or
ante-chapel. Only in this part of the keep was there a third storey, a
room above the chapel, possibly for the chaplain, reached via a
passage in the east wall from the spiral staircase in the north-east
corner. The same passage provided access to the third storey of the
forebuilding which, as mentioned, earlier was added c. 1300.

Castle Rising was founded in or around 1138 by William de
Albini II (later Earl of Sussex) who in that year married Alice of
Louvain, former Queen and widow of Henry I (1100–1135). His
father, William de Albini I, came over from Normandy in the reign
of William Rufus (1087–1100) and was given the manor of Rising
(among others) by the King. The castle of Rising, built by his son,
was probably an indication of his newly acquired prestige, following
the splendid match with a former Queen of England.

Norwich Castle (TG 232085)

The most striking feature of the keep at Norwich (virtually the only remnant of the castle) is the splendid decorative detail on the external walls, and although the whole surface was refaced in the years 1834–9, the original design seems to have been closely followed. The keep was a large one, c. 95 ft square, with walls 8 ft thick and some 75 ft high, so that in spite of its size its appearance is somewhat squat. Along the east side there was a forebuilding (destroyed in 1824), on the same general lines as Castle Rising with an enclosed flight of steps leading to a projecting vestibule in front of the main entrance at first-floor level. The existing forebuilding is nineteenth-century rebuilding. Internally there were three storeys (basement, entrance level and upper floor), with communication via two spiral staircases, one in the south-west angle and one in the north-east. Unfortunately the whole interior was gutted and refitted as a prison in the eighteenth century, so that not much can be said about the internal arrangements. There was an east-west cross-wall diving the keep into two equal parts, with two stone-vaulted rooms in the south-east quarter. The remaining floors were of timber. There was a chapel in the south-east angle, above one of the vaulted basement rooms, and a mural corridor running around most of the building on the second floor. The building was reroofed in 1894 and now houses a museum. The keep stands on a very large motte which must be largely, if not entirely, natural. There was a castle at Norwich as early as 1075, but at that stage it certainly did not include the existing stone keep, which was probably added in the first half of the following century, possibly by Hugh Bigod, who strengthened the castle in 1136.

SUFFOLK

Framlingham Castle (TM 286637)

Framlingham Castle, built, or rather rebuilt, c. 1190, is an early example of a castle without a keep, and also of one with regularly spaced wall-towers. Towers similarly arranged had first appeared at Dover Castle about 20 years earlier, although there they surrounded one of the last rectangular keeps to be built. At Framlingham there is no such final refuge; all the defence effort is

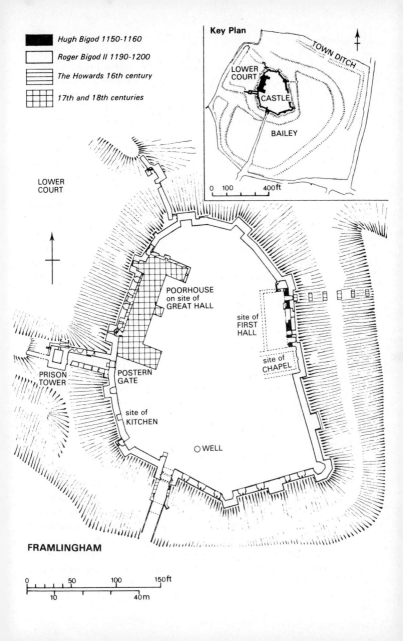

Hugh Bigod 1150–1160

Roger Bigod II 1190–1200

The Howards 16th century

17th and 18th centuries

Key Plan

TOWN DITCH

LOWER
COURT

CASTLE

BAILEY

0   100   400ft

LOWER
COURT

POORHOUSE
on site of
GREAT HALL

site of
FIRST
HALL

site of
CHAPEL

PRISON
TOWER

POSTERN
GATE

site of
KITCHEN

○ WELL

FRAMLINGHAM

0   50   100   150ft

10   40m

concentrated on the high curtain wall and the thirteen regularly
spaced towers. The post-Conquest history of the castle goes back to
c. 1100, although there is a tradition of an Anglo-Saxon fortification
on the site. Early in his reign Henry I (1100–1135) gave
Framlingham to Roger Bigod, who built the first castle. It was
probably of the ringwork-and-bailey type, with the timbered
ringwork following the line of the later stone curtain wall. Whatever
form it took, this first castle was dismantled by the command of
Henry II around 1175, after Hugh Bigod had been involved in a
rebellion against the King. It was Hugh's son, Roger Bigod, second
Earl of Norfolk, who began what was virtually a new castle around
1190, and this is substantially the castle which exists now, although
there are some remnants of the earlier structure.

The stone castle is roughly oval in plan (c. 300 by 250 ft), and
consists essentially of a curtain wall about 40 ft high and 8 ft thick,
and thirteen rectangular towers about 60 ft high. Internally nothing
remains of the contemporary domestic buildings. Against the east
curtain wall are some remnants of the hall of the earlier castle
(including two chimneys), but the remains of the Great Hall, built
for the 1190 castle against the west curtain, now lie beneath, or are
incorporated in, the Poorhouse, built by Pembroke College,
Cambridge, the then owners of the site, in the first half of the
seventeenth century.

One of the larger towers, on the south-west side, houses the
entrance, although the entrance arch and the coat of arms above are
later insertions of the sixteenth century. Most of the remaining
towers are of the open-gorge type, i.e. they have no wall on the side
facing the interior. Towers nos. 3 and 5 (counting the entrance
tower as no. 1 and going anti-clockwise) are solid up to wall-walk
level, but most of the others are open, although the spaces involved
were incorporated in the two-storey buildings which stood against
the curtain wall. Above wall-walk level the open backs of the towers
were originally closed by timber or timber-framed walls. Only one
tower (no. 4) at the south-east angle does not follow the rectangular
plan; the angle is bevelled so that it is five-sided rather than
four-sided. Most of the ornamental brick chimneys on top of the
towers are sixteenth-century additions, many of them built for

Framlingham Castle: the rampart walk

ornament rather than use since a number of them are dummies.

Apart from the section above the almshouse, the whole of the wall-walk is accessible. It is reached via a modern staircase within the almshouse. To the north of the stone castle are the substantial earthworks of the bailey, and part of the associated village enclosure.

Orford Castle (TM 419499)

All that remains of Orford Castle is the keep, but this is a splendid remnant of a once very important castle, and one of the most advanced of its day. It was a royal castle, built by Henry II (1154–1189) to strengthen royal authority in East Anglia where there were already many powerful baronial castles. The medieval Exchequer accounts tell us that the castle was begun in 1165 and completed in 1173, i.e. just a few years before Dover Castle (p 48), Henry's greatest castle undertaking. This is significant, for the bailey wall at Orford (now gone) was equipped with regularly

Section through keep at A-A of plans opposite

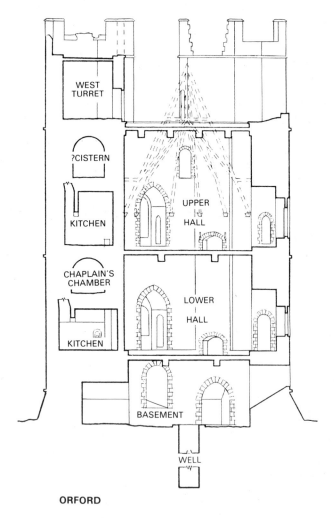

WEST TURRET

?CISTERN

KITCHEN

UPPER HALL

CHAPLAIN'S CHAMBER

LOWER HALL

KITCHEN

BASEMENT

WELL

ORFORD

Floor plans of keep

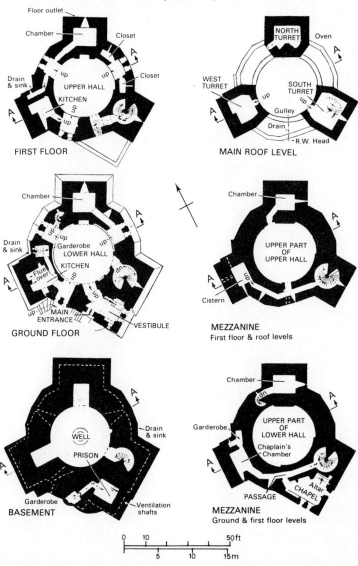

FIRST FLOOR

Floor outlet
Chamber
Closet
Closet
Drain & sink
UPPER HALL
KITCHEN
up
up
up
A
A

MAIN ROOF LEVEL

NORTH TURRET
Oven
WEST TURRET
SOUTH TURRET
Gulley
Drain
R.W. Head
up
A
A

GROUND FLOOR

Chamber
Drain & sink
Garderobe
LOWER HALL
KITCHEN
Fluer over
up
up
up
up
dn
MAIN ENTRANCE
VESTIBULE
A
A

MEZZANINE
First floor & roof levels

Chamber
UPPER PART OF UPPER HALL
Cistern
up
A

BASEMENT

WELL
PRISON
Drain & sink
Garderobe
Ventilation shafts
A
A

MEZZANINE
Ground & first floor levels

Chamber
Garderobe
UPPER PART OF LOWER HALL
Chaplain's Chamber
dn
PASSAGE
Altar
CHAPEL
A
A

0   10   50ft
5   10   15m

spaced rectangular towers which were a very new feature at this period, placing Orford quite clearly in the vanguard of new military architecture in the second half of the twelfth century. The evidence for these vanished features is an illustrated survey of the manor of Sudborne carried out by John Norden in the years 1600–1602.

The surviving structure belongs to that very small group of keeps which are neither round nor rectangular, but polygonal. In fact, Orford has so many sides (20) that it is for all practical purposes circular, and internally it is absolutely circular. The most striking aspect of its external elevation, however, is the three rectangular turrets spaced around its edge which rise some 20 ft above the main structure. The polygonal face of the tower is further obscured by the forebuilding which stands to about half the height of the keep. Internally there are three storeys (including the basement) in the main part of the tower and six storeys (again including the basement) in the turrets. There are two quite separate parts to the basement. The main part is a circular room, 30 ft in diameter with a well at the centre, reached via the spiral staircase in the south turret, and with side chambers in the north and west turrets. This was the main storage area of the castle. Quite separate from this complex was a rectangular prison or dungeon, which could be reached only from the vestibule above. Entry to the castle is via a flight of steps along the south-west side of the keep. These are modern (nineteenth century), but probably follow very closely the lines of the original flight. At the top of the steps is the doorway of the forebuilding, leading into a vestibule from which opens the doorway into the keep proper. This doorway leads into the Lower Hall which probably formed the common hall for the garrison and retainers. Above was the Upper Hall which was probably a somewhat more private apartment for the lord and his family and more intimate followers. These two halls, together with the basement, form the three storeys of the main part of the keep.

There was, however, a great deal of additional accommodation ingeniously contrived in the flanking turrets, in which there were two storeys fitted into each of the central main storeys (Lower and

Orford Castle: the keep

Upper Halls), plus an additional storey above main roof-level, making five in all, and six with the basement. Opening off the Lower Hall was a kitchen in the west turret and a private room in the north turret, with the south turret occupied at all levels by the spiral staircase. The kitchen and the north turret room, however, are only half the height of the Lower Hall, and another room is contrived above each of them, together with a chapel above the vestibule. From the chapel a mural passage led to a chaplain's room above the kitchen, and from the north-west window of the Lower Hall a spiral staircase led to another room in the north turret. This pattern is repeated in the Upper Hall; there is another kitchen in the west turret with a cistern above, reached by another mural passage above the first, together with two more rooms in the north turret. Each turret has an additional room above general roof-level, the south one giving access to the roof from below via the spiral staircase. In all, the Orford keep contained some sixteen rooms (not counting staircases), two of which were large circular rooms about 30 ft in diameter, and one of which was an even larger storage area.

5 South Midlands

The South Midlands region includes the counties of Gloucester, Hereford and Worcester, Warwick, Northampton, Oxford, Buckingham, Bedford and Hertford. Within this area there are remains of about 30 castles, plus fragments of another dozen or so. The outstanding sites are undoubtedly Kenilworth, Warwick, Goodrich and Berkeley. Of these, Kenilworth and Goodrich have rectangular keeps (together with much of later periods of work), while Warwick and Berkeley have shell-keeps (again accompanied by later work). There is another shell-keep at Berkhamsted and a circular keep at Longtown. There are fine twin-towered gatehouses at St Briavel's, Goodrich, Pembridge, Rockingham and Warwick, the latter accompanied by an elaborate barbican. These nine castles will be dealt with again in the main inventory. The remainder will be listed at the end of this section with a few brief notes. They include three sites with shell-keeps (Kilpeck, Waytemore, and Wigmore), two with rectangular keeps (Bennington and Oxford), two with circular keeps (Llancillo and Lyonshall), and two with polygonal keeps (Richard's Castle and Snodhill). The rest are mostly of later periods (from the mid-thirteenth century on), and in many cases are of the courtyard type, although often restored in recent times.

1. Barnwell (Northamptonshire): fine rectangular castle with twin-towered gatehouse. In private grounds.
2. Bennington (Hertfordshire): remains of rectangular keep on a motte.
3. Beverstone (Gloucestershire): substantial remnant of Edwardian castle, rebuilt in fourteenth century.
4. Brampton Bryan (Herefordshire): fine gatehouse of c. 1310. In private grounds.
5. Bronsil (Herefordshire): licensed 1460; rectangular, polygonal angle towers, intermediate towers and gatehouse.
6. Clifford Castle (Herefordshire): early thirteenth century, polygonal plan, angle towers and double-towered gatehouse. On private land.

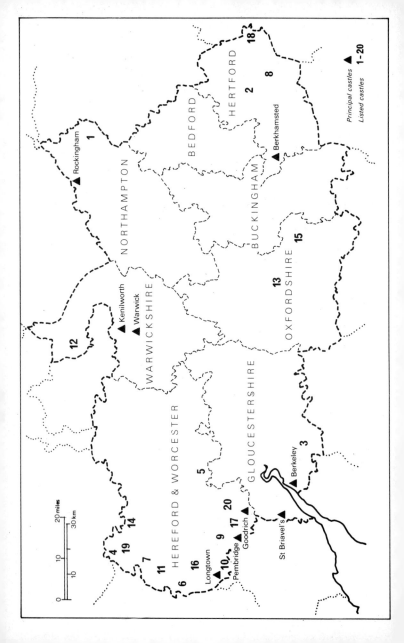

Principal castles ▲ 1 – 20
Listed castles ▲

18

HERTFORD

BEDFORD

2

8

Berkhamsted ▲

BUCKINGHAM

Rockingham ▲ 1

NORTHAMPTON

15

WARWICKSHIRE

13

OXFORDSHIRE

Kenilworth ▲
Warwick ▲

12

HEREFORD & WORCESTER

GLOUCESTERSHIRE

Berkeley ▲ 3

5

20
17

9

Goodrich ▲

St Briavel's ▲

Longtown ▲

Pembridge ▲

19

14

4

7

16

11

6

10

20 miles
30 km
10
10
0

7. Croft (Herefordshire): now a house, but retaining angle towers of rectangular castle of c. 1400.
8. Hertford (Hertfordshire): main remnant a fifteenth-century gatehouse.
9. Kilpeck (herefordshire): remains of a polygonal shell-keep on a motte
10. Llancillo (Herefordshire): remains of a circular keep on a motte.
11. Lyonshall (Herefordshire): circular keep with a stone bailey wall.
12. Maxstoke (Warwickshire): fine courtyard castle (1348). In private grounds.
13. Oxford (Oxfordshire): keep-like tapering tower, four storeys.
14. Richard's Castle (Herefordshire): overgrown motte-and-bailey with stump of octagonal keep on motte.
15. Shirburn (Oxfordshire): fine courtyard castle (1378). In private grounds.
16. Snodhill (Herefordshire): motte-and-bailey with remains of oval, polygonal keep on motte.
17. Thornbury (Avon): ambitious, unfinished courtyard castle, early sixteenth century.
18. Treago (Herefordshire): square, with angle towers, late fifteenth or early sixteenth century.
19. Waytemore (Hertfordshire): motte-and-bailey with remains of shell keep on motte.
20. Wigmore (Herefordshire): shell-keep on motte, with stone-walled bailey.
21. Wilton (Herefordshire): irregular quadrilateral with angle towers and double-towered gatehouse, c. 1300; also Elizabethan work and modern house.

GLOUCESTERSHIRE

Berkeley Castle (ST 684990)

There was a castle at Berkeley within a few years of the Conquest, and certainly before 1071, erected by William fitz Osbern, Earl of Hereford. This was of the motte-and-bailey type and the layout dictated the shape of the stone castle subsequently erected on the site. The first castle almost certainly had a timber superstructure and seems to have survived for nearly a century. Early in Henry II's reign (1154–1189) the manor of Berkeley was granted to Robert fitz Harding, and it was at this time that the castle was remodelled in stone. As at Farnham (p 59), it was decided that the nucleus of the new castle was to be a shell-keep and this was built around the existing motte, the edges of which were cut back to receive it. The height of the motte was lowered and the material spread to form a level surface within the shell, some 20 ft higher than the ground outside. The new shell-keep was c. 130 ft in diameter with walls 60 ft high, with flat pilaster buttresses on the south and west, and probably on the other sides as well, except the south-east, which must always have been masked by a forebuilding. There were also four semi-circular bastions (of which two and the upper part of a third survive), although these seem very early when rectangular towers were still being built at Dover, between 1170 and 1180. It may be that at Berkeley they belong to a late stage in the reconstruction which may have been spread over a number of years and was perhaps still in train c. 1180 when the semi-circular form might be envisaged. Certainly the curtain wall of the bailey was built later than the shell-keep, between the years 1160 and 1190, and appears to have been strengthened with rectangular towers. There was certainly a hall, of which some fragments remain, and presumably other domestic buildings as well, within the bailey. However, some 200 years later most of this early work was swept away when the greater part of the existing castle was built. Thomas III, Lord of Berkeley (1326–1361), remodelled the whole of the interior between 1340 and 1350. The showpiece was, and still is,

Berkeley Castle: the entrance to the hall block

the Great Hall on the south-east side of the bailey, on the site of the earlier hall. The forebuilding to the keep was also rebuilt at this time, but it must have followed the general lines of the earlier structure. Also of the fourteenth century is the Thorpe Tower, straddling the north wall of the keep. The castle was besieged in 1645, and any fourteenth-century buildings within the shell-keep were destroyed then. Apart from that, however, the greater part of the surviving castle represents the major rebuilding carried out in the mid-fourteenth century. The shell-keep is the major surviving remnant of the castle built in the time of Henry II.

St Briavel's Castle (SO 557046)

St Briavel's Castle is in private occupation and the remains can be viewed only from the outside. Since, however, the principal remnant is the double-towered gatehouse (added by Edward I, 1272–1307), which faces on to the road, there is no problem in seeing at least this part of the castle. The gatehouse is a typically Edwardian structure of two large, round-fronted towers linked above the entrance passage, and must have made a very powerful addition to the castle's defences, forming in effect a keep capable of surviving independently of the rest of the castle. The gatehouse was built in the years 1292–3 at the then cost of £477 (probably in the region of £100,000 in modern currency). The pre-Edwardian castle seems to have consisted of a keep, of which little remains, and a plain curtain wall with outer ditch which survives, more or less, around the whole site.

HEREFORD AND WORCESTER

Goodrich Castle (SO 577200)

There are records of a castle here (Godric's castle, hence the present name) as early as 1101–2 but nothing of this now remains. It is possible, however, that the existing rock-cut ditch is an enlarged version of the ditch of the first castle. The earliest surviving structure is the small but fine keep (only c. 30 ft square), built c. 1150, which must originally have stood within a bailey defended (at that time) by a wooden palisade behind the ditch on the south and east and at the head of the natural scarp on the north and west. About 50 years later, c. 1200–1210, the timberwork was replaced by a square, stone curtain wall with towers at the angles, and in this form the castle survived until the last decade or two of the century. The keep is a fairly simple affair of three storeys, with the original entrance at first-floor level later converted to a window, when access was contrived at ground-floor level via a door immediately below. There are original windows at third-storey level in the north and west walls.

Towards the end of the century (c. 1280–1300) a new 'Edwardian' castle was built, sweeping away all earlier remains except the keep, which is still a very prominent feature of the site. The new castle was built by William de Valence, a half-brother of the previous king, Henry III, and therefore the uncle of the reigning king, Edward I. The castle is generally rectangular in plan (c. 150 by 125 ft), not counting the angle towers. There are three of these, circular in plan, standing on square bases with spurs. The fourth angle, at the north-east, is occupied by the gatehouse. Unlike most Edwardian gatehouses, this is not symmetrical in plan. One side is formed by the large, D-shaped chapel tower but the other consists only of a small circular turret (c. 15 ft in diameter) at the end of a thickened section of curtain wall. The external window of the chapel, to the left of the bridge approach, is a fifteenth-century addition, as is the one on the courtyard side. The vaulted entrance passage, c. 55 ft long, originally with a two-leaved door and portcullis at each end, leads into one corner of the courtyard, around which the various buildings of the castle are grouped.

The west side of the courtyard is occupied by the remains of the Great Hall (c. 65 by 27 ft), with associated buildings to north and south, the latter concerned with domestic services. The basement and ground-floor levels of the south-west tower (c. 42 ft in diameter) were closely linked to the Great Hall, the basement probably providing food storage, and the ground floor acting as a buttery (for the service of drink). Between the south-west tower and the surviving keep is the kitchen, with remains of a great fireplace and flanking ovens. The kitchen and Great Hall doors are

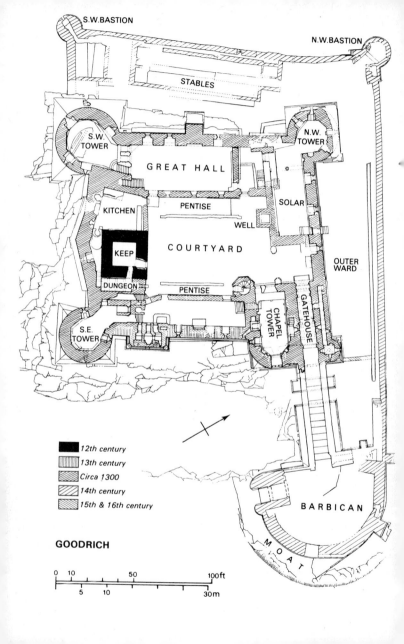

S.W.BASTION

N.W.BASTION

STABLES

S.W. TOWER

N.W. TOWER

GREAT HALL

SOLAR

KITCHEN

PENTISE

WELL

KEEP

COURTYARD

DUNGEON

PENTISE

OUTER WARD

S.E. TOWER

CHAPEL TOWER

GATEHOUSE

12th century
13th century
Circa 1300
14th century
15th & 16th century

BARBICAN

MOAT

GOODRICH

0 10   50   100ft

5   10   30m

immediately adjacent to each other in the south-west angle of the
courtyard. The buildings associated with the Great Hall to the north
formed the more private quarters for the owner of the castle. At
right angles to the Great Hall and separated from it by a lobby or
vestibule is the solar, a room in which the owner and his family
could enjoy a degree of privacy and relaxation not possible in the
communal atmosphere of the larger room. The rooms in the
north-west tower were an extension of the solar and of the
corresponding room below, at the level of the outer ward. There
was a small chapel above the vestibule for the owner's private use,
leaving the larger one in the chapel tower for general use. There was
thus a suite of rooms beyond the Great Hall to the north reserved
for the use of the owner and his family. This leaves only the east
range and the south-east tower to be accounted for, and the most
likely explanation is that this section of the castle provided the
accommodation for the garrison.

Goodrich Castle: the gatehouse

Externally, the most striking features of Goodrich are the great rock-cut ditch, c. 60–70 ft wide and 20–25 ft deep, on the southern and eastern sides, and the barbican in the entrance area. Opposite the gatehouse a U-shaped ditch runs off the outer edge of the main ditch, isolating a D-shaped island which forms a barbican (70 by 50 ft), reached by a bridge (originally a drawbridge) at one angle of the D. The barbican was originally surrounded by a curtain wall and formed an outer defence which had to be taken before the main castle could be approached. From the straight, western side of the D a stepped ramp leads towards the gatehouse, originally interrupted by two lifting bridges, although these gaps are now spanned by stone bridges. The barbican, on generally similar lines to the one built by Edward I in the Tower of London (p 42), was added shortly after the completion of the main castle, probably in the years 1310–1320. At the same time the Outer Ward, added below and to the north and west of the main enclosure, formed, as it were, half a concentric plan. The existence of the large ditch on the south and east made a fully concentric plan impossible, even if one had been desired.

Longtown Castle (SO 321292)

Not much remains of Longtown apart from the circular keep on top of a high mound, and some fragmentary walls. The castle occupies the western half of an earlier, rectangular earthwork of unknown date and purpose; the eastern half of the earthwork lies on the other side of the road from the castle. A substantial motte, c. 175 ft in diameter at the base and some 25–30 ft high, was built over the north-west angle of the earthwork, and on this stands the surviving keep, although it may not be the earliest structure on the summit. A possible mention of the castle in 1187 may be a little too early for a circular keep, and the existing stone building may have been preceded by a timber structure. The keep is a relatively squat affair, some 45 ft in diameter and only a few feet more than that in height. It stands on a high, bulbous plinth and is of two storeys only, with the walls, preserved nearly to their full height, running well above

Longtown Castle: the keep

the original roof line. Internally there were simply two superimposed circular rooms, c. 25 ft in diameter, the lower one the principal room, with three two-light windows and a fireplace; the upper one with a latrine and two loopholes. Externally there were three semi-circular buttresses, one of which (now gone) housed the spiral staircase which rose from entrance level to the battlements. The entrance, also gone, was at the top of the plinth and was reached by a flight of steps continuing those which ran up the side of the mound. Below the mound to the south are remains of the bailey wall and an entrance with two solid, projecting, D-shaped bastions flanking the approach. There is so little accommodation provided by the keep that there must have been buildings in the bailey, although there is now no trace of these to be seen.

Pembridge Castle (SO 448193)
The main lines of Pembridge are those of an Edwardian castle, not unlike Goodrich (p 148) in some ways. The earliest part of the castle is a circular keep, built c. 1200, which now occupies the west angle of the later quadrangular castle. The keep is of four storeys and has a modern parapet, but the rest is original. Presumably it was accompanied by a bailey, but if so this has been obliterated by the Edwardian castle built between 1250 and 1300. Much of the curtain wall of this is preserved, as are the gatehouse (which, like Goodrich, occupies one of the angles), the towers at the north and east angles, and the crypt of the chapel. The site of the hall is now occupied by a house, against the north-west curtain wall, adjacent to the keep. The larder and kitchen (rebuilt in the seventeenth century) formed an L-shape with the hall in the west angle of the courtyard, very much the same arrangement as at Goodrich. Beyond the kitchen is the double-towered gatehouse, and beyond the hall in the other direction is the chapel. There are no remains of the buildings on the north-east and south-east sides, but the solar range must have occupied the north-east, leaving the south-east range, close to the gatehouse, for garrison accommodation. The castle was held for the King in the Civil War, and was besieged in 1644. This probably accounted for much of the ruin which existed before the modern restoration began.

HERTFORDSHIRE

Berkhamsted Castle (SP 995082)

Situated as it is alongside the main railway line into Euston from the north, Berkhamsted is seen by thousands of people every day, even if the view is a fleeting one. The castle was built within 20 years of the Conquest by Robert de Mortain, although his son was subsequently dispossessed for rebellion in 1104. Berkhamsted follows the motte-and-bailey plan, with a wet moat around the whole castle and between the motte and the bailey. On the edge of the ditch is a large counterscarp or outer bank and beyond this, on the north and east, a second bank with platform-like projections on its outer side. This latter is probably a siege-work built when the castle was attacked and taken by Louis of France in 1216, after a fortnight's siege. The well-preserved motte supports the remains of a slightly oval shell-keep, some 60 by 50 ft with walls 8 ft thick. This probably replaced an original timber structure in the years 1155–1180 when there is known to have been considerable expenditure on the castle. About half of the bailey wall is preserved to a height of c. 15 ft, although most of the facing has gone. On it are the remains of three semi-circular towers which were probably built between 1200 and 1214, when again there is known to have been large expenditure on the site. The bailey wall itself may have been started in the earlier period (1155–1180), but those sections housing the D-shaped towers are probably of the later period (1200–1214). Judging by foundations, the north and south gates were simple rectangular towers straddling the curtain wall, with their ground floors taken up by the gate passage. They probably belong to the earlier rebuilding period. Straddling the west curtain wall are the remains of a large keep-like rectangular tower (c. 64 by 48 ft overall, including buttresses, one of them very large), which appears to be later than the wall on which it stands. There are references to the building of a three-storey tower in 1254 (by Richard of Cornwall), and this may be the one involved. It may have been intended as a replacement for the shell-keep on the motte, providing a secure residence half in and, as a means of escape, half out of the bailey.

NORTHAMPTONSHIRE

Rockingham Castle (SP 867914)

A motte-and-bailey castle was built at Rockingham within the first 20 years of the Conquest. The stump of the motte survives, now crowned by an ornamental garden, while the bailey is occupied by a fine Tudor mansion. As a royal castle, money was spent on Rockingham over a long period by Henry II, Henry III and Edward I. It is to the latter that the fine gatehouse, the most substantial medieval remnant, must be ascribed. Between 1280 and 1300 twin D-shaped towers were added to an earlier gatehouse of c. 1200, bringing Rockingham into line with other castles being built from new with twin-towered gatehouses in the later decades of the thirteenth century.

WARWICKSHIRE

Kenilworth Castle (SP 279723)

Kenilworth was built c. 1122 by Geoffrey de Clinton, Treasurer to Henry I (1100–1135). At that stage it was a straightforward motte-and-bailey castle with a timber superstructure. The remains of the motte are now buried beneath the keep, and the original bailey is represented by the existing Inner Bailey, surrounded by later stone buildings. Around the middle of the century the castle was rebuilt in stone, the principal structure being a great keep over the stump of the motte. The result of this is that the first of the two storeys involved is some 20 ft above external ground level, and this can be clearly seen from the north side, where the north wall above the high plinth is missing, removed in 1648 during the Civil War to render the keep useless thereafter. The keep is somewhat unusual in plan, with four massive angle turrets which are large enough to be described as towers. Although their upper portions are now missing, these must have risen to about 100 ft, some 20 ft above the main part of the keep. In spite of their size, the angle turrets are mainly solid structure, with a staircase occupying a small space in the north-east one, and latrines a similar space in the north-west.

The gatehouse at Rockingham Castle

A general view of Kenilworth Castle, with the outer curtain wall and keep

The lower rooms in the south-west turret are a later addition. Access to the keep was originally at second-storey level via a staircase against the west wall, but this was removed late in the fourteenth century when the annexe was added on this side. The existing large windows of the keep are not original. They were inserted in Elizabethan times by Robert Dudley, Earl of Leicester, who carried out extensive building works at the castle.

As built in the twelfth century, the keep was accompanied by a walled bailey, but the wall has been largely, if not entirely, obscured by later buildings. The most notable of these is the palatial Great Hall, built across the west end of the bailey by John of Gaunt late in the fourteenth century. The Hall was at first-floor level above a vaulted undercroft. The floor of the Hall has now gone, but much of the undercroft is preserved and from this, and from the surviving windows on the west side, some impression of the size and magnificence of John of Gaunt's building can be gained. This must have replaced the keep as the main residence, the keep probably then being used for the accommodation of military personnel. Associated with the Great Hall, and of the same date, were the Great Chamber and other apartments occupying the south side of the bailey. The tall block at the south-east angle represents additional accommodation built by the Earl of Leicester during his extensive rebuilding programme in Elizabethan times.

The castle came into Crown hands in 1173, and a great deal of money was expended on it in the reigns of King John (1199–1216) and Henry III (1216–1272). It was in this period that the Outer Bailey was added, together with the extensive water defences, now unfortunately gone. The bailey wall, with irregularly spaced buttresses, is well preserved on three sides (west, south and east); virtually the whole of the north side has gone, except for Leicester's Gatehouse which is another Elizabethan addition. On the whole of this long circuit (c. 2,300 ft) there were only three towers: Lunn's Tower at the north-east angle, the Water Tower at the south-east, and Swan Tower at the north-west. The first two are well preserved, but Swan Tower is now in ruins.

The main entrance to the castle was on the south side (Mortimer's Gate), and the approach to it was through the water defences which

were such an important part of Kenilworth's security. The entrance
(now in ruins) consists of an earlier rectangular gate-tower in front
of which a double towered gatehouse had been added, probably in
the first half of the thirteenth century. The approach to the entrance
is along a causeway which, together with the outer bailey wall,
originally formed a dam across the small valley in which the castle
stood, blocking the stream which flows through it. The result was
the creation of an artificial lake (the Great Lake), stretching away
to the west for about three-quarters of a mile, and providing a very
effective defence on the south and west sides of the castle, which
probably explains why there are no wall towers on these sides. The
water was also led into a double ditch on the north side, and into a
pool on the other side of the causeway, so that the castle was very
effectively protected by water. The castle was subjected to a long
(six-month) siege in 1266 during the Barons' War and in the end
surrendered only because of disease and starvation. The failure of
the attackers to overcome Kenilworth by force must have been due
in no small part to its elaborate water defences, completed only a
decade or two earlier. Indeed the water defences stimulated a novel
form of attack for an inland castle: a naval assault across the lake by
barges brought from Chester. But this, like the other forms of
attack, was unsuccessful.

The main structural events in the later history of the castle have
been mentioned already, involving mainly work by John of Gaunt
c. 1390, and by Robert Dudley, Earl of Leicester, in Elizabeth's
time (1558–1603). After slighting the castle in 1648, Colonel
Hawkesworth, a Roundhead officer, blocked up the entrance
passage in Leicester's Gatehouse and converted it into a dwelling
house for himself, this forming the final phase in the occupation of
Kenilworth Castle.

Warwick Castle (SP 283647)
Although most of the existing structure of Warwick is of the
fourteenth century or later, the original castle goes back to the very
earliest days of the Conquest. It was first built in 1068 and was
given by the king to Henry de Beaumont. Although not much of this
early castle now remains, its motte-and-bailey plan is clearly evident

in the layout of the existing castle. The motte, c. 250 ft in diameter, still stands at the western end of the castle, surmounted by the remains of an octagonal shell-keep. The probability is that the earliest structures were of timber and that the octagonal shell was their replacement, possibly early in the following century. The existing, generally rectangular bailey (c. 400 by 300 ft) may represent the original bailey, although it is not unlikely that the latter was extended eastwards when it was rebuilt in the fourteenth century. At this stage it was surrounded by a wide dry moat on three sides and by the River Avon on the fourth (south) side.

Warwick Castle owes its present appearance to the large-scale reconstruction started by Thomas Beauchamp, Earl of Warwick, in the second half of the fourteenth century. The work was still in progress when he died in 1369, and was eventually brought to completion by his son in 1394. The reconstruction was on a monumental scale, not least on the east front which is the great *tour de force* of Warwick Castle. The tall central gatehouse, fronted by a barbican, is flanked at the angles by two lofty towers, Guy's Tower, and Caesar's Tower, two of the largest and best preserved towers in the British Isles.

The main entrance to the castle is via a stone bridge, replacing an original drawbridge, on the east front, leading into the great fourteenth-century gatehouse. The outer part of this, about half the height of the gatehouse proper, is a barbican or outer entrance, which projects forward into the ditch. The entrance passage runs between two semi-octagonal towers, three storeys in height. Although their ground floors can be entered from the passage, their two upper storeys and the battlements can be reached only via a long sloping passage which starts inside the bailey, in the angle between the curtain wall and the south side of the gatehouse. This meant that even if an attacker carried the outer entrance he would still be confined to the ground floor. There was no immediate access to the upper floor and battlements without capturing the gatehouse proper and entering the bailey. On the inner side of the barbican, at first-floor level, was a gallery or balcony overlooking the middle section of the passage, from which attackers who had managed to get through the barbican could be assailed from the rear. Although

there is now no sign of it, this middle section of the passage, open to
the sky, almost certainly included another drawbridge in front of the
gatehouse proper and between the walls linking the latter to the
barbican. From the battlements at the top of these walls the enemy
could again be assailed as he attempted to fight his way towards the
inner entrance. The gatehouse proper (c. 70 ft high) is twice the
height of the barbican and the linking walls. It is generally
rectangular in plan with four angle towers, no two of which are
exactly alike. The towers are of five storeys and the rectangular
central block is of four. Access to the upper floors is via a staircase
entered from the south side of the inner entrance passage.

Having passed through the gatehouse, the visitor emerges into
the bailey or courtyard with the original motte at the far end and the
two great angle towers immediately to left and right. Caesar's
Tower to the left, at the south-east angle, is 85 ft high above internal

The hall block at Warwick Castle, seen from Guy's Tower

ground level and 133 ft high externally from the bottom of the
massive plinth on which it stands. It is tri-lobed in plan. Two tiers of
battlements at the top give the tower a very distinctive outline.
Within there are six storeys, the lowest, below the courtyard level,
forming a prison. The three storeys above it provided three suites of
apartments, each consisting of a main room (c. 20 by 15 ft) with two
windows and a fireplace, another chamber in the thickness of one
wall, and a latrine in the thickness of the opposite wall. Such suites
of rooms were part of a general trend in the fourteenth century to
provide more private accommodation for members of the family
and household. The two remaining storeys of the tower acted as a
guardroom and an ammunition store.

Guy's Tower, at the opposite end of the east front, is simpler in
plan and profile but no less massive than Caesar's Tower. It too
provided additional accommodation (four suites), and on a larger
scale. Apart from a guardroom in the top storey, the other four
storeys each consist of a main room (20 by 18 ft), with a mural
chamber in one wall and a latrine in the other. From the top of
Guy's Tower, as indeed from the top of Caesar's Tower and the
main gatehouse, there are splendid views over the town of Warwick
and the surrounding countryside.

Apart from the east-front group, the other major fourteenth-
century addition was the great suite of rooms, including the Great
Hall, built against the south curtain which is pierced by numerous
windows overlooking the River Avon. Although added to and
refurbished in modern times, this is still substantially the handsome
residential block added to the castle at the same time as Guy's and
Caesar's Towers and the gatehouse, and again is indicative of the
higher standards of comfort, convenience and privacy called for in
the late fourteenth century. There are two subsequent additions to
be noted. In the middle of the north curtain wall there is a squat
rectangular tower with two octagonal towers at its outer angles, and
with two more planned for the angles within the curtain, although
the structure was apparently never finished. It was designed for
artillery (hence the low elevation), and was begun by Richard III
(1483–5). In the following century the twin-towered Water Gate
was built on the south-western side, between the motte and the

great fourteenth-century residential block. Like its near neighbour, Kenilworth, the structures at Warwick cover the whole span of English medieval fortification, from 1066 to 1485 and beyond.

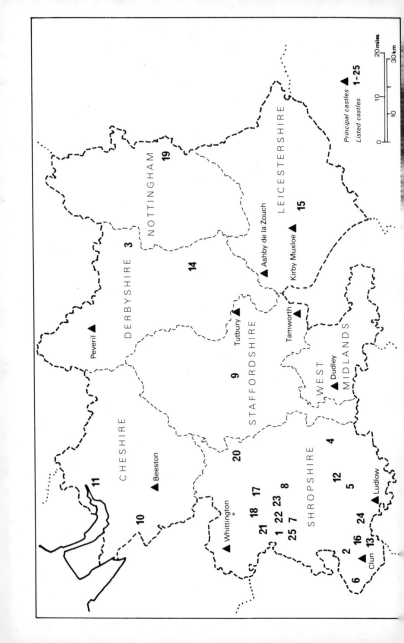

CHESHIRE

DERBYSHIRE 3

NOTTINGHAM 19

LEICESTERSHIRE

▲ Peveril

▲ Beeston

▲ Tutbury

Ashby de la Zouch ▲

14

9

Kirby Muxloe ▲ 15

STAFFORDSHIRE

Tamworth ▲

20

WEST

MIDLANDS

▲ Dudley

11

10

▲ Whittington

18 17

21

1 22 23 8

25 7

SHROPSHIRE

4

12

5

▲ Ludlow

2

6

16

24

13

Clun ▲

Principal castles   1-25 ▲
Listed castles   ▲

20 miles
30 km

10

10

6   North Midlands

The North Midlands region includes the following counties: Cheshire, Derbyshire, Leicestershire, Nottinghamshire, Shropshire and Staffordshire. Within the area covered by these six counties there are remains of about three dozen castles, many of them concentrated in the sensitive border area of Shropshire. Of this total, ten will be dealt with in the main inventory: Beeston in Cheshire; Peveril in Derbyshire; Ashby de la Zouch and Kirby Muxloe in Leicestershire; Clun, Ludlow, and Whittington in Shropshire; and Dudley, Tamworth, and Tutbury in Staffordshire. The rest will be listed at the end of this section and shown on the map opposite.

The Norman period is well represented, with a dozen rectangular keeps, including four (Clun, Ludlow, Whittington in Shropshire, and Peveril in Derbyshire) in the main inventory. The Whittington keep is now represented only by foundations but is surrounded by the remains of a later castle. Of the remaining keeps (Alberbury, Bridgnorth, Hopton, Horston, Moreton Corbet, Ruyton, Shrawardine and Wattlesborough), some are represented only by fragments. The most complete tower is Hopton which, although generally Norman in appearance, is in fact of fourteenth-century date. There is a circular keep on a motte at Chartley and foundations of another at Bryn Amlwg, among the listed sites. Shell-keeps are represented principally by Tamworth, although there was originally a shell-keep at Tutbury also. Listed sites with shell-keeps include Bolsover, Caus, and Lower Down.

The remaining sites in the inventory include one of the earliest tower-houses (Dudley, 1320) and one of the latest (Ashby de la Zouch, 1474). The two main towers at Tutbury (mentioned earlier in connection with its destroyed shell-keep), are also of the tower-house type and, like the rest of the existing stone castle, belong to the early fifteenth century. Beeston represents the concept of the early thirteenth-century keepless castle where reliance was placed on curtain walls, towers, and double-towered gatehouses, while Kirby Muxloe provides an example of the late medieval courtyard castle (1480–84), still surrounded by a wet moat, and also of the use of brick instead of stone, so long the material for castle building. Brief details of the listed sites are given below:

1. Alberbury (Shropshire): oblong keep, polygonal curtain wall.
2. Bishop's Castle (Shropshire): motte-and-bailey, fragmentary stone remains.
3. Bolsover (Derbyshire): oval wall around Jacobean tower is an original shell-keep.
4. Bridgnorth (Shropshire): remains of square keep and forebuilding.
5. Broncroft (Shropshire): small, square-towered rectangular castle, modernized in nineteenth century, now a private house.
6. Bryn Amlwg (Shropshire): foundations of round keep, towers and twin-towered gatehouse.
7. Caus (Shropshire): Motte-and-bailey, remains of shell-keep on motte and curtain wall around bailey.
8. Carlton (Shropshire): slight remains of a rectangular stone castle with surrounding moat.
9. Chartley (Staffordshire): remains of round keep on motte, and walled bailey.
10. Chester (Cheshire): original motte-and-bailey castle, principal stone remnant, the Agricola Tower.
11. Halton (Cheshire): fragments of thirteenth/fourteenth century castle on rocky knoll.
12. Holgate (Shropshire): foundations of rectangular building on motte, round tower in bailey.
13. Hopton (Shropshire): well preserved keep-like tower of twelfth-century type but probably of fourteenth-century date.
14. Horston (Derbyshire): remnants of a rectangular keep.
15. Leicester (Leicestershire): two gateways survive.
16. Lower Down (Shropshire): remains of a shell-keep on damaged motte.
17. Moreton Corbet (Shropshire): remains of rectangular keep, a gatehouse, and an Elizabethan range.

18. Myddle (Shropshire): fragments of fourteenth-century castle within square moat.
19. Newark (Nottinghamshire): fine Norman gatehouse on north, curtain wall and towers on west overlooking Trent.
20. Red Castle (Shropshire): fragmentary remains of thirteenth-century castle, four round towers, one square.
21. Ruyton (Shropshire): fragments of a square keep.
22. Shrawardine (Shropshire): motte-and-bailey, remains of square keep on motte.
23. Shrewsbury (Shropshire): motte-and-bailey, principal remains are a hall between two thirteenth-century round towers.
24. Stokesay (Shropshire): picturesque fortified manor house, two towers.
25. Wattlesborough (Shropshire): small square Norman keep and later domestic block.

CHESHIRE

Beeston Castle (SJ 538594)

Beeston Castle, built c. 1220, is one of the early examples of a castle without a keep. Its defence apparatus consists of two curtain walls, each strengthened by interval towers and a gatehouse. The castle occupies a magnificent position on an isolated hill rising high above the Cheshire plain, with a precipitous cliff below the curtain wall on the northern and western sides. Beeston was built by Randulph de Blundeville, Earl of Chester, on his return from a Crusade in 1220. The Earl was also the builder of Chartley Castle (p 166) and (probably) Bolingbroke Castle (p 126). From the foot of the hill a path, partly rock-cut, leads steeply upwards to the outer gatehouse at the eastern end of the castle. This has been destroyed virtually down to its foundations but its plan is clear: twin round-fronted towers with the entrance passage between. The square tower immediately to the south (left side) is a latrine tower added later to serve the needs of the garrison manning the outer gate. The outer gatehouse gives access to a large outer bailey (c. 800 by 500 ft) although this consists almost entirely of natural hill slope. The bailey was originally surrounded by a curtain wall some 2,200 ft long, of which about 750 ft survive, although not to any great height. At regular intervals there were open-backed, D-shaped towers, a series of which can be seen beyond the square tower along the southern and south-eastern sides.

Beyond the gatehouse the path continues upwards to the inner bailey, the nucleus of the castle on the highest part of the hill. The outer defence of the inner bailey is a great rock-cut ditch on the southern and eastern sides, with the precipitous cliff mentioned earlier defending the two remaining sides. Until a few years ago there was no public access to the inner bailey, but recently the Department of the Environment has built a new concrete footbridge across the ditch. The footbridge leads into the inner gatehouse, midway along the south curtain wall. It consists of two D-shaped towers, linked at first-floor level above the vaulted entrance passage. East and west of the gatehouse are two more D-shaped towers, and there is a third rectangular tower on the short eastern side. There are no wall-towers on the northern and western sides, a plain curtain wall understandably being considered sufficient above the precipitous cliff. In the absence of a keep the castle's accommodation must have been provided, first of all, by the gatehouse which was of keep-like dimensions (70 by 50 ft), although with fewer floors. In addition to the gatehouse, however, there were three towers, one of which at least was of keep-like proportions. These three towers, on their several floors, must have more than made up for any shortfall of accommodation occasioned by the absence of a keep.

The history of the castle was fairly uneventful. The Blundeville line died out in 1237 and the castle was taken into Crown service by Henry III. Edward I (1272–1307) did some work here, as part of his campaigns in North Wales. In the Civil War the castle was seized by the Royalists and held until November 1645 when the defenders surrendered with military honours. The imposing castle visible on the adjacent hill is Peckforton, built on medieval lines by the famous Victorian architect Anthony Salvin.

Beeston Castle: the gatehouse

DERBYSHIRE

Peveril Castle (SK 148826)

As it now stands, Peveril is an example of the very simple
keep-and-bailey type of castle, but in fact, as originally built late in
the eleventh century, Peveril was even simpler, for the keep was a
later addition. The first Peveril Castle was simply enclosed by a
plain curtain wall. There was a castle on the site by 1086, and as
there is no sign of earthwork (and, by implication, timber), it must
have been stone-built from the beginning. There are, indeed,
sections of herringbone masonry, a typical early Norman feature, in
the curtain wall and these suggest a date late in the eleventh or early
in the twelfth century. After the Conquest in 1066 William I made
William Peverel, a trusted knight, bailiff of the royal manors in
north-west Derbyshire. At the same time he was probably given
Peveril Castle by the King, for in the early days of the Conquest
virtually all castles were royal. Only later were the barons able to
build castles for themselves. The castle remained in the Peverel
family until 1155 when William (the younger) was disinherited for
poisoning the Earl of Chester. The castle then reverted to the
Crown and the King, Henry II (1154–1189), spent considerable
sums on it, including £135 towards the erection of the keep in 1175.
Henry himself stayed in the castle in 1157, 1158, and 1164, so that
in spite of the present bare and bleak appearance of the place, it
must then have boasted a degree of comfort sufficient to satisfy a
king. Other kings who stayed there included Henry III (in 1235)
and Edward III (in 1331).

The castle is approached from the north up a very steep path from
the village of Castleton, the final section of which slopes diagonally
upwards below the north rampart, to end at the entrance in the
north-east angle of the castle. Not much of this now remains, but
there is enough to indicate that the entrance was a decorated
semi-circular arch about 10 ft wide, no doubt originally closed by a
two-leaved door. This entrance appears to be an addition,
subsequent to the building of the north curtain wall. About 50 ft

Peveril Castle: the keep

along the north curtain wall to the west is a rectangular turret which likewise appears to have been added after the main wall was built, probably to command the final approach to the entrance. The north curtain, although much repaired and rebuilt, is substantially the original rampart of the late eleventh century, and together with two internal structures (below) forms the oldest part of the castle. The curtain wall on the two remaining sides (west and south-east) is later (early twelfth century), although very little remains on the south-eastern side. There are, however, in this section traces of two round towers added in the early thirteenth century.

The rectangular keep straddling the curtain wall was added in Henry II's time (1154–1189). Although quite small (c. 38 ft square) and of only two storeys, it had all the features associated with keeps of this period – pilaster buttresses (mid-wall and at the angles) rising to form angle turrets. It stands nearly to its full height. Access was at first floor level, probably via a wooden stairway; the ground floor was reached from above via a spiral stairway in the east angle turret and must have been used mainly for storage. The main room above was not very large, c. 20 by 18 ft, and probably did not provide permanent accommodation. It may have been reserved for use in time of extreme danger when the rest of the castle was threatened with disaster.

There are traces of more spacious accommodation in the north-west angle of the bailey, where there are the remains of a large hall of the early thirteenth century, with indications of a kitchen, buttery and pantry at the eastern end, and of private withdrawing-rooms at the western end and along the west curtain wall. This hall probably replaced an earlier hall and a chapel of the eleventh century, the remains of which are on the north-eastern side of the castle, near the cliff edge and the original south-east curtain wall.

LEICESTERSHIRE

Ashby de la Zouch Castle (SK 362166)

The same Lord Hastings who started, but did not complete, Kirby
Muxloe also built the great tower at Ashby de la Zouch which he
started in 1474 and, in fact, completed before his death. Although
the tower, or tower-house, was an addition, it was an addition to an
existing manor house rather than a castle. The manor house was
originally built in the twelfth century and rebuilt in the fourteenth,
and it is the stone-built fourteenth-century remains which now form
much of the site. Lord Hastings surrounded the whole of the
existing structure with a high curtain wall, and in the middle of the
south front he placed the tower-house which, in spite of its partial
destruction in 1648 during the Civil War, still dominates the site.
About half the tower has fallen away, but this does enable a view to
be gained of the internal arrangement.

The tower is (or was, when complete) rectangular in plan (48 by
41 ft), with a projecting square wing on the east side. It was
originally 90 ft high and is, in fact, only a little short of that today.
At the top there was a machicolated parapet and at the angles of the
two upper storeys were projecting octagonal turrets, richly
decorated. The whole tower was a handsome architectural
composition. Internally there were four storeys in the main tower
and seven in the square wing. Access was at ground-floor level via a
doorway protected by a portcullis, and this led into a vaulted
storeroom. The next room above, also vaulted, was a large kitchen.
Above the kitchen were the main living-room, the hall, and on the
top floor the great chamber, a more private withdrawing-room for
the family. There was a small chapel off the hall in the north-west
turret, and there were, of course, additional rooms in the
seven-storey east wing.

Kirby Muxloe Castle (SK 524046)

Kirby Muxloe belongs to a small group of English castles built of
brick with stone dressings, rather than entirely of stone. It was a
very late castle, started in 1480, and was never, in fact, completed.
Its builder was the politically ambitious first Lord Hastings, but

Ashby de la Zouch Castle: the tower-house

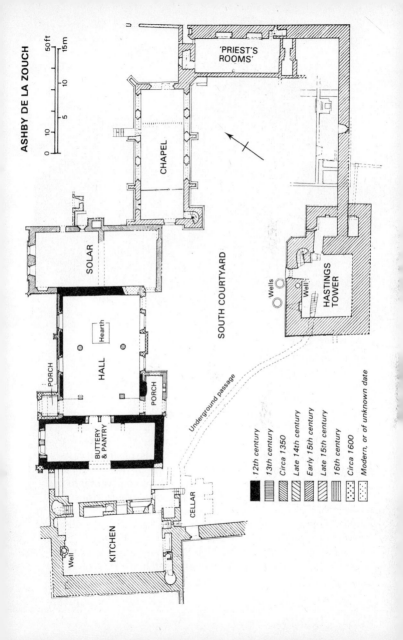

ASHBY DE LA ZOUCH

'PRIEST'S ROOMS'

CHAPEL

SOLAR

HALL

Hearth

PORCH

PORCH

BUTTERY & PANTRY

KITCHEN

Well

CELLAR

SOUTH COURTYARD

Underground passage

Wells

Well

HASTINGS TOWER

12th century
13th century
Circa 1350
Late 14th century
Early 15th century
Late 15th century
16th century
Circa 1600
Modern, or of unknown date

50ft

15m

10

10

5

10

0

Kirby Muxloe Castle: the gatehouse and moat

after his sudden fall from grace, and his execution by Richard III in
1483 work on the castle soon came to an end. Apart from
foundations, all that now remain are the gatehouse and the
south-west angle tower. However, the foundations are sufficiently
clear to illustrate the intended plan: a rectangular courtyard castle,
c. 250 by 200 ft, standing within a still surviving wet moat, c. 350 by
300 ft. There was, in fact, an earlier (fourteenth-century) manor
house on the site, and this was retained in the projected castle,
producing the same effect as at Herstmonceux (p 65) and Farleigh
Hungerford (p 117): a range subdividing the courtyard into two
parts. Externally, there were four rectangular angle towers (of
which one survives), and three intermediate towers, one each in the
middle of the north, east, and south sides, with the gatehouse (the
other survival) in the middle of the west side. The surviving angle
tower is of three storeys and 70 ft high to the top of its flanking
turret. Two of the three storeys of the gatehouse survive. It is

basically rectangular in plan with semi-octagonal towers at each end of the two long sides, producing a plan not unlike some of the late medieval tower-houses, such as Tattershall (p 127).

SHROPSHIRE

Clun Castle (SO 298809)

Clun is as much earthwork as stone castle, and might merit only a mention in the regional introduction were it not for the unusual position of the keep. The earthworks are of the motte-and-bailey type; the summit of the oval motte is c. 150 by 100 ft and about 30 ft high. There are two baileys side by side, to the east and south-east. The castle is first mentioned c. 1140–1150. The structure which existed then was probably still of timber although it is possible that the stone keep was added around this time. The castle is mentioned again in the years 1160–1164 and by this time one would certainly expect the rectangular keep to have been built. There is nothing particularly unusual about this structure; it is of four storeys with clasping buttresses at the angles, and is in rather a battered state. What is unusual is its position, built against the sloping side of the motte, one wall in the ditch, one (now missing) on top of the motte, with the two longer side walls running up the slope. Presumably it was felt that the motte would not provide a firm enough foundation and the keep was therefore built with its foundations on the natural ground surface beneath the slope of the motte. Two of the keep's four storeys are below motte-top level, the two upper storeys rising above it. The original timber palisade around the edge of the motte must have been replaced by a stone wall at this time, and some traces of this remain. There are also remains of two round towers on the same circuit, and these must be a thirteenth-century addition when round towers became popular. Because of the danger from loose masonry the motte top is not open to the public, but the rest of the site is freely accessible and virtually everything of significance can be seen. The keep at Guildford (p 41) is similarly sited on the slope of a pre-existing motte.

Ludlow Castle (SO 508746)

Ludlow is one of the great castles of the Welsh border and its Inner Bailey in particular has a range of splendid remains embracing most of the medieval period. The castle is roughly rectangular in plan with steep natural slopes on the north and west, and two lines of defence on the south and east. The outer defence consists of a curtain wall with a ditch in front and an outer entrance in the middle of the east side. These were built c. 1180, with round towers added in the following century. The entrance leads into the large Outer Bailey, with a range of later buildings to the left and a stone wall to the right, cutting off the northern part of the bailey which is not accessible to the public. However, the chief interest of Ludlow resides in its Inner Bailey which occupies the north-west quarter of the castle.

The entrance to the Inner Bailey is more or less opposite the outer entrance and, approaching it, the most prominent feature is the rectangular keep to the left. This, however, is not the original arrangement, for the keep itself was originally the entrance, with an entrance passage through the middle: evidence of the blocking of the outer arch can be seen on the front wall of the keep. The keep, in its original form of a gate-tower, was built by Hugh de Lacy (died 1121), or his nephew Gilbert de Lacy, together with the curtain wall and a series of rectangular wall towers on the north and west, overlooking the steep natural slope. At this stage the keep consisted of the entrance passage on the ground floor, with a lofty hall on the floor above reached by a stairway from the courtyard in the thickness of the east wall; leading off the hall is a sleeping-chamber (c. 16 by 8 ft) with a latrine at one end, and these rooms probably represent the principal accommodation of the castle at this time. Later, c. 1200, the entrance passage was walled up at either end and converted into a prison, and the upper part was transformed into something like a conventional keep. The lofty hall was subdivided horizontally into two storeys, and another storey was contrived within the existing walls which had risen well above the original roof. Thus, as converted the tower followed the lines of most keeps in having a basement (the prison), with three storeys above. Even this was not the end of the keep's structural history. Some time in

Ludlow Castle: the keep and the innter curtain wall

the fifteenth century the north (inner) end of the keep either fell or
was pulled down and the rebuilding involved a reduction in length
of 11 ft. From the top of the keep the whole layout of the castle can
be viewed as in a plan. In the thirteenth century the keep was
incorporated in a small rectangular court created by walling in the
south-west angle of the Inner Bailey.

The entrance is now to the right of the keep and leads into the
Inner Bailey. One of the most prominent features within is the
unusual round nave of the chapel of St Mary Magdalene with fine
Norman ornament, built early in the twelfth century. The chancel,
to the east, has been destroyed. Beyond the chapel, and occupying
the whole northern side of the bailey, is the hall range, built c. 1300.
It follows the classic domestic plan: hall in the centre (at first-floor
level) with a services wing at the lower (left) end, and a private or
family wing at the upper (right-hand) end. The principal room of

this wing is the Great Chamber, a room opening off the upper end of the hall. The buildings beyond the Great Chamber are rebuildings of the sixteenth century, but they probably replaced earlier buildings in the same position. Associated with these family rooms is the large projecting rectangular tower on the north curtain which was built c. 1330. It provided four storeys of private rooms, two each in the two lower storeys, with a single larger room on each of the two upper storeys. The rooms in the three lower storeys are reached from the corresponding floors of the Great Chamber and its adjacent buildings. The topmost, and most comfortable room, with fireplace, latrine and four windows, is reached directly from the hall below via a spiral staircase, and obviously represents a private retreat for the lord of the castle and his lady.

Whittington Castle (SJ 325311)
The outer gatehouse at Whittington castle faces on to the busy A5 trunk road at its junction with the A495 from Whitchurch and Ellesmere. Fortunately there is a car-park immediately alongside the castle which is a freely accessible recreation area. The nucleus of the castle is an Edwardian-type rectangular structure with boldly projecting circular angle towers and a double-towered gatehouse. Unfortunately, much of the facing stone of the walls and towers has gone, so that they are represented mainly by their rubble cores, although the main lines of the plan are reasonably clear. In fact, the Edwardian castle is not the earliest structure on the site. Just showing through the surface of its courtyard are remains of a rectangular keep c. 50 by 40 ft in plan, with walls c. 10 ft thick and a forebuilding on the north side. This was probably built around the middle of the previous century (c. 1150). The courtyard stands some 15 ft above the level of the surrounding ditch which is now dry, but water must originally have played a considerable part in the castle's defences (below). The castle walls rise from the ditch bottom, revetting the sides of the 15 ft high platform, but not now rising more than three or four feet above it, although originally they must have risen considerably higher to form free-standing curtain walls. The remains of the hall stand against the inner side of the north curtain wall. The south-west angle tower also does duty as a

gatehouse tower, a fifth tower being provided just to the north of it
to complete the entrance. The only other stone structures on the site
are a twin-towered outer gatehouse, facing the A5, and a linked
section of curtain wall with a round tower. These are in the Outer
Bailey, to the west of the rectangular structure (Inner Bailey) and
separated from it by the ditch. Originally the whole of the Outer
Bailey must have been similarly walled.

The water defences of Whittington have been referred to above.
There is still a body of water extending across the north of the
castle, immediately alongside the main road (A5), and it is quite
clear that water once played a considerable part in the castle's
defences. Most of the water has now gone but it is clear that some
engineering work must have been undertaken to dam up the waters
of a nearby stream and retain the waters so accumulated. In
particular, the rectangular Inner Bailey must have been completely
surrounded by water, and water at this depth would have extended
over a much wider area, giving an entirely new dimension to the
castle's appearance. The extensive earthworks to the south of the
castle indicate some fairly elaborate water engineering and a
detailed plan of the whole complex would probably be very
informative.

STAFFORDSHIRE

Tamworth Castle (SK 206038)

Tamworth Castle now stands in a park on the south edge of the
town, just north of the river. The main surviving feature is a great
sandstone shell-keep standing on a motte. The castle is first
mentioned in 1141 but the structure at that time may have been
simply a timber palisade around the summit. The earliest stone
structures are the shell wall and rectangular tower which were
probably built in the reign of Henry II (1154–89). The entrance,
close to the tower, leads into a small courtyard occupying about a
quarter of the space within the shell wall. The rest of the interior is
occupied by a house built and added to in the sixteenth and
seventeenth centuries, but this must have replaced earlier internal

buildings, contemporary with the building of the shell wall and rectangular tower. Tamworth as a place has a long history, going back to the time of King Offa who died in 796.

Tutbury Castle (SK 210293)

Tutbury is one of a very small group of castles built in the first five years after the Conquest, between 1066 and 1071. Its motte-and-bailey layout is still very evident in spite of much later building. The first castle must certainly have been timber-built. Like Dudley, it was demolished by Henry II c. 1175. Subsequently it was rebuilt in stone with a shell-keep on the motte and presumably a stone curtain wall along the top of the bank which had supported the original timber palisade. The shell-keep has now gone, replaced by a later folly. Apart from this, virtually all the surviving stone structure is a result of the extensive rebuilding begun c. 1400. Tutbury was the property of the Duke of Lancaster, Henry Bolingbroke, and when he came to the throne in 1399 as the first Lancastrian king, extensive rebuilding began at the castle, and continued intermittently for the next 60 years.

The castle is D-shaped in plan, with the motte (now supporting only a late folly) at one angle, and the entrance at the other. The main part of the entrance is fourteenth-century (1313–14), but the most obvious features to the approaching visitor are the two solid rectangular towers added to its front in the reconstruction begun under Henry IV. Apart from the curtain wall, about half of which is preserved although not to any great height, the principal remains are those of the North and South Towers. Not a great deal remains of the North Tower (c. 40 by 30 ft) but there is enough to show its plan, its height (four storeys), and its handsome windows on the side towards the bailey; at its north-west angle is a small turret housing a spiral staircase. The North Tower was one of the last features to be built (between 1450 and 1461), and was probably not started until the South Tower was completed. The latter, a larger and much better preserved tower, was started in 1441 and probably completed by c. 1450. It takes the form of two rectangular towers

Tamworth Castle: the shell-keep

side by side (55 by 33 ft and 40 by 25 ft) with a stair turret at the junction between the two. Spacious windows on the side towards the bailey indicate that, like the North Tower, this was intended for occupation. Both towers North and South, were clearly conceived on the lines of tower-houses being built in the north of England and in Scotland around this time – self-contained residences designed for safety and a degree of comfort not possible in the wall-towers of earlier castles.

One other feature worthy of note are the remains (foundations only) of the free-standing chapel in the middle of the bailey. This is the earliest surviving stone structure on the site, and was built in the twelfth century.

WEST MIDLANDS

Dudley Castle (SO 947908)
Dudley Castle, now incorporated in Dudley Zoo, is chiefly famous for its tower-house built between 1300 and 1321 by Sir John de Somery, described by W.D. Simpson as a 'baronial thug' who terrorized the Staffordshire countryside with a gang of hired villains. However, the history of the castle goes back to the earliest days of the Conquest. William fitz Ansculf's castle is mentioned in the Domesday Book, and is one of the relatively small number of castles built in the first 20 years after 1066. This early castle was inevitably of the motte-and-bailey type with a timber superstructure. It was attacked in 1138, during the Anarchy (the civil war from 1135–1154), and demolished by Henry II in 1173 in the aftermath of the same war. Another castle must have been built subsequently, since Sir John de Somery rebuilt it c. 1300, but his rebuilding was so extensive that it is difficult to ascertain just what filled the gap between 1173 and 1300.

There is, however, no doubt that existing remains on the motte are those of Sir John de Somery's tower-house, one of the earliest examples of this type of structure in Britain. Although now in a ruinous state, the main lines of the plan and elevation are quite

Tutbury Castle: the entrance

clear. The tower was a two-storey structure (unlike most other tower-houses which were multi-storey), and is oblong in plan with round towers at the angles. The upper storey consisted of a hall with two smaller chambers at the west end, and service rooms (pantry and buttery) at the east end. The kitchen and servants' quarters were at ground-floor level. There was a portcullis defending the entrance and an embattled parapet along the top of the walls. In this comfortable residence overlooking the rest of the castle, Sir John and his family could live in safety, secure against the doubtful loyalty of the hired cut-throats in the bailey below.

At the same time as he built his tower-house, Sir John also provided new quarters for his followers in the bailey. These included another kitchen, another hall, and another chapel; in other words, all the services and facilities to enable the family and the hired followers to live independently of each other within the same castle. These buildings occupy the eastern side of the bailey, although the fine frontages to the courtyard are mostly the result of later rebuilding in the sixteenth century.

Dudley Castle: the tower-house

Stokesay Castle: a fortified manor-house

Newark Castle: the entrance

7   South Wales

The South Wales region includes the counties of Dyfed, Glamorgan (Mid, West, and South), Gwent, and the southern half of Powys. Within this area there are remains of at least 80 castles. To some extent this reflects the size of the area involved (as compared, say, with North Wales), but to a greater degree it reflects the long-drawn-out conflict between the Welsh and the English in the centuries following the Conquest. Of this number, 18 castles are included in the main inventory, and the remainder in a list at the end of this section. Although there are a number of rectangular keeps (at Bridgend, Coity, Ogmore, Chepstow and possibly White Castle) none of them are of any great size or importance. The most significant is Chepstow which began as an oblong, two-storey, hall block and was converted into a keep by the addition of a third, tall storey in the second half of the thirteenth century. Circular keeps are rather more common, with examples at Pembroke, Castell Coch, Caldicot, Skenfrith, Bronllys and Tretower. Of these Pembroke is outstanding because of its domed roof and two tiers of battlements. Shell-keeps are represented only by Cardiff and Tretower, the latter surrounding the later circular keep just mentioned. As in North Wales, some of the best-preserved remains are of the Edwardian period (1272–1307 or thereabouts) and include Carew, Carreg Cennen, Kidwelly and Caerphilly, the last of which also splendidly exemplifies the concentric principle. Of the remaining castles, Grosmont is of the hall (rather than keep) and bailey type, similar to Chepstow as first built, while Raglan, built late in the medieval period (mid-fifteenth century), is of the courtyard type, as well as incorporating an elaborate hexagonal keep-like tower-house. The castles at Cilgerran, Llawhaden, Llanstephan and Manorbier, while varying somewhat in type, all belong to the thirteenth century and display the main characteristics of the period. Many of the features mentioned earlier form part of later and more elaborate castles such as Pembroke, Caldicot, Skenfrith, Chepstow, Coity, and White Castle, which likewise exemplify many features of thirteenth-century fortification.

The following sites in South Wales are not included in the main inventory; brief details are given with each and their location is shown on the map on p 194:

1. Aberedw (Powys): a small square castle with four round towers.
2. Abergavenny (Gwent): motte and stone-walled bailey; remains of four towers.
3. Aberystwyth (Dyfed): scattered remains of Edwardian concentric castle.
4. Benton (Dyfed): small castle with one circular tower.
5. Brecon (Powys): motte with remains of polygonal shell; towers in bailey.
6. Bwlch y Ddinas (Powys): built inside a hill-fort; square angle and gatehouse towers.
7. Caerleon (Gwent): large motte-and-bailey; one tower survives in bailey.
8. Candleston (Glamorgan): square tower, polygonal courtyard.
9. Cardigan (Dyfed): overgrown remains of round keep and bailey wall.
10. Carew (Dyfed): substantial remains of Edwardian castle.
11. Carmarthen (Dyfed): motte revetted with wall and round towers; twin-towered gatehouse.
12. Castell Coch (Glamorgan): restored, and picturesque, medieval castle.
13. Cefnllys (Powys): a possible hill-fort with remains of a stone castle within.
14. Crickhowell (Powys): motte-and-bailey; two towers remain in bailey.
15. Dinas Powis (Glamorgan): remains of a square tower and a bailey.
16. Dinham (Gwent): thirteenth-century rectangular tower and other rectangular buildings.
17. Dryslwyn (Dyfed): scattered stone remains inside probable hill-fort; now under restoration.
18. Dynevor (Dyfed): circular keep, irregular walled bailey.

19. Haverfordwest (Dyfed): substantial fragment of late thirteenth-century castle.
20. Hay (Powys): Length of curtain wall, a thirteenth-century gate, and a square tower.
21. Kenfig (Glamorgan): motte, walled bailey, and gatehouse.
22. Knucklas (Powys): small square structure, round angle towers, thirteenth century.
23. Laugharne (Dyfed): under reconstruction, mainly Tudor but two thirteenth-century towers.
24. Llanblethian (Glamorgan): remains of keep within ward with three towers and gatehouse.
25. Llandaff (Glamorgan): small castle, two small towers, and twin-towered gatehouse.
26. Llandovery (Dyfed): motte-and-bailey; D-shaped keep, twin-towered gatehouse.
27. Llanfair Discoed (Gwent): small square castle, two round towers, and part of gatehouse.
28. Llangibby (Gwent): unfinished castle; unusual keep, large gatehouse, three towers, and smaller gatehouse.
29. Llangynwyd (Glamorgan): plain curtain, double-towered gatehouse, and one tower.
30. Llantrisant (Glamorgan): inner bailey, curtain wall and round keep.
31. Llawhaden (Dyfed): substantial remains of thirteenth/fourteenth century castle.
32. Loughor (Glamorgan): remains of square tower and ring wall on motte.
33. Machen (Gwent): round tower and walled bailey.
34. Monmouth (Gwent): single ward, rectangular keep of twelfth century.
35. Morlais (Powys): remains of Edwardian castle, round keep, four other round towers.
36. Narberth (Dyfed): originally rectangular plan with projecting angle towers.
37. Neath (Glamorgan): twin-towered gatehouse and one tower.
38. Nevern (Dyfed): motte-and-bailey; small stone castle inside.
39. Newcastle Emlyn (Dyfed): quadrilateral (earthwork) inner ward with double-towered gatehouse.

40. Newport (Dyfed): gateway and three towers, two of them circular.
41. Newport (Gwent): one side of Edwardian castle with interesting water-gate.
42. Ogmore (Glamorgan): now mainly a ruined rectangular keep.
43. Oystermouth (Glamorgan): large rectangular tower, ward with double-towered gatehouse.
44. Penard (Glamorgan): small castle on rock, twin-towered gatehouse.
45. Pencelli (Powys): remains of a square (50 by 50 ft) keep, walls 10 ft thick.
46. Penhow (Gwent): small castle, oblong tower and ward.
47. Penmark (Glamorgan): inner ward with stone wall and round tower.
48. Penrice (Glamorgan): circular keep, triangular bailey with double-towered gatehouse.
49. Picton (Dyfed): small thirteenth-century castle, still occupied, but accessible.
50. Roch (Dyfed): a D-shaped tower, probably mid-thirteenth century.
51. St Donat's (Glamorgan): small concentric castle, rather irregular in plan, much altered.
52. St Fagan's (Glamorgan): stone castle with two wards (Welsh Folk Museum).
53. Tenby (Dyfed): some remains of castle; more of associated town walls.
54. Tinboeth (Powys): remains of square gate-tower, rest foundations.
55. Troggy (Gwent): possibly hall-and-bailey type; two towers remain.
56. Upton (Dyfed): small late thirteenth-century castle, similar to Picton.
57. Usk (Gwent): small square keep in inner ward; three thirteenth-century round towers.
58. Weobley (Glamorgan): a fortified manor house, thirteenth/fourteenth century.
59. Wiston (Dyfed): motte-and-bailey, polygonal shell on motte.
60. Ystradfellte (Powys): remains of stone-walled enclosure with traces of circular keep and a hall.

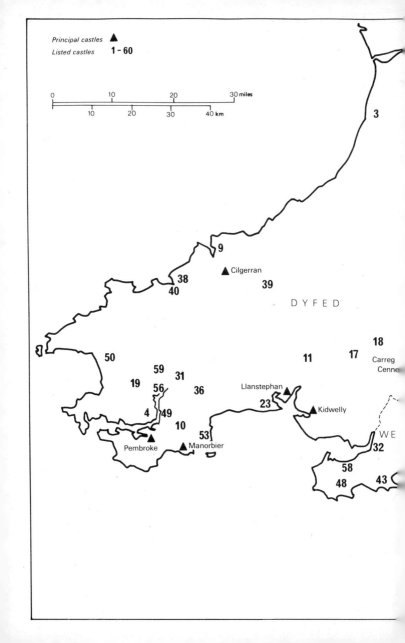

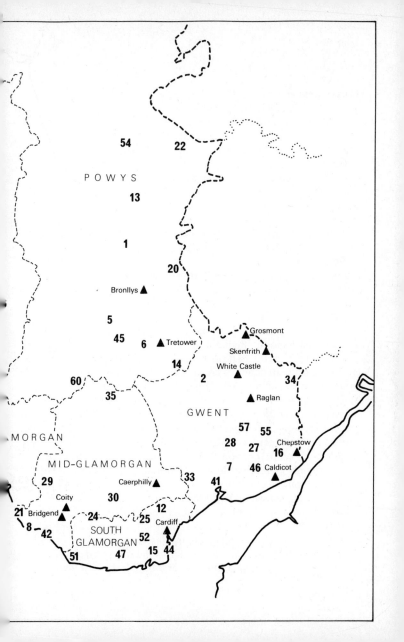

DYFED

Carreg Cennen Castle (SN 668191)
The present extensive remains of Carreg Cennen castle belong to
the Edwardian period (1272–1307), although there is a record of an
earlier Welsh castle on the site. This fell into English hands in 1277
at the opening of Edward I's first campaign against the Welsh
princes. In 1283, after the second Welsh campaign (1282–3),
Edward granted Carreg Cennen to John Gillard of Brimpsfield in
Gloucestershire and it was under him and his son, John Gillard the
younger, that the existing castle was built in the late thirteenth and
early fourteenth centuries. The castle built by the Gillards was
virtually a new structure, and as such inevitably followed the
'Edwardian' pattern: rectangular plan, projecting angle towers,
double-towered gatehouse etc. It was built in three stages (Inner
Ward, Barbican, and Outer Ward), although all three stages fall
within the two or three decades around the turn of the century
(1300).

The rectangular Inner Ward, the nucleus of the castle, was
probably built between 1283 and 1295 or thereabouts. Its south
curtain wall stands immediately above the steep cliff; on the west,
north, and part of the east sides there is a rock-cut ditch beyond the
curtain. The main defences are concentrated on the north front
where there is a circular (NW) angle tower, a rectangular (NE)
angle tower, and a double-towered gatehouse. The gatehouse
passage had machicolations, a portcullis, and a double door at the
outer end, and another portcullis at the inner end so that it could be
isolated from attack from within as well as from without, in the
manner of a keep; the rooms on either side of the passage were
guard-chambers. At first-floor level, passages in the thickness of the
north curtain wall communicated with the north-west and
north-east angle towers. The circular north-west tower was
probably of three storeys. The ground floor is accessible from the
courtyard, but the first floor could apparently be reached only via
the mural passage from the gatehouse just mentioned.

The domestic range on the east side of the courtyard was of two
storeys, with the principal rooms at first-floor level. The lower

Carreg Cennen Castle – a well-preserved Edwardian castle

rooms were probably used for storage and for servant accommodation. The only access to the range was via a flight of stone steps (the remains of which still exist), leading up to a door at the north-west corner of the hall. There was another door opposite, at the north-east corner, and the space between the two formed a screens passage, separated from the main body of the hall by a screen. On the opposite side of the screens passage was the kitchen, forming the north end of the range. To the south of the hall are two solars, reached by a passage in the thickness of the east curtain wall. The southernmost of the two (the lord's solar) had a fireplace, two windows (one to the courtyard and one through the south curtain wall), and probably a garderobe or latrine. The chapel, in the rectangular tower in the middle of the east curtain, formed part of the domestic range. It was reached via a mural staircase rising from the door at the north-east corner of the hall mentioned earlier.

The domestic range cut off the north-east angle tower from the courtyard, although its ground floor is now accessible via the kitchen basement. Originally it was accessible only from above, via a staircase which led down from the north-east door of the hall, mentioned earlier. The room contained a fireplace and a garderobe and presumably provided living-quarters for some member of the household. The room above was similarly equipped, and possibly the third storey also; the second-storey room was linked by the mural passage to the gatehouse. Thus hall and kitchen were flanked to the south by private family accommodation (the two solars), and to the north-east by what was probably accommodation for senior members of the household (the three floors of the north-east tower).

Within a few years, the castle was further strengthened by the building of an elaborate barbican (much of which is preserved) in front of the main entrance. This takes the form of a long, walled passage starting beyond the north-east corner of the castle and running, with two right-angled changes of direction, along the north side just beyond the ditch, to end between the twin towers of the gatehouse. There was no other way into the gatehouse so that approach was effectively constricted to a passage less than 10 ft wide over a distance of some 130 ft. The passage is stepped up gradually from the level of the Outer Ward to that of the gatehouse threshold. Movement along it was barred by two towers, five pits (plus another in the gatehouse), and a series of drawbridges and gates which would have made progress extremely difficult for an attacker. Within another few years (probably in the first decade of the fourteenth century) a second addition was made to the castle. To the north, north-east, and east an outer curtain wall with solid round towers was built, forming the Outer Ward and more than doubling the area of the castle.

The castle saw use during the Wars of the Roses and was slighted in 1462. Thereafter it gradually fell into ruin, eventually being handed over to state guardianship in 1932 by its owner, Earl Cawdor.

Cilgerran Castle (SN 195431)

Cilgerran Castle stands at the end of a naturally defended triangular promontory at the junction of the River Teifi and Plysgog stream. It consists of an Outer Ward, of which little remains, and an Inner Ward which includes the principal surviving structures: the gatehouse, the two great circular towers, and the three linking sections of curtain wall. These are of early thirteenth-century date and form the main defences of the Inner Ward. They were probably erected by William Marshall, Earl of Pembroke, shortly after 1223 when he recaptured Cilgerran from the Welsh. The remaining visible structures are of the late thirteenth century, except for the north-west tower at the end of the promontory which was added towards the end of the following century. c. 1377, when the castle was put in order against a feared invasion by the French. The present-day entrance to the site is at the south-west angle of the Outer Ward, with traces, on the ground, of the late thirteenth-century curtain wall on the left above the very steep natural slope, and the remains of the outer ditch stretching away to the right, beyond the custodian's hut. From the entrance a path leads straight to the Inner Gatehouse, via a modern wooden bridge.

The Inner Gatehouse is a rectangular, three-storey structure, with the entrance passage protected by two portcullises (the grooves for which are visible), with a two-leaved gate between, secured by a draw-bar (the holes for which are likewise visible). To the right of the gatehouse are the thirteenth-century defences, the main features of which are the two large circular towers, East Tower and West Tower. The West Tower provides four storeys of circular rooms, each c. 23 ft in diameter. As originally built, it was entered at first-floor level (probably via a wooden staircase), like a keep, for the keep idea was still strong in the early thirteenth century. In the fourteenth century the present ground-floor door was inserted, together with a spiral staircase to provide more convenient access to the rooms above. The East Tower is somewhat smaller (c. 40 ft in diameter), but is built on very much the same lines, with four storeys of circular rooms, c. 22 ft in diameter. It has two doorways, one giving access only to the ground floor, and the other to a spiral staircase leading up to the other three storeys, the floors of which

Cilgerran Castle

are unfortunately missing. In the curtain wall immediately adjacent
to this tower is a postern gate, originally protected by a portcullis,
leading out to the inner ditch, and to the postern gate in the
surviving section of the outer curtain wall – through which
defenders could make their way (hopefully unobserved) around to
the front of the castle and take any would-be attackers by surprise.

The surviving defences on the two remaining sides of the
promontory are mostly of late thirteenth-century date, i.e. probably
about fifty years later than the gatehouse, the round towers, and the
associated curtain wall. The remains of the tower at the end of the
promontory are of the fourteenth century (c. 1375). The
north-eastern side appears to have fallen away. If this is so, then the
new tower must have represented a considerable addition to the
castle's defences. The surviving walls within the courtyard indicate
the existence of buildings against the north-eastern and

north-western curtains. The kitchen appears to have been built against the latter, and the hall or main residence against the north-eastern curtain, but the remains are fragmentary and it is hard to be any more precise.

Kidwelly Castle (SN 409070)

The somewhat unusual D-shaped plan of Kidwelly was dictated by the layout of an earlier, earthwork castle erected by Roger, Bishop of Salisbury, between 1106 and 1115. This was of the motte-and-bailey type, and the mound which still exists in front of the main gatehouse is almost certainly the remains of the motte. Of greater significance, however, are the remains of the bailey, consisting of a rampart underlying the existing stone outer curtain wall and a ditch, which is in fact the original ditch, re-used for the Edwardian castle. The result is a castle in which the inner defences, built from new, follow the conventional rectangular Edwardian plan, placed within an outer enclosure of D-shaped plan inherited from the earlier castle. The D-shaped plan itself is a result of utilizing the steep slope above the river Gwendraeth as the eastern side of the enclosure, with a semi-circular bank and ditch protecting the three remaining sides. This early castle had a chequered history, changing hands half a dozen times in the long-drawn-out struggle between the Welsh princes and the Normans. Around 1250 the castle was back again in English hands, in the person of Patrick de Chaworth. He was killed shortly afterwards and it was his son, Payn de Chaworth, who began building the new castle c. 1275.

Entry to the castle is through the main gatehouse at the southern end of the site. The mound, some 30 ft in front, is probably the remnant of the earlier motte. The entrance passage leads into the Outer Ward, with the southern defences of the Inner Ward immediately in front. The Inner Ward is square in plan (c. 100 by 100 ft) with four circular, projecting, angle towers, each c. 30 ft in diameter. The entrance to the Inner Ward is a simple archway, originally closed with double doors and a portcullis, midway in the south curtain wall. This leads into the inner courtyard with the remains of the main domestic buildings on the right occupying the whole eastern wall. These form a comprehensive suite of rooms including the north-east tower, the whole east range, the south-east tower, the chapel tower, and, in the angle between the entrance and the east range, the kitchen. The east range consisted of the hall with the solar or withdrawing-room to the north, both at first-floor level, with a low ground floor below, probably used for storage. Beyond the solar to the north, the rooms of the north-east angle tower probably provided further private rooms for the use of the lord of the manor and his family. Similarly, at the southern end, the rooms of the five-storey south-east tower formed a further extension of the domestic accommodation. The basement, entered from the hall basement, was probably again used for storage, while the first floor, at hall level, seems to have been used as a buttery.

Immediately adjacent to the south-east tower and projecting above the steep natural slope is the semi-octagonal chapel tower, with a smaller square tower on its south side housing a sacristy at the same level and a priest's room below. On the opposite side of the hall from the chapel tower is the kitchen, and this completes the suite of rooms on the east side of the Inner Ward. The only other building to note is another, larger kitchen in the south-west corner; this was an addition of the Tudor period, c. 1500, and was designed to serve the needs of the later hall in the Outer Ward (below).

The outer defences were built in the first decade or two of the following century (c. 1300–1320). They consisted of a small north gatehouse, much ruined and not accessible, a massive south gatehouse, and four D-shaped wall-towers, all six features linked by a semi-circular curtain wall. In addition, two straight lengths of curtain wall on the east side linked these defences to those of the Inner Ward. The dominant feature of the outer defences, and indeed of the whole castle, is the south gatehouse which is of keep-like dimensions (80 by 50 ft) and is three storeys high. Its potential independence of the rest of the castle is demonstrated by the arrangements in the entrance passage, where there were originally double doors and a portcullis at each end. The rest of the ground floor is divided into five somewhat irregularly-shaped rooms which probably provided guardrooms and barrack accommodation for some at least of the garrison. Two further rooms, below the two front rooms of the gatehouse, were probably used for storage

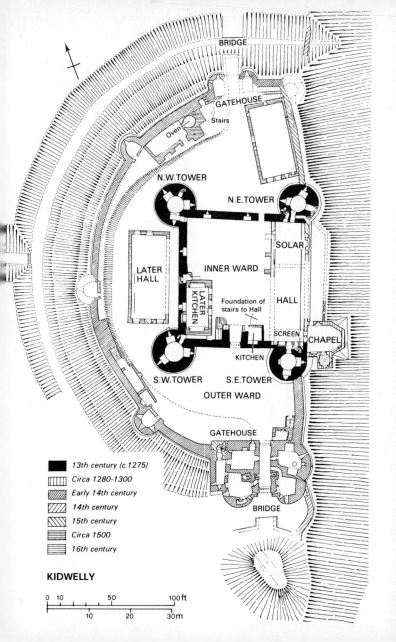

BRIDGE

GATEHOUSE

Stairs

Oven

N.W. TOWER

N.E. TOWER

SOLAR

LATER
HALL

INNER WARD

HALL

LATER
KITCHEN

Foundation of
stairs to Hall

SCREEN

CHAPEL

KITCHEN

S.W. TOWER

S.E. TOWER

OUTER WARD

GATEHOUSE

BRIDGE

	13th century (c.1275)
	Circa 1280-1300
	Early 14th century
	14th century
	15th century
	Circa 1500
	16th century

KIDWELLY

0 10   50   100ft

   10   20   30m

and/or as prisons. As originally built, the only staircases to the upper floors were housed within the five ground-floor rooms, again stressing the keep-like function of the gatehouse.

The two upper storeys of the gatehouse contain a suite of rooms which duplicates that in the Inner Ward. Along the north side, overlooking the Outer Ward is the hall, with a kitchen at its eastern end and three other smaller rooms occupying the towers and the rectangular west wing. Above the hall and kitchen is the solar or private family room, with three smaller rooms corresponding to the three below. There was thus a great deal of accommodation contrived within the gatehouse which would have enabled it to function as an independent unit, a small self-contained fortress, should the need arise. The original cramped staircase arrangements proved inadequate and inconvenient, and two additional staircases were provided. About a century after the gatehouse was built an additional staircase turret was built in the north-west angle. This rises from within one of the ground-floor rooms and provided access to the hall, the solar above, and the battlements, where the turret rises well above general roof-level. Later again, c. 1500, a more spacious external staircase was added in the angle between the gatehouse and the east curtain wall, providing easy access from the Outer Ward to the hall.

This staircase was almost certainly the work of Sir Rhys ap Tudor, to whom the castle was granted by Henry VII (1485–1509), the first of the Tudor kings. Apart from this Sir Rhys did a considerable amount of building in the castle. The later kitchen, mentioned earlier, is one of his buildings, as is the later hall which it served on the west side of the Outer Ward, with its gable ends still standing high. Another building of similar size, and with similar remains, stands in the north-east angle, although its use is uncertain. There is also a bakehouse against the north-west curtain wall, and a building of unknown use against the curtain on the south-west side. Little was added after this period, and eventually the castle went out of use and fell into decay. Its restoration began in 1927.

Llanstephan Castle (SN 351101)
The earliest certain reference to Llanstephan Castle is in 1146 when the Welsh princes Cadell, Maredudd, and Rhys captured it from the

English. At that time the castle was of the ringwork (Upper Ward) and bailey (Lower Ward) type, with earthwork and timber defences. Within a decade or so the castle was back in English hands and seems to have remained in them from then on. Towards the end of the century the castle was in the possession of the de Camville family, and a William de Camville is recorded as having borrowed money in 1192 to fortify Llanstephan. This is probably when the first move was made to replace the timber defences with a stone curtain wall. This is preserved along the west side of the Upper Ward, although it has been raised in height at least once, and strengthened on the inside by an arcaded construction added about the middle of the thirteenth century. The early curtain wall was quite thin (c. 4 ft) and rose only about 5 ft above the interior, although the external height above the ditch bottom would have been considerably greater. The inner gate, a square tower, was added c. 1225. It is of three storeys and is preserved very nearly to its full height.

In 1257 Llanstephan was once more in Welsh hands, but only briefly, and was soon back in de Camville hands, under William de Camville II and, from c. 1275 on, Geoffrey de Camville; and it was under these two lords that Llanstephan received its Edwardian additions and assumed the form in which it stands today. Whatever the previous defences of the Lower Ward had been, they were now replaced, first of all by a fine curtain wall and D-shaped towers, with the addition, within a few years (c. 1280), of an Edwardian-style double-towered gatehouse. Because of the steep natural slope not much is called for on the south but a plain curtain wall, but on the remainder of the circuit there is an evenly spaced range of additional defences: East Bastion, North Tower, Gatehouse and West Tower. The East Bastion is simply a thickened section of curtain wall, rising a little higher than the rest, with the external appearance of a tower, in a position where a full tower was considered unnecessary. On the inner side, at ground level, are four wide recesses which originally opened into a large building along the north-east curtain, and this was almost certainly the hall. All trace of it has now gone and the existing remains along this side are those of a Tudor barn.

The hall probably abutted the North Tower which is much larger than West Tower, and seems to have contained a residential suite of two rooms above a basement which was entered separately from the rest of the tower and was probably used only for storage. The two rooms above contained a fireplace and two windows each, with latrines housed in a flanking turret. A turret on the opposite side housed the spiral staircase. When built c. 1260–70, the North Tower probably acted as a private retreat, beyond the upper end of the hall, for the lord of the castle and his family. The West Tower is a much smaller affair, its upper portion now largely gone. It contained one small private room with a fireplace, probably for some senior member of the staff.

These features (curtain wall, East Bastion and East and West Towers) were probably built between 1260 and 1275. Within a year or two, c. 1280, the Great Gatehouse was added, almost certainly following the main lines of the East Gatehouse of Caerphilly Castle (p 211), built a few years earlier. The gatehouse is formed of two D-shaped towers linked above the entrance passage, with two circular turrets at the inner angles. The rooms on either side of the entrance passage were probably guardrooms and barracks, but the two floors above each consisted of a single large room occupying virtually the whole available space. Each room has two large windows on the inner side, overlooking the Lower Ward. In many ways the most interesting aspect of the gatehouse is its later treatment. The entrance passage is now walled up at both ends, converting the structure from a gatehouse into a tower-house, and this was done in Tudor times, probably between 1500 and 1600. At the same time a new and smaller entrance (the existing means of access) was built alongside. The converted gatehouse thus became the principal residence of the castle. This may have been when the original hall was swept away. Certainly new buildings (including the barn mentioned earlier) were built along the north-east and north curtain walls at this time.

Manorbier Castle (SS 064978)
Manorbier Castle is famous as the birthplace, in 1146, of Gerald de Barri, better known as *Giraldus Cambrensis*, Gerald of Wales, who wrote vivid accounts of twelfth-century life in both Wales and

Ireland. The castle in which he was born was probably first built between 1130 and 1140 and was a mixture of timber-and-earth construction and stonework, sited on a promontory. The defences, following the line of the existing curtain wall except at the west end (below), were at this stage of earthwork and timber, except for a single rectangular stone tower immediately north of the existing, and later, gatehouse. This was presumably designed to protect the entrance (probably a simple gate) which preceded the gatehouse. The tower was entered at first-floor level, like a keep, although its walls are quite thin. Nevertheless, it may have been intended to survive independently of the rest of the castle.

The main structural feature of this early castle was the stone-built hall block, still substantially intact, which runs across the west end of the castle. The hall is at first-floor level, and is reached by a stone staircase against the front of the building. The entrance to the first floor is about halfway along the block, with the hall originally occupying about two-thirds of the space, divided by a cross-wall (now mostly gone) from a buttery (a room for the storage and service of drink). The hall rose through two storeys, but the buttery originally had another room above (the old solar or withdrawing-room). The block is surmounted by battlements which appear to be original, providing a second line of defence above and behind the earth and timber defences.

The castle seems to have remained in this state (stone hall, stone gatetower, earth and timber defences) for nearly a century, until c. 1230, when the defences were rebuilt in stone, more or less in the form in which they survive today. The surviving curtain walls, which are well preserved, cover the north, east and south sides of the castle, with round towers at the north-east and south-east angles and a new entrance alongside the early tower (the gatehouse was slightly later). At the west end, however, there is no surviving curtain wall, the western end of the castle being formed by the hall block, a later building, and a spur wall to the south-west angle. However, it seems probable that there was originally a west curtain, some 20 or 30 ft beyond the hall, possibly with south-west and north-west angle towers, matching those at the eastern end. This is very much the pattern of defences one would expect in a castle of the early thirteenth century.

Soon after the completion of the stone defences the chapel was built (c. 1260) to the south-east of the hall block, leaving only a narrow gap between. This was soon filled by the block which now links the two, forming a water-gate at ground-floor level and two rooms above, one of which became the solar or private family room: this was in a much more convenient position than the old solar which had been situated at the lower, service end of the hall. The well-preserved chapel, like the hall, is built on an undercroft and is reached by an external flight of stone steps. Although the new family quarters were now conveniently situated between hall and chapel, they lacked latrines, which needed to discharge outside the curtain wall. To provide these, the spur wall was built from the new solar block to and beyond the curtain to form the Spur Tower, the rectangular projection at the south-west angle of the castle. All this building activity effectively cut off the small western end of the castle from the rest, and at a later stage, probably when defence needs were less pressing, the west curtain wall (and angle towers if any) were dismantled and the hall, new solar block and Spur Wall became the western end of the castle.

Internally, the kitchens and other associated services were situated in the north-west angle, adjacent to the hall block, but the remains are fragmentary. The buildings along the south curtain (where they are not completely modern) are later (sixteenth and seventeenth centuries) and include the remains of a stone barn. Externally, there are some remnants of the curtain wall of the Outer Bailey to the east of the main structure, with the remains of a stable block, just beyond the ditch in front of the main gatehouse.

Pembroke Castle (SM 982016)
Pembroke Castle is splendidly sited on the promontory formed by the junction of the Pembroke River and Monkton Pill. Equally splendid are the surviving remains, which belong to two main periods: the Inner Bailey to c. 1200, and the Outer Bailey to c. 1250. However, there was a castle on the site about a century earlier and this was of the earthwork-and-timber type. The ditch fronting the Inner Bailey (now filled in) was almost certainly the ditch of the early castle, with an earth rampart behind surmounted

Pembroke Castle

by a timber palisade which probably extended around the edge of
the promontory as well. Around 1200 these earth and timber
defences were rebuilt in stone, and a range of stone buildings was
erected within, presumably replacing the existing internal timber
buildings. This rebuilding produced the present Inner Bailey,
dominated by the great circular keep, still preserved to its unusual
domed top, although all the internal (wooden) floors have long
since gone. The keep is unusually massive in construction, 78 ft high
with walls some 15 ft thick. It was of four storeys, with entry
originally at first-floor level (now blocked), via a drawbridge from a
detached stone stair. Communication down to the basement and to
the upper floors is by means of a single spiral staircase in the
thickness of the wall to the right of the entrance. This is now

reached by a later doorway at ground level (the present entrance to the keep), from which all the upper levels can be reached. At the top, the spiral staircase leads out on to the battlements which form two tiers, one at the head of the outer wall in the normal way of all keeps. At Pembroke, however, there is a second tier, above and within the first, surmounting the stone dome which rises within the outer rampart walk. From the top of the keep there is a splendid view of the whole castle and its setting on the promontory defined by the two rivers.

Other buildings of the Inner Bailey include two halls in the north-east corner, one of which projects beyond the curtain wall and has beneath it, carved out of the solid rock, a chamber called Wogan Cavern, reached by a staircase from the hall above. This was probably used for various purposes, as a water-gate, as a storage area, and as a possible means of escape by river should the castle be in danger of falling. In the south-west corner, alongside the entrance, are the foundations of what was the chapel, with alongside it the Western Tower which probably acted as a guardroom and barracks for some of the garrison. Not much remains of the inner curtain but foundations, together with those of a D-shaped tower flanking the entrance. The well-preserved circular Dungeon Tower near the keep is a slightly later addition, possibly added when the outer defences were built.

The Outer Bailey was formed c. 1250 when a much larger area of the promontory was enclosed by a curtain wall (still substantially intact), linking a series of circular towers and a great rectangular gatehouse with a D-shaped tower flanking the entrance, which is further defended by a barbican, and two circular stair turrets on the inner face, towards the bailey. The entrance passage originally contained a formidable range of defences: a portcullis (at the outer end), followed by a machicolation, followed by a two-leaved door, with arrow loops on either side; beyond the door was another machicolation, another portcullis, another two-leaved door and two more arrow loops; beyond the second door was a third machicolation. Nor was this all. Above the inner end of the passage, between the two stair turrets, is a gallery facing into the bailey from which an enemy could be assailed from above and behind if he attempted to emerge from the passage. One of the circular towers (Barbican Tower) is so close to the gatehouse that it must be considered part of the entrance defences. Like the keep in the Inner Bailey it has a stone-domed roof, and must have been designed to overlook the entrance to the barbican in front of the gatehouse. The tower on the opposite side of the gatehouse (the Henry VII Tower), approached by a flight of stone steps, is so named because it is reputed to be the birthplace of Henry Tudor, the future Henry VII (1485–1509), founder of the Tudor dynasty. The Barbican Tower, the Gatehouse and Henry VII Tower were all linked by mural passages. Of the other towers, Northgate Tower at the north-east angle is so named because it overlooked the original north gate in the town wall, and Westgate Tower similarly covered the west gate of the town.

GLAMORGAN (MID-, WEST AND SOUTH)

Caerphilly Castle (ST 155871)
Caerphilly is a large and complex site, magnificently preserved, particularly with regard to its water defences which were such an important element in its composition. The castle was built by Richard de Clare, Earl of Gloucester and Hereford, and was begun in 1268, although the building of such an elaborate castle would obviously have been spread over a number of years, perhaps 10 or 15. The castle was built to protect the Earl's territories (including Glamorgan) from the encroachments of the Welsh princes who were particularly active and aggressive in the thirteenth century. The castle consists of three main portions and can be best understood by considering these in turn: the screen wall, the castle proper, and the outwork.

The key to the understanding of Caerphilly is the screen wall which is, in fact, a dam. The castle is approached from the east (the town side) via a bridge across the still-wet moat. Stretching away on either side is the screen wall or dam, over 1,000 ft long, blocking the mouth of the valley and retaining behind it the waters of two streams to form an artificial lake within which the main castle still stands. The dam is, in fact, a complete stronghold in itself, with a range of towers, gatehouses, and curtain walls comparable to any castle. Stretching away to the right of the main entrance is a long curtain wall with three projecting semi-octagonal towers and a twin towered gatehouse at the north end. Behind the curtain wall is a platform or terrace about 25 ft wide. This forms the north section of the dam. The central section is a much more spacious platform (c. 200 by 150 ft) with the central gatehouse at its north-east corner still forming the main means of access to the castle. There were originally two drawbridges here, separated by a diamond-shaped barbican, the platform for which is still visible. Stretching away to the left, beyond the curving bastion at the other angle of the central platform, is the south platform (c. 350 by 80 ft) fronted by massive, closely-set, rectangular buttresses, with a D-shaped tower and a twin-towered gatehouse at its rounded, southern end. A walk, either north or south, around the ends of the dam, will reveal the entrance arrangements there, the back view of the screen walls and platforms, the extent of the existing lake, and the relation of these features to the castle proper.

From the central platform a modern wooden bridge (replacing an original bridge with a lifting section) leads across to the east gatehouse of the castle. This is in fact the east outer gatehouse, for apart from its other complexities, the central portion of Caerphilly Castle is also a concentric castle, with an outer curtain wall and two outer gatehouses (east and west) completely embracing an inner curtain wall with two further, and larger, gatehouses, four circular angle towers and a D-shaped interval tower (Kitchen Tower). The outer curtain rises directly from the lake and the outer ward forms a wide terrace, c. 40 ft wide around the central part of the castle. Apart from the gatehouses there are no towers, although the curtain bows out at the angles to command the adjacent stretches of wall.

The outer gatehouse is directly opposite the east inner gatehouse, largest of the four, the front of which was, like much else in the castle, restored in the earlier part of the century. This consists of two large D-shaped towers, with circular stair-turrets at the rear. Its entrance passage contained a formidable array of defences, two double doors (one set facing outwards, the other inwards, towards

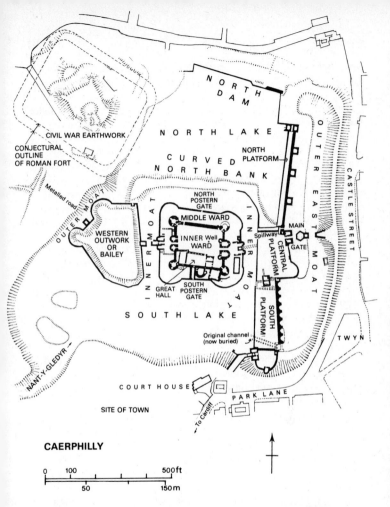

CAERPHILLY

```
0    100              500 ft
|____|____|____|____|____|
     50              150 m
```

the inner ward), each fronted by a portcullis and machicolations. The only access to the flanking towers was through the doorways on either side of the passage between the inner and outer doors, so that the gatehouse could be effectively isolated from the rest of the castle and could act as an independent keep. The upper floors of this gatehouse probably provided the quarters for the constable, in a position where he could exercise control over the defence of the whole castle.

The passage through the east inner gatehouse leads into the Inner Bailey, with the west inner gatehouse directly in front across the courtyard, and the Great Hall to the left along the south curtain wall. At the east end of the hall there are two rectangular rooms which were probably the buttery and pantry, with the lord's solar (private room) and chapel above. This, the lower, service end of the hall, was not the most convenient situation for the lord's quarters and a new suite of rooms was soon added at the upper, west end, in the south-west angle of the bailey. The kitchens were in the D-shaped tower on the other side of the curtain wall and they too were later added to, with an annexe to the east. To the west of the Kitchen Tower the transverse block, running between the inner and the outer curtains, provided, in its lowest storey, a stepped passage from the hall to a postern gate on the lake – a means of escape should the castle be about to fall, or a means of supply during a siege. Of the four angle towers, the one on the south-east is the most noticeable because of the dangerous-looking angle at which its surviving portion leans, a result of deliberate slighting during the Civil War. Most of the north-eastern tower has gone, but the one at the north-west angle has been almost fully restored and probably represents the original state of all four, with minor variations. Entry is at courtyard level, with a latrine to the right, staircase to the left, and ground-floor room in front with three arrow loops. There is a basement below the wooden floor, (presumably reached originally via a trap-door), and two storeys above, each equipped with a fireplace and intended therefore for occupation. The same staircase also provides access to the wall walks and galleries of the west and north curtain walls.

The west inner gatehouse is a smaller and less elaborate structure than the one on the east. In front of it is the west outer gatehouse, which is generally similar to the east outer gatehouse. The outer gatehouse leads to the modern wooden bridge which provides access to the third portion of Caerphilly, the western bailey or outwork. This is roughly as big as the main castle but is simply

Caerphilly Castle: the Inner Bailey

surrounded by a curtain wall (never finished), backed by an earth rampart. It was intended as a refuge for the townspeople in time of danger. On its north-west side the curtain forms two rounded bastions flanking an original entrance, reached by a bridge with a lifting section, from the bank of the lake. This, rather than the more elaborate east entrances seems to have been the most generally used means of access to the castle.

Caerphilly is undoubtedly one of the finest pieces of medieval military architecture in the British Isles and the careful restorations during this century has re-established much of its original appearance.

Cardiff Castle (ST 180767)

Three major building periods are represented in the impressive remains of Cardiff Castle: Roman (c. AD 300), medieval (c. 1100), and modern (from 1766). The earliest structure was one of the Roman forts of the Saxon shore, built around AD 300 as a defence against the growing menace of Saxon raids, mainly on the south and east coasts but also on the west, as at Cardiff. These were usually square in plan, and the present outer wall of Cardiff Castle, although heavily restored, follows almost exactly the line of the Roman wall and incorporates in its lower courses at least some of the original Roman structure.

Some 800 years later the Normans built a new fortification within the surviving ruins of the Roman work, probably reduced by then to a bank and ditch. They built a large motte in the north-west corner, still surrounded by a wet ditch, and utilized the Roman work as a bailey. This early castle was built in 1081, and at this date a timber rather than a stone superstructure to the earthworks has to be envisaged. The stone castle is probably due to rebuilding in the following, twelfth century. The motte was now surmounted by a fine and well-preserved polygonal shell-keep, and a new stone-walled bailey was contrived in the western half of the original Roman enclosure. Most of the western and half of the southern walls of the Roman fort were rebuilt to form two sides of the bailey, and new walls were built running from the shell-keep to these sides to form a trapeze-shaped inner bailey. At the same time the surviving Roman bank (on the north, east and part of the south sides) was added to and a new, relatively thin wall was built on top. This formed an outer bailey. The entrance to the new castle was in the Black Tower in the middle of the south side. The semi-octagonal tower through which the shell-keep is now entered is a later addition, possibly of the fifteenth century. In the same century occupation shifted from the shell-keep to more spacious apartments on the west curtain wall, including the great octagonal tower and some of the adjacent buildings.

Around the middle of the sixteenth century William Herbert (later Earl of Pembroke) added the Herbert Tower just south of the octagonal tower, but the major changes in the castle began after 1766 when it came into the possession of the Marquis of Bute. The third Marquis, who succeeded in 1848, and his architect, William Burges (the team responsible for the restoration of Castell Coch, p 191), were particularly active and the existing shape and appearance of the castle is largely due to their efforts. Three great new towers (Bute Tower, Guest Tower, and Clock Tower) were built close to the two existing towers (Octagon Tower and Herbert Tower), forming the group of five tall towers which are now such a striking feature on the south-west side of Cardiff Castle. It was in this period, in 1898, that the foundations of the Roman walls were discovered on the east side of the castle and it was first realized that the site was much older than had previously been suspected. From this time began the restoration, under the third Marquis and his successor, of the Roman walls on the north, east and part of the south sides, giving now some impression of what one of these great Roman forts must have looked like. Of particular interest in this respect is the restored Roman north gate of the fort. Like many another medieval castle, Cardiff has a history stretching back to early times, but in few castles are the earlier structures so well represented, even if in restored form.

Coity Castle (SS 923816)
Records indicate that there was already a castle at Coity in the years 1090–1106 but this can hardly refer to the existing stone structure. The circular inner bailey of the latter suggests an original ringwork of earth and timber some 150 ft in diameter, with a surrounding ditch, and this is probably the castle referred to above. Like many such castles this was rebuilt in stone in the twelfth century. The presumed timber palisade was replaced by a circular (actually many-sided polygonal) stone curtain wall, with a rectangular keep on the north-west side and an entrance tower on the north-east. The existing curtain wall on the north-west half of the circuit is a later rebuilding, but the original curtain survives on the south-east, with a later addition on top bringing it to its present height. The keep is ruinous but still stands in two upstanding portions to third-storey level. No doubt there were other buildings within the bailey at this time, but the surviving remains against the south curtain wall are of buildings of the fourteenth century. These include the ruins of a first-floor hall and other associated domestic buildings. At the same time the rectangular outer bailey, surrounded by a curtain wall with rectangular towers, was added on the west side.

One of the most interesting features of Coity is the oval tower which projects into the ditch from the south curtain of the Inner Bailey. This was built in the thirteenth century so it must then have been associated with the buildings (hall etc.) which preceded those

referred to above which were built, or rebuilt, in the fourteenth century. Its great projection (over 20 ft) would have provided covering fire for a large part of the south-eastern curtain and, with the keep and the entrance tower, would have formed a more or less evenly spaced arrangement of towers. Apart from its military function, however, it seems to have been built with domestic needs in mind, as a specialized latrine block. It is (or was) of four storeys, although the top-most storey has now mostly gone. The bottom storey, with a drainage outlet to the moat, was, in fact, a latrine pit or chamber some 15 ft deep. Above this were three generally similar storeys given over to latrines and, when the need arose, defence. The storey above the pit had three latrines, the next one two, and the ruined top storey apparently one. These floors were linked to the adjacent domestic buildings on the inner side of the curtain wall.

Newcastle, Bridgend (SS 902801)

Newcastle is a fairly simple structure, virtually of one period as far as its visible stone remains are concerned. There is a reference to a castle at Bridgend as early as 1106; if it was on the site of the existing castle then it has left no visible remains, although at such a date it would almost certainly have been timber-built anyway. The existing castle was built in the reign of Henry II (1154–89). It consists of a polygonal curtain wall (most of the outer facing of which has gone) enclosing an area or courtyard about 100 ft in diameter. Straddling the wall are the remains of two rectangular towers and these, with the curtain wall and a few fragments of internal buildings, constitute the entire castle. The entrance (an arched passage through the 7 ft-thick curtain) is immediately alongside the southern tower, often called the keep although it is, in fact, marginally smaller than the one on the north-west. The ground-floor door into the (so-called) keep from the courtyard is a sixteenth-century alteration, as is the window alongside the fireplace inside. The tower was originally entered only at first-floor level, possibly by a timber stair on the site of the existing

Coity Castle: the gate-tower

Newcastle Bridgend: the arched entrance alongside the south tower

sixteenth-century flight of stone steps. The room at first-floor level contains a fireplace, as does the one above, so that the tower could well have been used as a keep. The existing relatively large windows are again sixteenth century, replacing much smaller original windows. The larger western tower is less well preserved (most of the eastern wall has gone), but like the other it was entered at first-floor level. Against the inner face of the east curtain are two walls of what may have been the hall of the castle. The building to the south of it, in the south-east angle, is of sixteenth-century date and of uncertain purpose, as is the undated building north-west of the hall.

Caldicot Castle (ST 487885)

The original motte-and-bailey plan of Caldicot is still very evident in the earthworks on which the existing stone castle stands. This was probably preceded by a timber castle, built c. 1100 by the Sherriff of Gloucester who held the manor of Caldicot at that time. During the following century ownership passed to the de Bohuns, Earls of Hereford, and it was under them that Caldicot was transformed into the splendid castle which still exists today. The rebuilding began in the last decade of the century (1190–1200) and the first part to be built was the fine circular keep on the motte in the north-west corner of the site. This is of four storeys and is entered from the motte top at second-storey level. The three upper storeys are well appointed rooms with fireplaces and at this stage the keep probably formed the principal accommodation in the castle. The bottom storey, buried in the motte and reached from above, was probably used only for storage. A noticeable feature of the keep is the solid semi-circular turret on its west side, facing the exterior.

When the keep was complete, work began on the curtain walls and towers of the large bailey, probably in the years 1200–1210. Linking the various sections of curtain wall are four towers and a gatehouse. The large, semi-circular south-east angle tower (to the right as one faces the gatehouse) still retains some of its battlements and, below them, the holes for the timber-covered platforms built out from the wallhead in time of siege to allow missiles to be dropped directly down on to the heads of attackers. To the left of the gatehouse is a smaller circular tower at the south-west angle. There is an interval tower in the middle of the west curtain which contains a postern gate with a right-angled bend in its passage.

About a century later (c. 1310) two considerable additions were made to the castle. The lesser of these was the fine semi-octagonal tower built (or rebuilt) on the north side of the castle. This is preserved to its full height and has a heavily machicolated parapet, making temporary timber structures unnecessary in times of siege. At ground level it provided another postern gate (or alternative entrance) in times of emergency. The second and greater addition was the handsome gatehouse which still stands on the south side of the castle and is the means of access for visitors. At this period (early fourteenth century), a twin-towered Edwardian-type gatehouse might have been expected, but Caldicot follows a style of its own. It is oblong in plan, with an entrance passage through the middle and tall twin rectangular latrine towers at either end. In the entrance passage there were two portcullises and two twin-leaved doors. Unlike the Edwardian gatehouses, it had no great hall on the upper floor, simply a comfortable suite of rooms for the lord of the castle. Quite clearly the principal accommodation of the castle had now shifted from the keep to the gatehouse, and domestic comfort (albeit with the needs of defence still in mind) was the guiding principle behind the building of the new gatehouse.

The de Bohun ownership ended in 1377 and the castle passed to the Duke of Gloucester and then the Dukes of Buckingham, the third of whom was executed in 1521. Subsequently Caldicot fell into decay and its present excellent appearance is due to restoration in modern times.

Chepstow Castle (ST 533941)
Chepstow was built by William fitz Osbern, a kinsman of the Conqueror, in the years 1067–71 and it appears to have been stone-built from the beginning. The nucleus of this early castle was an oblong hall block, with the hall at first-floor level above a vaulted basement. The hall block is placed lengthwise along the narrowest part of a ridge, leaving only a narrow passage on its north side for communication between the two baileys which flanked it: Upper Bailey to the west and Middle Bailey to the east. The walls of both baileys have been rebuilt in later periods, but some portions of the early walling remain. Early in the thirteenth century the castle was extended in both directions. The Lower Bailey, with a double-towered gatehouse, was added at the eastern end, and a barbican was built beyond the outer ditch at the western end. In the second half of the century there were three major additions to the castle. The hall block was given a tall, third storey, transforming it, in effect, into a keep. A large D-shaped tower (Marten's Tower) was added at the south-eastern angle, providing an independent,

Chepstow Castle: the gatehouse

self-contained residence (a tower-house). The third addition was a great domestic range on the north side of the Lower Bailey, no doubt replacing the accommodation formerly provided in what had now become the keep. Apart from minor modifications, repairs, and maintenance, the castle has remained largely unaltered since 1300, although the south curtain wall was rebuilt c. 1650.

Entry to the castle is at the east end through the double-towered gatehouse built between 1200 and 1250. This leads into the Lower Bailey, with Marten's Tower on the left, built in the second half of the century and named after Henry Marten, who was imprisoned there 1660–1680. The tower is of keep-like proportions (55 by 42 ft with walls 12–15 ft thick), and by means of portcullises it could be isolated from the Lower Bailey and the curtain walls on either side. It has a basement below courtyard-level and three spacious rooms above (c. 25 by 18 ft), together with a chapel and garderobes, and must have formed a comfortable, commodious, and secure self-contained residence within the castle, possibly for the lord and his family in times of danger. To the right of the gatehouse are the substantial remains of the great domestic range added about the same time as Marten's Tower. This is unusual in that it contains not one but two complete suites of rooms, two halls, two solars etc., and may have been built originally for the visit of Edward I and his queen Eleanor in December 1284, although no doubt it was subsequently used by the lord and his family for their own domestic needs.

The gate at the north-west angle of the Lower Bailey leads into the Middle Bailey, one of the two original baileys of the castle. Beyond the Middle Bailey are the remains of the keep (the original hall block) with the northern and western walls still standing virtually to their full (three-storey) height. Although the roof and all floors have long since gone, much of the architectural embellishment of the walls in the hall can still be seen from the basement. Access to the western part of the castle is via a narrow passage or gallery, blocked by gates, between the north wall of the keep and the cliff edge, surmounted by a wall some 15 ft away. This passage leads into the Upper Bailey, the second of the original baileys of the early castle. Beyond the ditch at its western end (originally the western limit of the castle), is the barbican, added c. 1250–1300, a small enclosure with a curtain wall, a gatehouse and two wall-towers (the northern one almost gone), which had to be taken before any approach could be made to the Upper Bailey and its defences.

Grosmont Castle (SO 405244)
The earliest surviving part of Grosmont (the stone-built hall) belongs to the thirteenth century, so that references in the twelfth century must be to the timber-built castle which preceded the existing structure. These references mention work in 1162–3 and 1185–6, so presumably the castle was already in existence then and may have been built in the first half of the century. At this time Grosmont was a royal castle, administered on the king's behalf by the Sheriff of Herefordshire. It would have consisted of a timber palisade with internal timber buildings, surrounded by the same

Grosmont Castle

D-shaped ditch (or an earlier version thereof) which surrounds the existing castle.

In 1201 King John (1199–1216) granted Grosmont Castle (together with White Castle, p 232, and Skenfrith Castle, p 230) to Hubert de Burgh, and it was he who, in the next few years, began the conversion of the castle from a timber to a stone structure. The first building erected (c. 1210) was the long, two-storey hall block which still occupies the entire eastern side of the site. The two doorways near the centre of the west wall (the courtyard side) lead into what were the two basement rooms beneath the hall which was at first-floor level (the floor and the roof above have gone). The southern basement, which had a fireplace, may have been the kitchen. In such hall blocks the first-floor accommodation is usually divided into the hall proper and the solar or withdrawing-room. There is no indication of such a division at Grosmont, but since it is unlikely that one did not exist, it may be presumed that in this case it was of timber, an arrangement not unknown elsewhere. The hall occupies the straight side of the D-plan. At this stage the curving portion was still defended by a timber palisade and this remained in position for another decade or two.

In 1233 the castle was attacked by the Welsh, and although it was not taken it may well have been this event which led to the rebuilding of the timber defences in stone. In any case, the main defences were certainly rebuilt between 1220 and 1240. A gatehouse and three round towers, with linking curtain walls, were built in a semi-circle around the western half of the castle, with the already built hall occupying the eastern portion. The western tower is of four storeys, and the two others were probably the same, although they have been altered by later rebuilding. Additional accommodation was provided by buildings against the curtain walls.

In this form the castle continued for another century or so, until c. 1330, when the last major addition was made. A three-storey range (its outer, northern wall now gone) was built outside the north curtain wall and part of the north wall of the hall. Its building involved the destruction of most of the north tower. A prominent surviving feature of this new block is the chimney which served fireplaces in the new second- and third-storey rooms, built partly over the remains of the north tower. At the same time the south-west tower was enlarged on the inside and a similar addition was made to the curtain wall immediately adjacent to it. The gatehouse was also extended forwards by some 24 ft at this time, to enclose the drawbridge pit.

This was the last phase in the castle's structural development. The only subsequent event worthy of note is the siege by Owen Glendower in 1405, which, like the earlier attack in 1233, was unsuccessful. Thereafter the castle seems to have fallen gradually into decay.

Raglan Castle (SO 415084)

The building of Raglan Castle was undertaken (c. 1435) by Sir William ap Thomas, an adherent of the Duke of York, who led the opposition to Lancastrian rule which eventually developed into the Wars of the Roses, although by this time ap Thomas was dead

(1445). The castle was completed by his son, the first Earl of Pembroke, in the years 1450–1469, although there were some alterations and additions around the turn of the century (1490–1525).

Access to the castle area is through an outer (early seventeenth-century) gatehouse with flanking, semi-octagonal towers, although these are not well preserved. Directly in front is the gatehouse of the castle proper, while to the left is the Great Tower (the Yellow Tower of Gwent), one of the outstanding features of the site. This is a great hexagonal tower of keep-like proportions, four (possibly five) storeys high, with very thick walls (10 ft), although at this date it is probably best considered as a tower-house (p 37). The top and two of the six sides of the tower have now gone (destroyed in 1646), but the main lines of its structure are clear. Access was, and still is, at first floor level, originally via a wooden bridge, later by a stone bridge and a forebuilding, now by a modern bridge. This leads into a small lobby in the thickness of the wall with a spiral staircase to the left providing communication both up and down to the various floors, each of which consisted of a single hexagonal room. Below entry-level is a room which was (or at least could be used as) a kitchen, with a large fireplace and a well. The room at entry-level was the hall or main living-room, and the room above was the lord's camera or private apartment. The fourth storey was a bedroom and so probably was the fifth, if one existed. There was a garderobe (latrine) on every floor. The range of rooms and services make it clear that this was a self-contained residence and it is, therefore, justifiably described as a tower-house. The surrounding terrace is of the same shape, with an outer wall strengthened with semi-circular turrets at the angles, and beyond this is the still-wet moat which isolated it from the surrounding area and from the rest of the castle.

The Great Gatehouse, with its flanking semi-hexagonal towers, stands close to one edge of the moat, and is preserved virtually to its full height. Its entrance passage (originally protected by two portcullises and three double doors), leads into one of the two courtyards in the castle, the Pitched Stone Court, so called because

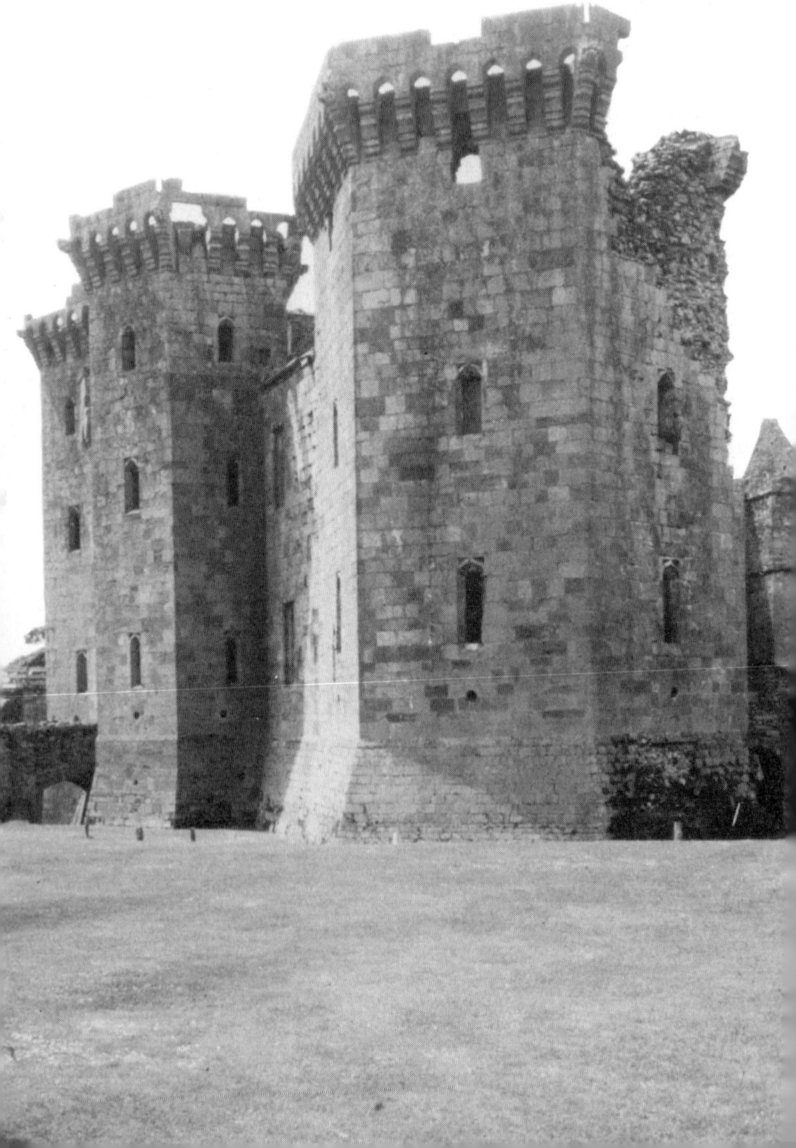

of its well preserved (and heavily cambered) cobbled surface. The surface dips down to a gully parallel with the surrounding walls, designed to take the run-off from the adjacent roofs and from the centre of the courtyard. This particular cobbled surface dates from the sixteenth century when the courtyard was enlarged, but about 15 ins beneath it is an earlier cobbled surface, probably of the mid-fifteenth century when Raglan was first built. From the Pitched Stone Court the back view of the gatehouse is very different from the front. The most noticeable features are the very large rectangular windows lighting a large room occupying the first floor of the gatehouse, probably used as a gallery (in the sense of a long gallery) for the entertainment and relaxation of guests. To the left of the gatehouse (looking from the courtyard) is the hexagonal Closet Tower, with a prison in its basement and three storeys above. The first two storeys were comfortable living-rooms, with fireplaces, garderobes and windows, probably forming a suite for the steward, the lord of the manor's chief officer. The top storey seems to have had some specialist storage function and may have been a treasury. From the Closet Tower the Office Wing (not a great deal of which remains) runs along the north-east side of the court as far as the Kitchen Tower, another large hexagonal tower. The Office Wing housed the bakery and brewhouse at ground-floor level, with (probably) domestic accommodation on the floors above.

The left side of the Pitched Stone Court from the entrance is occupied by the hall and its associated offices. The wall facing the courtyard is preserved virtually to its full height and has a three-storey porch, with three large windows to the left, the one at the upper end of the hall being a fine oriel window. The rest of the range (to the right of the porch) is occupied by the buttery, and a passage leading round to the range at the far end of the court which contained the pantry and a connecting passage leading to the kitchen in the Kitchen Tower mentioned earlier. This completes the circuit of the Pitched Stone Court, except for the area between the upper end of the hall (the oriel window end) and the gatehouse, which contained the private apartments for the lord and his family,

Raglan Castle: the gatehouse and the east angle tower

and was the means of access to the Great Tower across the adjacent moat.

The remains around the Fountain Court, on the far side of the hall range from the Pitched Stone Court, are more fragmentary than the latter, and were in any case far less varied in character. They consisted mostly of apartments, i.e. accommodation for various members of what was clearly a very large household. Against the south-west side of the hall are the foundations of a chapel, and of a porch, opposite the one in the Pitched Stone Court. In one corner of the Fountain Court, adjacent to the moat, is the South Gate, a rectangular tower built in the first period of the castle's construction (1435–45); the remaining buildings belong to the second period (1450–69). The Fountain Court takes its name from a marble fountain which once stood at its centre but has now gone.

Although not much of it now remains, Raglan once contained a fine long gallery, added by William Somerset, third Earl of Worcester, who was in possession from 1548–89. The long gallery (126 ft long) ran above the chapel and the porch and ended in the semi-hexagonal tower projecting beyond the curtain wall to the west, where some of its fine windows can still be seen. There were similar windows along the gallery overlooking the Fountain Court.

Skenfrith Castle (SO 457203)

Skenfrith, which in its existing form was built c. 1200, embraces both the early tradition of castles with keeps (in this case in circular form), and the later tradition of castles which relied on curtain walls and angle towers. References to repairs carried out in 1163 and 1183, however, indicate that there was an earlier castle on the site, and this presumably involved a timber tower on the existing motte and a timber palisade on the general line of the existing stone curtain wall. Even at that stage the castle would appear to have been surrounded by a wet moat (now dry) on three sides, fed from the River Monnow on the fourth, and this presumably explains the choice of site.

Around 1200 the castle was rebuilt in stone, and it is the surviving portion of this castle which is visible today. The relatively low motte

Skenfrith Castle: the circular keep

was surmounted by a circular keep. Because the artificial motte would probably not have been strong enough to support the weight of a heavy stone structure, the foundations of the new keep were carried down through the motte to the natural ground beneath to provide a solid support. The keep itself (c. 35 ft in diameter) is of three storeys above a basement, with communication (although not to the basement which must have been reached by a trap-door) via a spiral staircase housed in the semi-circular projection on the east side. The upper portion of the keep is now missing.

Whatever defences the bailey previously had, they were now (1200) replaced by the existing stone curtain wall and towers, forming a trapeze-shaped plan. A gap in the middle of the north curtain wall indicates the position of the original entrance, which does not appear to have been very elaborate; there certainly is not sufficient room for a twin-towered gatehouse. Apart from the curtain, the main defence features were four boldly projecting circular angle towers, c. 25 ft in diameter, which permitted flanking fire along the adjacent walls. The north-west tower has almost completely gone but about two-thirds of each of the others is preserved. The best preserved section of curtain wall is on the east side, towards the river, where it stands up to wall-walk height. There was a postern or water-gate on the east, in the form of a vaulted passage through the thickness of the curtain wall. The west curtain wall was further strengthened by a solid, D-shaped tower or bastion. Within the west curtain are the foundations and lower walls of a suite of rooms which must have added greatly to the range of accommodation within the castle, which would otherwise have been confined to the keep and the angle towers.

Skenfrith was never a very elaborate castle, but its plan, with four rectilinear walls, foreshadows the much more regular planning of the thirteenth century and leaves behind the somewhat irregular layout of the preceding periods.

White Castle (SO 380168)

The early name of White Castle was Llantilio Castle, but by the thirteenth century it had acquired its present name, a result of the white plaster coating with which the stonework was once covered (cf. Conway Castle, p 265). White Castle is divided into three sections. The middle section (the Inner Ward) is oval in plan and is surrounded by a deep wet moat. To the south is a crescent-shaped hornwork, also surrounded by a moat linked to the one just mentioned. On the opposite side (the north) is a large Outer Ward, surrounded by a dry moat not connected with the other moat systems. The existing stone remains are of the mid-twelfth century (and later), but there was probably a castle here c. 1100 which must have been timber-built. Around the middle of the century the first stone structure (the rectangular keep) was erected. In fact this must have been built before 1155, for there is in the Exchequer records no mention of expenditure which could account for its construction after that date. Very little remains of this keep apart from about half its foundations, but it is a convenient point from which to start any account of White Castle's structural history.

The castle is entered via the Outer Gate on the north-east side. About 120 ft beyond is the bridge across the wet moat, leading to the gatehouse at the northern end of the Inner Ward. At the southern end are the remains of the rectangular keep (c. 35 ft square). At the time (pre-1155) this was the only stone structure on the site, so that the rest of the defences must have been still of timber as described earlier. The existing stone curtain wall was not built until some 30 years later (1184–6), and then it was a plain curtain, the wall-towers and gatehouse being later again. Thus by the end of the twelfth century the castle consisted of a keep and stone-walled bailey, with a timber palisade outwork to the south, and a similarly defended Outer Ward to the north. At this stage the entrance was alongside the keep and was reached via a wooden bridge (now gone) from the outwork, which would have to be taken by an enemy before the entrance could be approached. When the main entry was switched to the north end in the following century, the old entrance was retained as a postern gate.

The castle seems to have remained in this state for about three-quarters of a century until troubles in Wales in the 1260s and 1270s led to a major refortification of the site, incorporating the latest ideas in military architecture. The old keep was pulled down and a new section of curtain wall was built across its remains. The curtain as a whole was strengthened by the addition of six circular towers, two of them forming a gatehouse at the northern end of the site, which thus became the main means of access. From the top of the gatehouse an excellent panoramic view can be obtained of the whole castle layout. Against the curtain walls both to east and west are the low walls or foundations of a range of thirteenth-century buildings, including a kitchen, a hall, a solar, and a chapel, the chancel of the latter housed in the south-east tower. As thus reconstructed the Inner Ward was very much a structure of the thirteenth century, when curtain wall with towers (including towered gatehouses) replaced the old keep concept.

The outwork seems to have remained very much as it was, with its timber palisade, but there were new stone structures at the northern end of the site in the larger Outer Ward, probably intended to accommodate a large body of troops in time of war. Whatever existed before was now replaced by a stone curtain wall with four evenly spaced towers (three round, one rectangular), and the Outer Gate mentioned earlier. The moat surrounding the Outer Ward was (and is) dry: its bottom stands well above the level of the deep moats surrounding the Inner Ward and the outworks, and water could never have flowed from one system to the other.

The pacification of Wales by Edward I (1272–1307) robbed White Castle of much of its military importance, although it continued in use for another couple of centuries. By the sixteenth century, however, it was derelict, but has now (since 1922) been restored to its existing state by the Department of the Environment and its earlier equivalents.

POWYS

Bronllys Castle (SO 149346)
Apart from the earthworks (a motte and a large rectangular bailey) virtually the only surviving remnant of Bronllys is the

White Castle: the twin-towered gatehouse

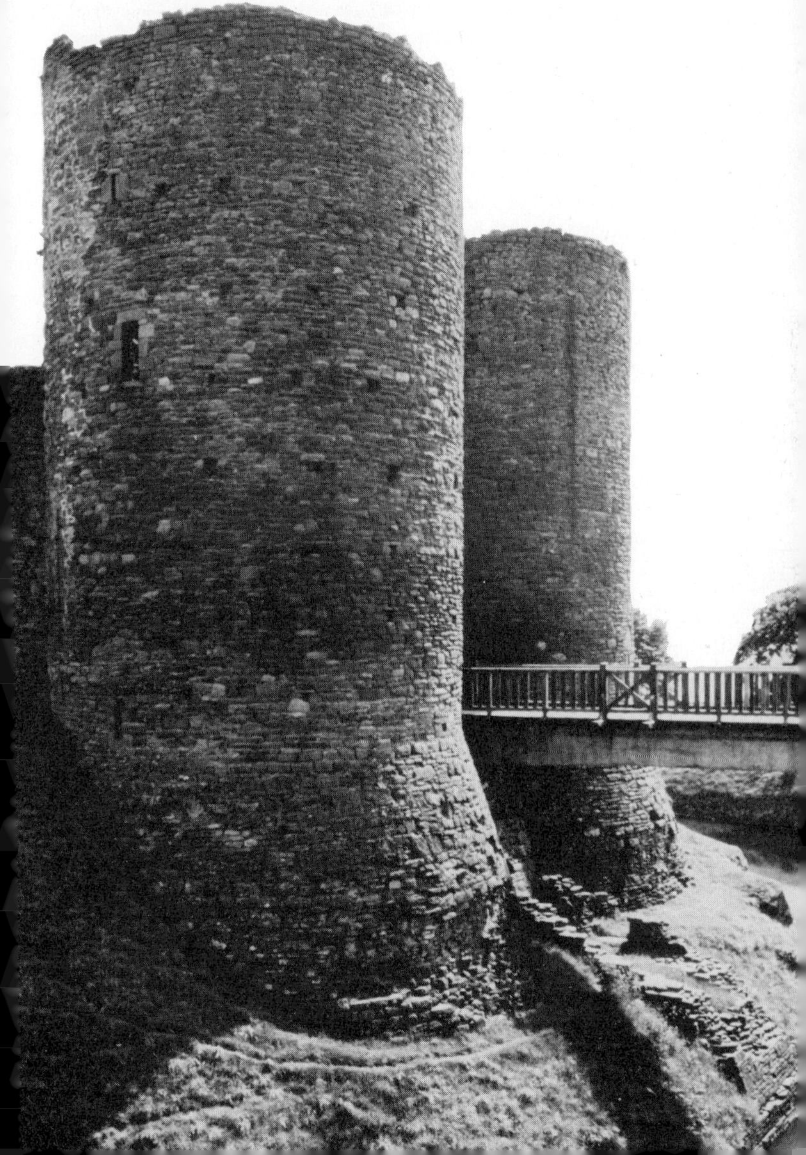

well-preserved circular keep which surmounts the motte. Access is at first-floor level via a modern wooden stair; there is no indication of the original means of access which may likewise have been of wood. The first floor has two windows but no fireplace. From a trap-door in one of the window recesses there was access to the basement below. From one side of the other window recess, a stair in the thickness of the walls leads up to the second floor which also has two windows, and a fireplace. Another mural stair, on the opposite side to the one below leads up to the third floor, which has three windows, a fireplace and a latrine chamber. Quite clearly the main accommodation was in the two upper rooms, the top one no doubt serving as the lord's private retreat from the more general living-room below. There is a reference to the castle in 1175, when a fire is mentioned. The existing stone tower can hardly be as early as that and the reference is presumably to the timber castle which preceded it. There is a further reference in 1223 when Henry III (1216–1272) and Hubert de Burgh were at Bronllys, and this is much more likely to refer to the surviving stone keep.

Tretower Castle (SO 184212)
Tretower Castle is approached through Tretower Court, a fine manor house built around a courtyard which probably succeeded the castle as the main accommodation of the lord of the manor. Certainly part of the building (the north range) goes back to the fourteenth century when the castle, although still in use, was probably considered too cramped and uncomfortable for normal domestic purposes. The castle is of the motte-and-bailey type, although the motte is quite low beneath the later stone structure: whether it was ever much higher is doubtful. As first built, probably c. 1100, there were timber palisades around the top of the motte and around the roughly rectangular bailey, with timber internal buildings in both. Around 1150 the first stone structure was built, a shell-keep with a range of internal stone buildings. The shell (c. 70 ft in overall diameter) is somewhat irregular in plan, since on the south and west it follows the line of the L-shaped domestic block, with a further projection to the south to accommodate the kitchen. On the north and east, much of which is now gone or reduced to

foundations, it followed a more regular line around the edge of the motte in a series of straight sections, and included the entrance, housed in a square structure (with a pit) which probably rose as a tower above the shell wall.

Most of the internal buildings were destroyed when the circular keep was built inside the shell in the first half of the thirteenth century. They consisted principally of a hall along the south and a solar along the west side, in an L-shaped arrangement, both at first-floor level on low basements. Better preserved is the kitchen to the south of the hall and on a level with its basement. This is reached by a passage in the thickness of the wall to the left of the entrance, and presumably continued in use as the kitchen after the keep was built. The way in which the kitchen block projected beyond the curtain wall can best be seen from outside the shell wall, to the south. From the same position can be seen the arrow loops on either side of the fireplace and, above and to the left, two blocked windows of the first-floor domestic buildings. The south-west angle of the curtain has collapsed, but in the surviving lower corner can be seen the beginnings of a spiral staircase which provided access to the rampart walk.

Between 1200 and 1250 the walls of the domestic buildings facing the courtyard were destroyed to make way for a new circular keep (c. 36 ft in diameter) preserved virtually to its full height, which takes it well above the level of the surrounding curtain walls. The keep is of three storeys above a basement, although the upper parts are not now accessible. Access is at first-floor level, above the basement. On the left side of the entrance passage a mural staircase rises to the (non-accessible) upper floors. The first floor has a fine fireplace and two deeply recessed windows with window seats. From the left side of the window recess opposite the entrance another mural staircase leads down to the basement. The second floor is generally similar to the first (fireplace, two windows), but the top floor lacks a fireplace. The two principal living-rooms, therefore, must have been the first and second floors, acting as hall and solar.

Thus as completed by c. 1250 the castle formed a sort of concentric arrangement: the original twelfth-century shell wall

South Wales

closely surrounding the thirteenth-century tower which rose high above it. The arrangement was completed by a stone-walled bailey to the east, with circular angle towers, some remnants of which are incorporated in the adjacent farm buildings.

Tretower Castle: the keep and shell wall

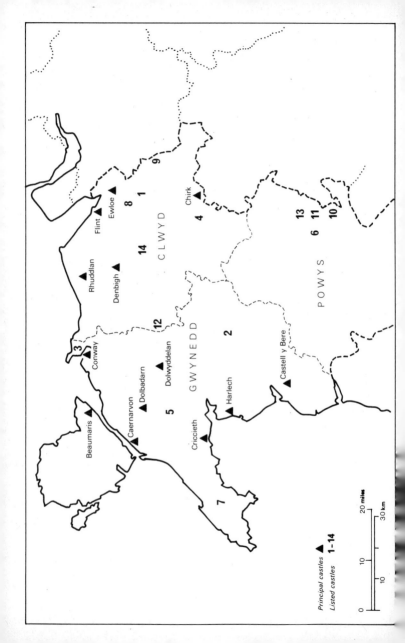

Flint

Ewloe

Rhuddlan

Denbigh

Chirk

CLWYD

POWYS

Conway

Caernarvon

Dolbadarn

Dolwyddelan

GWYNEDD

Beaumaris

Criccieth

Harlech

Castell y Bere

Principal castles ▲

Listed castles 1–14

0   10   20 miles

10   30 km

8 North Wales

The North Wales region includes the modern counties of Clwyd, Gwynedd, and the northern part of Powys, replacing the old counties of Flintshire, Denbighshire, Caernarvonshire, Anglesey, Merionethshire, and Montgomeryshire. Within this area there are remains of about two dozen castles, some of them outstandingly well preserved, including the group built by Edward I in the years between 1277 and 1307. Although the Edwardian castles are the most spectacular, they are by no means the only visible castle remains in the area. Prior to the Edwardian period the Welsh had built a number of castles of their own in the course of the long, see-saw struggle with the English for the control of North Wales. These included Dinas Bran and Ewloe (Clwyd), Castell y Bere, Criccieth, Dolbadarn and Dolwyddelan (Gwynedd), and Dolforwyn (Powys). After the conquest of the area Edward I adapted three of these for his own needs: Castell y Bere, Criccieth, and Dolwyddelan. There were also a number of pre-Edwardian English castles built in the course of the same struggle, principally by Edward's father, Henry III (1216–1272): Dyserth and Degannwy (Clwyd), and Montgomery (Powys).

   As part of his effort to bring North Wales finally under English control Edward I (1272–1307) waged two campaigns, one in 1277 and one 1282–3. As part of the first campaign he built (or extensively rebuilt) castles at Flint, Rhuddlan, Hawarden, and Ruthin. The peace achieved at the end of 1277 was short-lived, and a more decisive campaign was conducted in the years 1282–3. Arising out of this second campaign a much more ambitious castle-building programme was launched, embracing no less than eleven castles, in addition to the four already under construction. This second group included the four outstanding sites in North Wales, Conway, Caernarvon, Harlech, and Beaumaris, together with Holt, Chirk, Denbigh, Criccieth, Dolwyddelan, Castell y Bere, and Caergwrle.

   About a dozen castles in the area have keeps of one sort or another, including all of the Welsh castles mentioned above. There are rectangular keeps at Criccieth, Dinas Bran, and Dolwyddelan; there are D-shaped keeps at Castell y Bere, Ewloe, and Carndochan; and there are circular keeps at Dolbadarn, Dolforwyn, Flint, and Hawarden. Of other types of castle there are examples of concentric castles at Rhuddlan, Aberystwyth, Harlech and Beaumaris, and of curtain-wall and tower castles at Conway and Caernarvon. A particular feature of castles in North Wales are the great double-towered gatehouses, including those at Denbigh, Caernarvon, Harlech, and Beaumaris.

The castles not included in the detailed inventory are listed below and shown in the map on p 240:

1. Caergwrle (Clwyd): small Edwardian castle; remains of three towers and a curtain wall.
2. Carndochan (Powys): D-shaped keep; bailey with two round-fronted towers.
3. Degannwy (Gwynedd): built by Henry III (1216–72), but very little now above ground; plan from excavation.
4. Dinas Bran (Clwyd): stub of a rectangular keep, and a double-towered gatehouse.
5. Dinas Emrys (Gwynedd): square tower on Dark Age fortified site.
6. Dolforwyn (Powys): round keep and rectangular bailey, built by Llywelyn ap Gruffydd.
7. Garn Fadrun (Gwynedd): within Iron Age hill-fort of same name; mentioned as new in 1188.
8. Hawarden (Clwyd): round keep on motte, remains of bailey wall; built or rebuilt in Edwardian period (1272–1307).
9. Holt (Clwyd): rather puzzling remains of pentagonal castle built in late thirteenth century.
10. Montgomery (Powys): begun 1223 by Henry III; three baileys along a promontory site.
11. Nantcribba (Powys): small stone castle with four round towers on top of conical rock.
12. Pentrefoelas (Clwyd): large motte with traces of a ring wall; bailey doubtful.

13. Powys (Powys): built late thirteenth century, heavily rebuilt
    late seventeenth century; principal remnant a double-towered
    gatehouse.
14. Ruthin (Clwyd): Edwardian castle, now in hotel grounds,
    accessible to hotel guests only.

CLWYD

Chirk Castle (SJ 268381)
Chirk Castle was the result of a new lordship created by Edward I in
pursuance of his policy of securing a firm hold on North Wales after
the troubles of 1277 and 1282–3. In June 1282 he granted the
territory to Roger Mortimer the younger, and work on the castle
began some time between 1282 and 1300; there is some
disagreement as to the exact starting date. Whenever it started, the
work was still incomplete when Roger Mortimer fell from grace
under Edward II in 1322. In fact, the castle as originally conceived
was never completed, the existing structure representing just over
half of the original plan. Instead of the projected southern portion,
a simpler southern range without towers was eventually added, just
south of the east and west interval towers. Chirk has been
continuously occupied since the fourteenth century and contains
some fine internal rooms of the post-medieval period.

   The medieval aspects of the castle can best be understood from
the outside. The approach for visitors is from the north, on which
side there are three towers, north-west angle, north-east angle, and
a half round mid-wall tower. These now rise only to the same height
as the curtain wall but they would originally have risen about half as
high again, if and when completed. The entrance is an arched
passage through the thickness of the curtain wall; there is no
gatehouse as such, but the mid-wall and north-east angle towers are
so close anyway that they virtually provide the same cover as
normal flanking towers. Before entering, it is worthwhile looking at
both the east and west sides of the castle which tell the same story.
About 75 ft south of both angle towers is a D-shaped interval tower,
presumably marking the half-way point in the planned east and west

Chirk Castle: continuously occupied since the fourteenth century

curtain walls. The original plan is curtailed just south of these two towers, and the structure is completed by the later block mentioned above. Presumably, however, the intended plan called for a southern half matching the surviving one to the north of the interval towers, with south-west and south-east angle towers and an interval tower, producing a large castle, nearly twice the size of the existing structure.

The arched entrance passage in the north curtain leads into a rectangular courtyard which, although splendidly preserved, contains little that is medieval, apart from the west curtain wall and the north-west angle and west interval towers, where the thickness of the original walls can be seen in the window openings. The entrance to the interior of the castle is in the north range and visitors can see a series of post-medieval rooms in the eastern half of the north range, on the first floor of the east range, and along the ground floor of the south range.

As a medieval structure Chirk is not now particularly impressive; the lack of tall towers gives it an unexciting elevation. However, an appreciation of its unfinished state can leave the visitor to imagine what a magnificent castle it might have been had the original plan been fully carried out.

Denbigh Castle (SJ 052658)

Like Chirk, Denbigh was a lordship castle, built by a trusted baron on land granted by Edward I as part of his grand strategy for controlling North Wales. The lordship was granted to Henry de Lacy, Earl of Lincoln, on 16 October 1282, and work began almost immediately.

The castle is built in the south-west angle of the surviving town wall, and its defences fall into two parts. The south and west sides are formed by the town wall and inevitably follow the style of its defences, with round towers and relatively thin (6 ft) curtain walls. As visitors will quickly appreciate, this is scarcely a weakness since there are formidable natural defences on these sides below the walls. On the two remaining sides, north and east (the town side), the castle's defences were completed by building a much thicker (10 ft) curtain wall, with much larger towers, octagonal or semi-octagonal in shape, and an impressive gatehouse. The area thus cut off from the town enclosure forms the castle and is roughly oval in plan (c. 350 by 250 ft internally). Much of the castle is in a ruinous condition but there is more than enough left to show that in its original state it must have been a most impressive structure.

Entry is via the original gatehouse at the north end of the castle. The first point to note is the use of octagonal towers, as at Caernarvon. The second is the decorative pattern of stones above the entrance arch. The third is the statue in the same position, the figure of a seated man, which may, in fact, be a representation of Edward I himself. The most unusual aspect of the gatehouse, however, is its plan which again recalls that of Caernarvon. The Denbigh gatehouse consists not of the usual two towers, but of three, arranged in a triangular fashion, two to the front and one to the rear, within the castle, but linked by walls to the others to form a single massive triangular block some 120 ft long and 90 ft wide. The entrance passage between the two outer towers leads, not, as in most castles, directly to the courtyard, but into an octagonal hall at the very heart of the triangular block, with the third tower directly in front. Entry to the courtyard was via a second passage, opening from the right of the octagonal hall, which could be closed off by means of a portcullis. This meant that an enemy who had passed through the outer entrance passage would find himself in a confined space (the octagonal hall), under fire from surrounding arrow loops, and with no means of gaining the courtyard once the inner portcullis was lowered. The gatehouse is a most impressive piece of military architecture and is one of the outstanding features of Denbigh. Access to the upper floors of the gatehouse is through a door just south of the inner entrance to the courtyard. This leads to a double staircase, a spiral one (leading upwards), but now largely gone, and a straight one leading off it to the east, which now gives access to the top of the surviving curtain wall south-east of the gatehouse. Although the top of this wall is now open to the sky it was originally a covered gallery (similar to the ones at Caernarvon), with the original rampart walk (not preserved) at a higher level.

Only a limited section of the wall top is accessible, although from it there is a panoramic view of the interior, particularly of the domestic buildings against the east curtain wall immediately below, which can be examined next. Returning to the courtyard, the site of the chapel (now entirely gone) was in the angle between the gatehouse and the curtain wall to the south-east. There was a second chapel (also gone) near the Bishop's Tower on the west side of the courtyard. Beyond the chapel site is the well (50 ft deep) and beyond that the Great Kitchen Tower, one of the great semi-octagonal towers on the east curtain wall. Only the ground floor of this three storey tower is now accessible, but this contains the features which give the tower its name. To left and right on entering are two huge fireplaces, each 16 ft wide, in which the cooking for meals in the adjacent Great Hall was carried out. Access to the two upper floors (now gone) was via a spiral staircase reached from a doorway to the left of the entrance to the kitchen. Immediately beyond the Kitchen Tower are the remains of the Great Hall, now only foundations and lowermost courses. Beyond the upper (dais) end of the hall is another semi-octagonal tower (White Chamber Tower). This stood three storeys high originally and the two upper floors formed part of the suite of rooms which formed the lord's private apartments. The rest of the suite was formed by the Green Chamber, another large rectangular block, bigger than the Great Hall, against the curtain wall south-west of the White Chamber Tower. The basement of this is preserved and is divided into two parts, both entered by short flights of steps down from the courtyard; they were probably used for storage purposes, one of them possibly as a wine or meat store.

Immediately south of the Green Chamber is the Postern Tower which marks the point where the thick curtain wall meets the thinner town wall. Alongside the tower is an elaborate postern gate or rear entrance to the castle. A walled passage, S-shaped in plan, runs down the steep southern slope and emerges at the foot of the cliff below the southern defences. From here it is possible to walk around the southern and western sides of the castle and examine the natural defences from the viewpoint of an attacker. Returning up the S-shaped passage it is possible, before re-entering the courtyard, to examine the mantlet which is another interesting feature of Denbigh. The mantlet is, in effect, a terrace outside the main defences which has a lighter line of defences on its outer edge, preventing anyone gaining a foothold at the top of the cliff. The effect is that of a concentric castle.

Not a great deal is preserved around the south and west sides apart from the curtain wall and towers which are part of the town wall circuit. At the north-west angle the second junction of castle and town wall is marked by the Red Tower, octagonal in plan, which seems to have been somewhat later than the other octagonal structures and to have replaced an earlier circular tower at this point. A lean-to structure seems to have stood against the curtain wall in the position now occupied by the custodian's office and the museum, which should be included in any visit.

The town wall of Denbigh is well preserved and should be seen as part of the whole picture, although space does not allow any description here. The twin-towered Burgess Gate is about 150 yards north of the castle. The town walls can normally be seen by

consulting the custodian of the castle. If they are not accessible at
the time, then they can be seen, in part at least, from the outside, by
following them from the Burgess Gate around the northern and
eastern sides.

Ewloe Castle (SJ 288676)
Ewloe is a delightful castle, the more so because visitors receive a
bird's-eye view of it as they reach the outer edge of the ditch which
protects it on the approach side. Quite unexpectedly, instead of
looking upwards, one is looking down into the castle from above,
from the top of the bank which flanks the ditch to the south.
Because this increases the vulnerability of the castle still further,
this bank may, in fact, be a siege work of Edward I, built during his
campaigns of 1277 and 1282–3. All the existing stonework appears
to belong to the thirteenth century, but it is probable that there was
an earlier timber-built castle of the motte-and-bailey type here. The
shape of the stone-revetted mount on which the stone keep stands
suggests that it was originally a motte, with the stone-walled Lower
Ward as the original bailey. The fact that it later supported a stone
keep suggests that the motte may well have been partly, if not
entirely, a natural mound being formed by scarping (steepening) the
sides and levelling the top of an existing knoll.

The keep in question, D-shaped in plan, was built c. 1210. It is
approached by an outside stair which must originally have been
protected by a wall on the outer, south side, against missiles from
across the ditch. At the head of the stairs is the doorway into the
main room, the floor of which has gone. To the right of the doorway
is a mural staircase up to the top of the tower which has lost its
battlements. The tower had only two storeys, one of which was a
basement, reached by a trap-door from above. The main floor could
only have provided very limited accommodation and may have been
used simply as the private quarters of the lord and his family rather
than as a keep in the full sense of the word. The main domestic
services, and the chapel, may have been in the Lower Ward where
there was a little more room. Since the keep is the only stone
feature of this date (1210) it was presumably accompanied by
subsidiary timber defences, perhaps of the original castle, perhaps

Ewloe Castle: the keep

rebuilt or built new to fit in with the new stone structure. Whatever the arrangement, the stone keep is unlikely to have stood alone without subsidiary features.

The rebuilding of the rest of the castle in stone appears to have been the work of Edward I's great opponent in North Wales, Llywelyn ap Gruffydd, leader of Welsh opposition to English rule, in the years around 1257. Both motte (Upper Ward) and bailey (Lower Ward) were walled in stone and a new round tower (West Tower) was built on a knoll of rock at the western end of the site. Like the keep, this was a two-storey structure, entered at first-floor level with a basement below reached by a trap-door. There must have been other buildings in the Lower Ward but they appear to have been timber-built and there are no visible remains. The only surviving visible feature is the original well which has been cleared of its centuries-old accumulation of rubbish and debris.

Ewloe is only a mile or two from Flint Castle, and with the building of the latter, from 1277 onwards, Ewloe ceased to have any military significance and has little or no subsequent history.

Flint Castle (SJ 247734)

Flint Castle, on the western shore of the Dee estuary, was the first new castle built by Edward I in North Wales and was begun while the 1277 campaign was in progress. Like the other castles in the system it could be supplied by sea, and this was an important part of Edward's strategy for controlling North Wales. Like the other castles again, it was the work of James of St George, Edward's master-builder, who was responsible for so much of the rich heritage of castles in North Wales. Work began in 1277, and by the time the castle was completed in 1284 the cost was around £7,000 – equal in modern terms to between $1\frac{1}{2}$ and 2 million pounds.

Not much remains of the Outer Ward on the south side of the castle, apart from the wall revetting the inner side of the ditch along the south and part of the east side. This wall, now flush with the ground level of the ward, would originally have risen to form the outer curtain wall of the castle, perhaps to a height of 20 or 25 ft above the interior. Across the Outer Ward is the original (and present) entrance to the castle, where there would have been a drawbridge in the position of the modern timber bridge. To the left is the south curtain wall, the best preserved of the four curtain walls, with a ditch in front, and the south-west angle tower at the end. To the right is the Great Tower or keep, completely isolated by its own circular ditch from the rest of the castle, while the curtain wall to the right of the entrance curves round beyond the ditch in conformity with its shape. The Great Keep cannot be reached from outside the castle. It is necessary to enter the Inner Ward and turn right to reach another bridge across the circular ditch around the keep. This is the present arrangement and it is also the original arrangement. Not a great deal remains of the Inner Ward. Most of the curtain walls have gone and only the north-east angle tower is anything like complete.

Flint Castle: the south-east angle tower

The Inner Ward followed the main lines of Edwardian planning and was rectangular in shape (185 by 165 ft overall) with boldly projecting circular angle towers at three of the angles and the detached keep at the fourth.

It is this detached keep at the south-east angle of the Inner Ward which has given rise to a great deal of discussion. This discussion has centred mainly on the reason behind the plan of the lower storey. This consists of two walls, inner and outer, with a circular gallery or passage between, running the whole circuit of the tower. The gallery is at a slightly higher level than the central room or basement (c. 25 ft in diameter) and communication between the two is by means of three doorways and three short flights of steps. The central room is reached directly from the main entrance of the tower at the end of the bridge across the circular moat, and this may be part of the explanation of the plan. To anyone crossing the bridge and reaching the entrance the obvious way to continue was down the flight of steps directly in front. This looks like the main means of access to the tower as a whole. In fact, entry to the upper part of the tower is via a flight of steps in the thickness of the wall to one side of the entrance passage, but this could easily be missed by an onrushing attacker who would be most likely to continue down the steps directly ahead and into the central room. It has been suggested that this was, in fact, the purpose behind this particular arrangement. Would-be attackers would find themselves in a dead end, and could then be assailed by defenders issuing from the surrounding gallery via the three doors. In the present state of our knowledge this appears to be the most acceptable explanation of the unusual plan of the circular keep at Flint Castle.

From the stairs to one side of the entrance passage it is possible to reach the first floor of the keep, or what remains of it, i.e., the part above the inner and outer walls and the passage between. The portion above the central room is now open to the sky. Presumably there was a third storey above, bringing the keep more or less to the same height as the other towers, but no trace of this now remains.

Rhuddlan Castle (SJ 025779)
There are, in fact, two castles, or remains thereof, at Rhuddlan.

About 200 yards south-east of the stone castle are the earthworks of an earlier motte-and-bailey castle. This was built as early as 1073 by Robert of Rhuddlan on behalf of Hugh, Earl of Chester, and was the base from which Robert extended Norman power over much of North Wales.

The new stone castle, begun in 1277, the same year as Flint, was a very different affair from the latter. It was built on the concentric plan, the first of three in North Wales, the other two being Harlech (p 275) and Beaumaris (p 255). The entrance to the site is from the north via Castle St. The entrance to the actual castle is via the Town Gate on the north-west side. There were originally twin square towers and a drawbridge here, but little now remains beyond foundations. To the left as visitors face the castle is the dry moat, with its inner and outer walls lined with stone. The outer wall was originally surmounted by a timber palisade forming an additional outer obstacle. The inner wall originally rose above the ditch to form the outer of the two curtain walls, although very little survives above Outer Ward level. This outer curtain was strengthened by surviving buttresses and turrets, the latter containing flights of steps down to sally-ports which opened into the ditch bottom. From the Town Gate the ditch runs round the north-west, north-east, south-east and south sides of the castle, the last section being, in fact, separate from the rest and forming the dock on the River Clwyd which was such an important factor in Rhuddlan's situation.

From the Town Gate a cobbled path leads across the Outer Ward to the West Gatehouse of the Inner Ward. This is almost rectangular in plan, with a massive curtain wall some 9 ft thick which, apart from two breaks on the north-west and north-east, is preserved to the height of the original rampart walk, although the crenellated parapet which rose above this is missing. The twin-towered West Gatehouse is matched by another twin-towered gate at the east angle, with single towers at the two remaining north and south angles. The towers of the West Gatehouse and the South Tower are preserved to their full height (one storey higher than the curtain walls), although again their battlements are missing. Unfortunately their otherwise fine appearance is marred by the lower courses having been robbed of facing stones. The remains of

Rhuddlan Castle: the West Gatehouse

the North Tower and the East Gatehouse are less complete but still substantial. Although the interior of the Inner Ward is now a clear open space, it has to be visualized as originally lined with two-storey timber-framed buildings against the curtain walls, leaving an open courtyard in the centre.

On three sides of Rhuddlan the outer curtain (or what remains of it) follows the inner curtain at a more or less regular distance of about 80 ft. On the side towards the River Clwyd, however, the outer wall swings away to take in a triangular section of sloping ground, with a rectangular tower, Gillot's Tower, at its apex. This protects the entrance to the dock formed, as mentioned earlier, by an extension of the moat down the slope, originally to the river's edge so that ships could sail in and unload under the protection of the castle's walls. Both Gillot's Tower and the dock are now set back a little from the water's edge.

Accompanying the castle was a new walled town, surrounded by timber-and-earthwork defences, and remains of the earthworks can still be seen on the north-west side. The existing streets of Rhuddlan reflect the original Edwardian plan, with the High Street dividing the town into two parts, and two streets at right angles further subdividing each side into blocks which still form the basis of the present layout.

The works at Rhuddlan include not only a castle but also a very considerable engineering achievement – the rechannelling of the River Clwyd on the east bank of which the castle stands. Rhuddlan is about 2½ miles from the sea, and in order to ensure the delivery of sea-borne supplies and reinforcements, Edward I put in hand (in 1277) work which would allow ships to sail right up to the castle.

GWYNEDD

Beaumaris Castle (SH 607763)
Beaumaris was a late addition to Edward I's strategic plan for North Wales, and was begun in April 1295. Although building work went on for 35 years, until 1330, the castle was never finally completed, most of the towers being roofed at a lower level than originally planned. Also missing, as a result, are the turrets which some of the more important towers would almost certainly have had, as at Conway, Caernarvon and Harlech. Nevertheless, the castle was, and is, an impressive example of medieval fortification and was one of the masterpieces of James of St George, Edward's master military engineer in North Wales and elsewhere. Beaumaris is probably the most eloquent expression of the concentric principle and in it the medieval castle reached its fullest development.

Entry to the castle precinct is at the south-west angle of the moat, still water-filled on the south, west and north; before entering the castle proper it is worth walking along outside the moat and viewing the west side of the castle from the exterior. Immediately in front across the moat is the west outer curtain wall with angle towers at north-west and south-west, and three evenly spaced interval towers between. The outer curtain on the east side is exactly the same,

except that the moat has been filled in; this section is outside the castle precinct and can be viewed freely from the public park on this side. Returning to the south end of the moat, the castle proper is entered by a wooden bridge in the position of an original bridge with a lifting section. Immediately to the right is the dock which allowed supplies to be brought in by sea, an important consideration in all the Edwardian castles in North Wales.

The wooden bridge leads to the south gate, and after passing through this the barbican of the southern gatehouse is immediately to the right. However, before moving into the Inner Ward, it is worth walking right round the Outer Ward, between the two curtain walls, to see how the two lines of defence relate to each other. Turning left from the South Gate and proceeding in a clockwise direction, visitors encounter, on the right (the Inner Ward side) and in succession, the circular south-west angle tower, a D-shaped tower mid-way along the west curtain, the north-west angle tower, the great twin-towered Northern Gatehouse in the middle of the north curtain, the north-east angle tower, the D-shaped Chapel Tower midway along the east curtain, the south-east angle tower and, finally, the Southern Gatehouse, similar to one on the north side, except for the addition of a barbican in front. The main features to the left on the same circuit (the outer curtain wall) have been mentioned already as far as the east, west and south are concerned. Apart from the north-west and north-east angle towers, the only other features on the north side of the outer curtain are two more interval towers and the North Gate which was never completed. The Inner Ward is virtually square in plan (220 by 210 ft) although the boldly projecting towers and gatehouses produce an overall dimension of c. 300 ft square. Completely embracing this structure is the Outer Ward which is basically square, although each of the four sides bows out to accommodate the projecting features of the Inner Ward, producing overall dimensions of c. 375 by 375 ft.

The Inner Ward can be entered by either the South or North Gatehouse. In front of the South Gatehouse is a rectangular barbican, a small fortified enclosure which had to be overcome

Beaumaris Castle: the gateway through the outer curtain

before attack could be made on the gatehouse proper. The entrance
passage through the gatehouse is, or was intended to be, 65 ft long;
the inner side of the gatehouse within the curtain wall was one of
the parts of the castle which was never completed. It was almost
certainly intended to have three doors and three portcullises, at the
inner and outer ends of the passage and halfway along: the same
arrangement as in the completed North Gatehouse. Visitors emerge
into the Inner Ward between the low walls of the incomplete
gatehouse, the plan at least of which can be examined.

The Inner Ward is now a clear open space within the 15-ft thick
inner curtain wall. Any buildings planned or intended against the
inner face of the curtain wall were never started or, if started were
quickly abandoned. To the right, in the middle of the east curtain, is
the Chapel Tower, one of the showpieces of Beaumaris Castle. The
chapel, at first-floor level, is now reached by a modern flight of
wooden steps. It would originally have been reached by steps from
within the hall planned, but not built, at this point. The walls of the
chapel are arcaded and the ceiling is vaulted. The rooms above were
almost certainly intended to be the chaplain's quarters. From the
chapel entrance, passages or galleries run north and south in the
thickness of the wall and these continue around the four sides of the
Inner Ward, providing one means of communication between the
various towers and the two gatehouses. The other means of
communication was, of course, the rampart walk, and from this
vantage point one can get a clear view of the whole castle, its layout,
and its surroundings. In particular, it can be clearly seen how the
outer curtain wall is completely dominated by the inner curtain and
this is one of the principles underlying the concentric arrangement.

Between them the two great gatehouses provide a great deal of
accommodation and this may be connected with possible royal use
of the castle. Beaumaris provides no less than five suites of rooms,
each having its own hall and chamber (private room), together with
ancillary rooms. Each gatehouse contains, or was intended to
contain, two suites: the fifth suite was planned against the east
curtain wall adjacent to the chapel, although never actually built.
This was probably intended for the constable of the castle, leaving
the other four suites to be accounted for. It has been suggested that

these were in anticipation of the time when the castle might need to accommodate not only the King's and Queen's households (needing a suite each), but also the households of the Prince of Wales, heir to the throne, and his wife, the future queen (two more suites). Although the provision of so many suites need not necessarily be connected with the double-gatehouse arrangement, it would have been difficult to provide so much accommodation around the courtyard, and the provision of two gatehouses may have been seen as the best answer to the problem. In addition, the gatehouses, which could be isolated from the rest of the castle in the manner of keeps, would have provided much safer accommodation for the royal occupants than suites built against the curtain walls.

Caernarvon Castle (SH 478627)
Caernarvon Castle was a work of 'unparalleled architectural magnificence' (W.D. Simpson's words), because Edward I intended it to be a centre of royal government and a palace for the Prince of Wales. Work on the castle began in June 1283, and on the town wall in the following year. By 1294 some £12,000 had been spent (c. £3,000,000 in modern terms), when the Welsh rose in revolt and seized and held Caernarvon for six months, doing considerable damage to both castle and town walls. Work was resumed in 1295 and between then and 1301 another £5,000 was spent. By 1330, when work was still going on, the total cost of castle and town walls was in the region of £27,000, a colossal sum for those days (c. £6,750,000 in modern terms). The size of this bill is a reflection of the architectural elaboration of Caernarvon Castle. The same plan carried out in the style of Conway Castle (p 265) would have cost considerably less.

Caernarvon follows the same general plan as Conway: a series of towers linked by curtain walls and divided internally into two baileys. Caernarvon is, however, considerably larger (600 ft long as compared with Conway's 400 ft, and correspondingly wider), and, as already indicated, much more elaborate architecturally. Before entering (by the King's Gate on the north side) it is worth walking completely round the castle and viewing the external elevation which is one of Caernarvon's most impressive features, particularly

on the south, where the curtain wall is at its highest. This section provides three tiers of firing positions, two in galleries in the thickness of the wall, and the third from the rampart walk above. On the less exposed north side, facing into the town, it is noticeable that the linking curtain wall is both lower and thinner. On the same circuit Caernarvon's thirteen towers can also be examined. These vary in both shape and size; no two are exactly alike. Although usually described as octagonal, some of them have more and some of them have less than eight sides, and as a group they are best described as polygonal. In size they range from the Watch Tower (20 ft in diameter) to the great Eagle Tower (c. 70 ft) surmounted by triple turrets. About two-thirds of the latter's circumference can be seen to project beyond the curtain walls in the manner of a keep. Abutting its north side is one end of the town wall. The other end originally abutted the north-east tower, although there is now a gap where the present roadway passes through. Four of the towers form two gatehouses: the King's Gate mentioned already, and the Queen's Gate, at the eastern end of the castle. This now looks somewhat odd, with its threshold high above external ground-level, but it has to be remembered that the latter is, in fact, the bottom of the original ditch, the outer edge of which has been removed to make way for later buildings. Originally the Queen's Gate would have been approached by a bridge (with a lifting section), from the outer edge of the ditch which was more or less at the same level as the threshold. One final point can be made about the present external appearance of the castle. The wide quay forming a terrace along the south side is not an original feature. As built, the waters ran virtually up to the foot of the castle walls, and this indeed was one of the ideas underlying the siting of the castle.

Entry to the castle is via the King's Gate in the middle of the north side, the portion falling within the town walls. Unfortunately the gatehouse was never completed, but the plan was that it would provide access to both east and west baileys. The main entrance passage between the twin towers, some 60 ft long, was equipped with no less than six portcullises and five sets of double doors. Much

The Eagle Tower at Caernarvon Castle

of this passage survives. It was intended to lead into an octagonal hall or vestibule (a fragment of which survives), from which two further passages, also equipped with doors and portcullises, led off at right angles, one into the east bailey and one into the west bailey. A generally similar arrangement exists at Denbigh Castle (p 245), and there are other similarities between the two sites which suggest the hand of the same man, James of St George (p 29), Edward's masterbuilder of castles. The gatehouse block was originally intended to extend right across the castle, dividing it into two parts, east and west baileys, communicating with each other via the octagonal hall at the heart of the gatehouse block.

The east bailey (to the left as one enters the castle) is now a level grass lawn, but this is a fairly recent event. The Edwardian stone castle was not the first on the site. There was an earlier motte-and-bailey castle built in the early days of the Conquest, with the motte occupying the area of the east bailey. Surprisingly enough, the motte was retained in the Edwardian castle and, in fact, survived until 1870 when the area was levelled. The presence of a motte within a confined space must have made for considerable inconvenience and there must have been some strong reasons for retaining it. Douglas Simpson has suggested that Edward intended to add even more to the architectural impressiveness of the castle by building a tall tower on the motte, in the manner of Windsor Castle. The tower was never built, but the motte remained, filling the east bailey for another 600 years.

In the west bailey are the foundations of the hall, but the principal feature here is the great Eagle Tower at the western extremity, with most of its circumference standing beyond the castle wall. Its floors have been restored and it is possible to ascend to the roof, above which rise its three turrets, and get a panoramic view of the whole castle. At this date (late thirteenth century) the Eagle Tower is best regarded as a tower-house (p 37) rather than a keep and was probably intended as the self-contained residence of the constable of the castle, Sir Otto de Grandson.

In a large and complex castle such as Caernarvon there is much to explore which cannot be described here, but the rampart walk of the great southern curtain should not be missed. This is the topmost of the three tiers of firing positions mentioned earlier. The two others are in two superimposed galleries in the thickness of the wall below, and these likewise should not be missed. Also worth examining are the multiple firing positions in the north-east curtain between the Granary Tower and the North-east Tower. Integral with the castle are the town walls which are well preserved, with two double-towered gates (the West or Golden Gate and the East or Exchequer Gate), and eight circular towers, enclosing a D-shaped area to the north of the castle.

Castell y Bere (SH 667085)

Castell y Bere was one of three Welsh castles captured and re-used by Edward I during his second campaign in North Wales (1282–3); the other two were Criccieth (p 270), and Dolwyddelan (p 273). Castell y Bere was built by Llywelyn the Great in 1221 and the existing remains are substantially those of his castle. The English occupation involved very little change in the Welsh stronghold and was, in any case, short-lived. Edward's forces captured Castell y Bere in 1283 and appear to have used it virtually as it stood. Twelve years later, in 1285, the Welsh rose in revolt and laid siege to the castle. The exact outcome is not known but Castell y Bere does not appear again in the Exchequer accounts, and there is excavation evidence of burning and destruction in the late thirteenth century. The implication is that the castle was destroyed or badly damaged in 1294–5 and was subsequently abandoned as a fortification.

The castle occupies a rocky ridge running generally north and south. Few of the walls are preserved to any great height and this, and the irregular rocky nature of the site, make the castle a little difficult to follow, but Castell y Bere is basically a keep-and-bailey castle. The bailey is triangular in plan with towers at two corners and another tower close to the third corner. The keep on the end of the ridge, was originally separated from the bailey by a space of some 60 ft but was later linked to it by the only substantial piece of Edwardian work on the site, a four-sided walled yard which filled the intervening space. Apart from this virtually everything else visible belongs to the original Welsh castle.

The approach to the castle is from the north-east via a rising path which runs along the east side (with the long side of the triangular bailey above), around the south end (where the keep is located), and up the west side as far as the main entrance in the middle of the south-west wall of the bailey. The entrance is, in fact, preceded by a barbican or outer enclosure which had to be overcome before the inner entrance could be approached. Running across the barbican is a flight of stone steps which originally had a drawbridge at either end. To the right of the staircase are the remains of a small rectangular tower. At the head of the stone steps is a modern wooden bridge, leading across the site of the inner drawbridge and so through the south-west bailey wall and into the castle proper.

Immediately to the left of the entrance are remains of a round tower, one of the three towers protecting the bailey. It was probably so placed to cover the entrance rather than the west angle of the bailey, some 30 ft beyond, which was well defended by nature anyway. About 40 ft in from the entrance are the remains of the castle well, which yielded material (green-glazed jugs, leatherwork etc.) of the Edwardian period when excavated. To the right of the entrance the bailey wall climbs the slope to the Middle Tower, rectangular in plan, which marks the south angle of the bailey. From the Middle Tower the long straight east wall of the bailey runs north along the highest part of the ridge to the North Tower, D-shaped in plan, which marks the north angle of the bailey. From the North Tower the north-west wall of the bailey runs on a slightly irregular course to the west angle mentioned earlier, thus completing the circuit of the enclosure. Apart from the keep (South Tower), the North Tower is the largest on the site (c. 63 by 35 ft); only the ground floor is preserved, but the tower originally housed a chapel at first-floor level, together with (probably) accommodation for the chaplain. The remains of the stone steps are preserved to the left of the entrance to the basement. The rectangular Middle Tower at the opposite end of the bailey likewise retains only its ground floor, entered by steps on its north (bailey) side. A separate flight of steps to the left gave access to the upper floors.

The south walls of the Middle Tower and the barbican mark the south edge of the bailey defences. Beyond the Middle Tower, and at a lower level, is the yard enclosed by a wall in Edwardian times, and beyond that, the South Tower, D-shaped in plan, which was, in fact, the keep. Although again only its lower walls are preserved, this was quite clearly a substantial original structure some 75 by 40 ft, with walls c. 10 ft thick. It may be presumed to have been at least three, and possibly four, storeys high. It was entered in the middle of the short, straight north side, a few steps leading down to the ground floor, and a staircase in the thickness of the wall to the right leading (originally) to the upper floors. The Edwardian addition which linked the two parts of the castle (keep and bailey) together was presumably intended to prevent an enemy from isolating one part from the other by commanding the original 60 ft gap between them.

Conway Castle (SH 784774)

Conway was one of the castles built by Edward I as a result of the second Welsh uprising in 1282–83, when he decided to establish a firm grip on the whole of North Wales. Like the other castles involved in this strategic scheme, it could be supplied by sea, standing as it does at the mouth of the River Conway, making it independent of land-borne supplies. Work on the castle and town walls, which were a single project, began in March 1283. Within five years, by the end of 1287, the work was more or less complete, at a cost of just over £14,000 (an outlay in modern terms of about £3,500,000). Before (or after) visiting the castle it is well worth walking around the town wall which is virtually complete, with three double-towered entrances and 21 wall-towers. Conway is among the best preserved town walls in Europe and admirably complements the splendid castle which stands on a natural knoll of rock at its south-east angle.

It is this knoll which dictates the plan of the castle. The essential features of Conway are the eight more or less evenly spaced round towers, linked by a high curtain wall, forming a slightly irregular oblong lying east and west. The towers form two rows of four, a north row in a straight line and a south row slightly bowed out to the south. A cross-wall, similar to the main curtain wall, divided the interior into two sections, an inner ward to the east, defined by the four eastern towers which are surmounted by turrets, and an outer

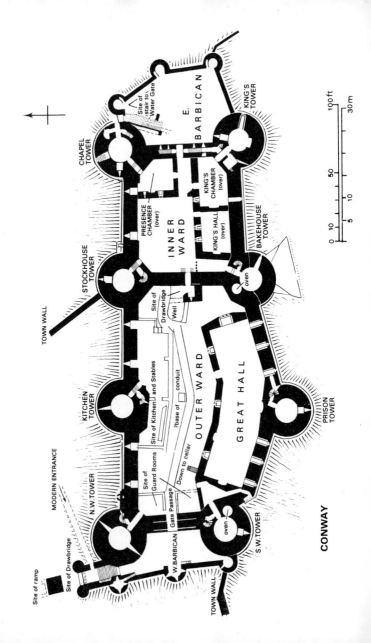

CONWAY

ward to the west. Communication between the two is via a narrow entrance originally with a drawbridge in front. There are two main entrances, one each in the short east and west curtain walls, each with a barbican in front. Such are the main features of Conway Castle. The overall plan was so arranged that the west entrance, serving the outer ward, falls within the town defences, while the east entrance, serving the inner ward, stands outside them, allowing movement in and out of the castle independent of the town and whoever controlled it.

Present-day access to the castle is via a path up the steep slope below the north-west tower, but the original approach was at right angles to this, up a stone ramp, the upper end of which survives about 30 ft to the right of the path. The gap between the ramp and the outer entrance was spanned originally by a drawbridge. A modern gap in the outer entrance wall leads visitors back on to the original route into the castle. A flight of steps to the left leads up to the barbican in front of the west entrance. To the right is the barbican wall with three small towers overlooking the ditch between town and castle. To the left are the great north-west and south-west towers, with the entrance in the short curtain wall between. These two towers, which communicated by means of the rampart walk, formed a suite of rooms for the constable (or commandant) of the castle, placed in charge of it by the king. From this key position the constable could survey both castle and town and make any decisions needed with a clear picture of the overall military situation.

The entrance passage (originally equipped with inner and outer gates secured by drawbars, with a portcullis between) leads into the outer ward which occupies about two-thirds of the castle's interior. To right and left on entering there were originally rectangular guardrooms. The north guardroom covered the entrance to the ground floor of the north-west tower, which was probably used for storage, or possibly, since it opened off the guardroom, for garrison accommodation. The two upper floors were part of the constable's accommodation, as mentioned earlier, as were the two upper floors of the south-west tower. The ground floor of the latter, entered from a small triangular yard between the Great Hall and the tower, contained a large oven and was probably a bakehouse. Although only foundations now remain, the north side of the outer ward was occupied by the kitchen and by stables. The ground floor of the adjacent Kitchen Tower was probably used as a larder, while the two upper floors probably provided private accommodation for senior members of the staff. The major surviving (albeit ruined) feature of the outer ward is the Great Hall which occupies most of the bowed-out south side, hence its unusual canted plan. Only one of the eight stone arches which once supported the roof survives; these, however, were a replacement, in 1346–7, of the original wooden arches built in 1284–6. The hall has three fireplaces, three two-light windows on the courtyard side, a single three-light window in the east wall and six single-light windows with deep embrasures in the thickness of the south curtain wall. The Prison Tower, which projects from this side, was entered from a passage opening from one side of the adjacent window embrasure to the east. From the passage steps led down to a doorway some four feet above the original floor level. Below this, however, was another storey which formed the dungeon proper, a dark pit entered only from above by means of a trap-door. The Prison Tower had four storeys; basement and dungeon, with two floors above similar to those in the other towers.

At the far end of the outer ward is the well which acts as an obstacle in front of the gate to the inner ward. There was originally a drawbridge between it and the cross-wall, on one side of the rectangular gatehouse through the remains of which one still enters the inner ward of the castle. The south and east sides of this ward are occupied by the remains of an L-shaped suite of rooms for the king's use, leaving a small courtyard in the north-west quarter. The important rooms were at first-floor level, approached by outside staircases and by stairs within the thickness of the east curtain wall. The ground floors probably provided servant and storage accommodation. The first-floor suite consisted (from west to east) of a vestibule, the King's Hall, and the King's Chamber in the south range, and, in the east range, the Presence Chamber – a state room for important meetings and reception of distinguished visitors. The

Conway Castle: the rampart walk

south-east tower (King's Tower) contained the king's bed-chamber and the north-east tower (Chapel Tower) the king's chapel. The layout of the east end of the castle is similar to the west: an entrance passage midway between the two end towers with a barbican in front, providing for movement in and out of the castle beyond the town walls. Conway castle can be examined not only from ground level, but also from the rampart walk, the whole circuit of which is accessible. Also accessible are the turrets at the top of the two eastern towers which provide a bird's eye view of the whole castle and a panoramic view of the walled town and its surroundings. Conway must rank high in any list of castles and is undoubtedly one of the finest castles in the British Isles, and indeed, in Europe as well.

Criccieth Castle (SH 500377).
Criccieth was one of the Welsh castles captured and added to by Edward I in his second North Wales campaign (1282–3) and converted to English use. The main upstanding remains are those of the English structure; the surrounding Welsh remains are only a few feet high. Criccieth occupies the summit of a promontory above Cardigan Bay. The original Welsh castle was in existence in the time of Llywelyn the Great, grandfather of Edward's opponent Llywelyn ap Gruffydd, and was probably built around the end of the twelfth and the beginning of the thirteenth century. The remains consist of a roughly triangular curtain wall (c. 300 by 150 ft), with a gate-tower at the south-east angle, a rectangular keep (c. 65 by 40 ft) at the south-west angle, and another rectangular tower at the north angle (the Engine Tower) from which missiles, probably large stones, could be hurled at attackers approaching from the landward side. Although the plan is clear, none of the Welsh structures are preserved to any great heights, although the keep was originally of three storeys.

The English portion of the castle was built inside the existing Welsh castle so that there were inner and outer walls on the north, west and south, but only a single wall on the east, the English wall overlying the Welsh wall at this point. The principal feature of the new structure (and still the most prominent feature of the site) was

the double-towered gatehouse, a regular component of an
Edwardian castle. There was also an additional rectangular tower
projecting diagonally through the east curtain wall. The original
approach to the south-east entrance of the castle ran below the east
curtain wall, and it was presumably to exercise greater command
over this that the Leyburn Tower was built, so named after the
second constable of Criccieth, Sir William de Leyburn, appointed
by Edward I on December 23, 1284, after a short tenure of the
same office by Henry of Greenford who had assumed office as soon
as the castle had been captured.

Dolbadarn Castle (SH 586598)
The most prominent feature of Dolbadarn Castle is the circular
keep which still stands some 40 ft high. It forms part of a small and
fairly simple castle at the north end of the Llanberis pass,
commanding an old route from Caernarvon to the upper Conway
Valley. The castle appears to have been built at two main periods,
both before the English conquest in 1282–3. The first castle
consisted of a stone curtain wall surrounding the summit of the
small rocky knoll. This castle was of the simplest kind, a plain wall
enclosing a triangular space, c. 250 ft long and 100 ft wide, and was
probably built during the twelfth century. Early in the thirteenth
century, in the time of Llywelyn the Great, one of the greatest of the
Welsh princes, the circular keep and one or two other structures
were added, probably between 1220 and 1240, when Llywelyn
died. The keep is of three storeys, and is entered at first-floor level.
The existing stone steps are modern but probably follow the lines of
an earlier medieval flight. There was probably a small forebuilding
in front of the entrance. Internally there are no steps down to the
basement which must have been reached through a trap-door. The
first and second floors provided two living-rooms (c. 27 ft in
diameter) equipped with a fireplace, a garderobe (latrine), and, in
the case of the second floor, a sleeping-compartment, housed in the
turret-like projection on the east side of the keep which also
contains the latrines. Communication between the two storeys and
the battlements was provided by a spiral staircase in the thickness of
the keep wall to the right of the entrance. At the southern angle,

and in the middle of the west curtain, are the remains of two rectangular towers added around the same time as the keep. Running from wall to wall across the northern end of the courtyard are the remains of a large rectangular room (50 by 27 ft) which was probably the hall, or principal living-room, with the keep acting as a private suite for the lord of the castle. There are remains of another large room at the east angle, and indications of several smaller rooms against the curtain wall.

After Edward I's conquest of North Wales Dolbadarn quickly lost its importance; timber was removed from it for Caernarvon in 1284 and by the following century the castle was in decay and was never subsequently rebuilt.

Dolwyddelan Castle (SH 722523)

Dolwyddelan was one of the Welsh castles captured and re-used by Edward I in the 1282–3 campaign. The castle was symbolically important as the birthplace of the greatest of the Welsh princes, Llywelyn the Great, Prince of Wales (1200–1240) and grandfather of Edward's opponent, Llywelyn ap Gruffydd; it was captured in January 1283. Work began immediately on making good any damage and adapting it to English use. The castle is of a fairly simple type, not unlike Criccieth (p 270), and consists of an irregular polygonal wall with two rectangular towers, one of them a keep which still dominates the site, although the upper portions are late medieval and modern. The keep is the earliest part of the castle and was probably built c. 1190–1200. At that stage it had only two storeys, and was surrounded by a timber palisade. Early in the following century the timber defences were replaced by a stone curtain wall, the remains of which still surround the castle. Later in the century, possibly c. 1250, the rectangular West Tower was built in the north-west angle of the curtain wall. This seems to have been damaged in the English attack but was repaired almost immediately. The roof of this tower may have supported catapults for throwing missiles, since an inventory of the castle made in 1284 mentions two wooden catapults for a tower.

Dolbadarn Castle: the circular keep is its most prominent feature

Dolwyddelan Castle: rectangular keep

The keep stands to its full (albeit restored) height and is accessible to the battlements, from which there is a commanding view of the valley below. In the fifteenth century a third storey was added in the roof space within the existing walls. The present roof and the battlements are nineteenth-century restorations, but they must follow the original lines very closely.

Llywelyn ap Gruffydd stayed in the castle during 1281, and after its capture Edward I stayed there in 1283. The castle seems to have survived as such until about 1500, when the then owner built himself a more comfortable residence lower down the valley. After this the castle inevitably decayed, and was rescued from total ruin in the nineteenth century by the work mentioned above. The monument was placed in state guardianship in 1930.

Harlech Castle (SH 581312)

Harlech Castle (begun 1283) stands on a cliff overlooking the coastal plain, with natural defences on the north and west. On the south and east there is a rock-cut ditch which must have provided much of the stone for the construction of the castle. There are three baileys or enclosures, the two innermost forming a concentric arrangement. The most massive part of the castle is the Inner Bailey, roughly rectangular in plan, with a high curtain wall preserved to the level of the rampart walk, linking four circular angle towers and a great double-towered gatehouse on the east front. Surrounding this is the narrow Middle Bailey which is, in effect, a terrace with its own fairly low outer curtain, completely embracing the structure within. Beyond the Middle Bailey on the north and west is the Outer Bailey, a much more irregular enclosure taking in the rocky slope in these sides and providing access to and from the Sea Gate below, which enabled Harlech to be supplied by sea when the sea level was somewhat higher than it is now.

The castle is entered on the eastern side via a modern timber bridge and steps. These lead up to the outer entrance, flanked by two small projecting circular turrets. Immediately beyond is the main gatehouse, but before passing through this it is worth making the circuit of the Middle Bailey so as to see the exterior of the Inner Bailey wall on all sides, and to appreciate its relationship to the wall of the Middle Bailey. Having done this the Inner Bailey can be entered by the main gatehouse. This is a massive building, c. 75 by 65 ft in area, not counting the angle towers. The entrance passage, some 50 ft long, had three portcullises, two double-leaved doors and eight machicolations (lines of openings in the roof of the passage through which an enemy could be attacked from above). There were guard-chambers on either side, from which the upper floors could be reached. These must have provided some of the best accommodation in the castle, possibly for the constable and his family. James of St George (p 29) was the architect of the castle; he was also one of its early constables. He was appointed in 1290 and held the post for just over three years, so that it is quite possible that Master James lived in the gatehouse that he himself had designed. The external staircase against the back of the gatehouse is not part of the original design.

Beyond the gatehouse the remains of the internal buildings are ranged around three sides of the courtyard: north, west and south. The principal range was on the west side, opposite the gatehouse, and included the hall, the kitchen, and associated domestic offices. Buildings along the other walls included a chapel and a granary. Apart from the main entrance through the gatehouse there are two other gates, one on the west side, via what was originally the screens passage at the lower end of the hall, and another on the north side, opposite another, twin-towered, postern gate leading from the Middle Bailey to the Outer Bailey. The whole plan of the castle can be studied from the rampart walk at the head of the main curtain wall which is fully accessible. From the same position one can see how great was the command of the inner curtain over the surrounding parts of the castle.

The castle was besieged during the Welsh uprising of 1294–95 (as a result of which the castle at Beaumaris was added to the North Wales system), but successfully resisted the attack. In 1404, after another siege, the castle eventually came into the hands of Owen Glendower during another Welsh uprising. He remained there until 1408, using it as both home and capital, and held a parliament there. The castle was again besieged in the Civil War and eventually surrendered to the Cromwellian forces. By this time much of the castle was in ruins and remained so until 1914 when it was placed in the care of the then Office of Works (now the Department of the Environment).

The main gatehouse at Harlech Castle

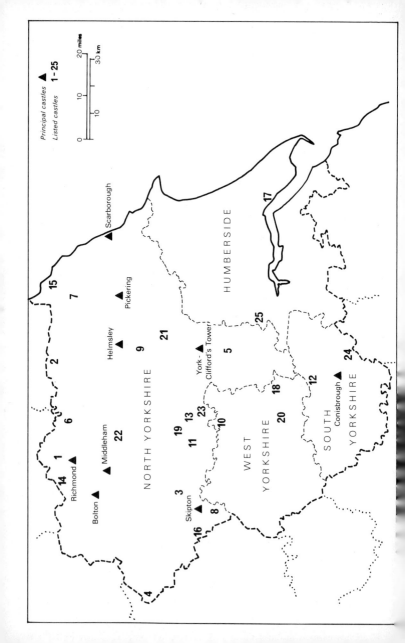

The Yorkshire region consists of the countries of North Yorkshire, West Yorkshire, South Yorkshire and Humberside. Within this area there are remains of about two dozen castles, plus another dozen or so which can be described as fortified manor houses or tower-houses. Of these the nine major castles will be dealt with in the main inventory; the rest will be listed at the end of this section and shown on the map opposite.

Rectangular keeps are well represented among the nine chosen sites with fine examples at Helmsley, Middleham, Richmond and Scarborough. There is a circular keep at Conisbrough and an unusual quatrefoil keep at York (Clifford's Tower), with the remains of another at Pontefract. Middleham, in its later phases, also exemplified the courtyard principle, but the outstanding northern example of this type is Bolton Castle. There are less complete examples at Sheriff Hutton, Wressle, Harewood, Danby and Snape. The only example of a shell-keep among the nine castles is at Pickering, although there are other examples in Yorkshire, at Tickhill and Burton in Lonsdale. Skipton displays the Edwardian characteristics of curtain wall and circular towers, although not the rectangular plan. Brief details of the remaining castles are given in the list which follows:

1. Aske Hall (N. Yorkshire): fifteenth-century pele tower behind east wing.
2. Ayton Castle (N. Yorkshire): a three-storey tower-house.
3. Barden Tower (W. Yorkshire): a tower-house, early Tudor.
4. Burton in Lonsdale (N. Yorkshire): remains of a shell-keep on a motte.
5. Cawood (W. Yorkshire): surviving gatehouse of Archbishop of York's castle, 1426–51.
6. Cowton (N. Yorkshire): late fifteenth-century tower-house.
7. Danby (N. Yorkshire): Bolton-type castle, diagonally projecting angle towers.

8. Farnhill House (W. Yorkshire): early fourteenth-century fortified manor house.

9. Gilling Castle (N. Yorkshire): mainly Elizabethan, but over remains of large tower-house.

10. Harewood (W. Yorkshire): courtyard castle, licensed 1367.

11. Haywra (N. Yorkshire): foundations of stone tower in moated site.

12. Hooton Pagnell (W. Yorkshire): fourteenth-century gatehouse remains.

13. Knaresborough (N. Yorkshire): mainly a tower-house, built 1307–12.

14. Mortham Tower (N. Yorkshire): centre of the house is a tower-house.

15. Mulgrave (N. Yorkshire): remains of rectangular keep and curtain wall.

16. Nappa Hall (N. Yorkshire): a fortified manor house, c. 1460.

17. Paull Holme (Humberside): a brick tower-house, probably late fifteenth-century.

18. Pontefract (W. Yorkshire): remains of quatrefoil keep and curtain walls.

19. Ripley Castle (W. Yorkshire): fifteenth-century gatehouse.

20. Sandal (W. Yorkshire): motte-and-bailey, remains of fine gatehouse.

21. Sheriff Hutton (N. Yorkshire): remains of late fourteenth-century courtyard castle.

22. Snape Castle (N. Yorkshire): ruins of a Bolton-type courtyard castle.

23. Spofforth Castle (W. Yorkshire): fortified manor house, licensed 1308.

24. Tickhill (S. Yorkshire): fragmentary remains of a shell-keep.

25. Wressle (Humberside): remains of a late fourteenth-century courtyard castle.

Bolton Castle (TA 033918)
Bolton Castle was built for Lord Scrope, Chancellor to Richard II (1377–99). The castle appears to have been started around 1375 although the licence allowing him to build a castle was not actually

granted until 1379, by which time much of the castle had been completed. Bolton is the prime example of the northern courtyard type (p 35) in which rectangular angle towers were preferred to the circular towers of the southern courtyard castles such as Bodiam (p 63). Bolton Castle is famous, among other things, as the prison of Mary Queen of Scots in 1568–9, from where she was moved to Tutbury Castle (p 183).

Before entering, the castle should be examined from the outside where the details of the plan can best be seen. The site is oblong, with rectangular towers at the angles and rectangular turrets halfway along the north and south walls. The towers project only a few feet beyond the adjacent walls. The original entrance is at the east end facing the village, immediately alongside the south-east angle tower. It consists of a vaulted passage through the east range of buildings and had portcullises at both ends. The four ranges of buildings are three storeys high, the angle towers two storeys higher. The north-east angle tower has almost completely gone, but the other three are preserved virtually to their original height. The south-west tower is still roofed, and in use, as is the west range adjoining it.

The modern entrance to the castle is at the west end, via a flight of steps to the first floor of the south-west tower. From here one can ascend to the upper floors and roof of the tower, from which an excellent view of the whole castle and its surroundings can be obtained. Descending from the battlements, the chapel and chaplain's chamber (both now roofless) can be seen at second (top) floor level in the adjacent section of the south range. Descending to the ground floor, visitors emerge in the south-west corner of the rectangular courtyard. This is one of only five doorways in the courtyard (including the main entrance), and all of them were originally equipped with portcullises, so that even if an enemy were to break through the inner portcullis of the main entrance passage, he would still find his way into the surrounding buildings barred by the portcullises on the only four doors which gave access to them.

The ground-floor rooms around the courtyard, apart from the guardroom in the south-east tower, provided such services as storage, stables, bakery, brewery etc. The main rooms were housed on the first and second floors. The hall, two storeys in height and now roofless, occupied the western half of the north range. The eastern half of the range and the north-east (kitchen) tower formed the kitchen, buttery and pantry, always sited at the 'lower' end of the hall. At the 'upper' (west) end of the hall, in the north-west tower, the west range and the south-west tower, were a series of private apartments for senior members of the household. Beyond the south-west tower was the chapel (already mentioned) in the western half of the south range. The east range, between the Kitchen Tower and the entrance, was the accommodation for the military personnel.

This survey of rooms and functions still leaves the south-eastern part of the castle unaccounted for. This consists of the south-eastern tower, the section of the south range between it and the chapel and the section of the east range over the entrance passage. In this part of the castle are duplicated many of the functions already provided elsewhere in the castle (kitchen, hall, solar, etc.) and this provides the clue to the nature of this section. It was an entirely separate section of the castle, isolated from the rest by blank walls. It forms, in effect, an L-shaped tower attached to, but capable of surviving independently of, the rest of the castle. This sort of subdivision within the main structure is not uncommon in fourteenth- and fifteenth-century castles. It is generally ascribed to the effects of 'bastard feudalism', the use of hired mercenary troops whose loyalty was suspect; but it may more simply reflect a distaste for sharing the castle's facilities with a rather rough and uncouth body of men whose services were nevertheless necessary. This suite of rooms is reached by the door in the south-east corner of the courtyard, immediately adjacent to the original entrance passage. It consists of three rooms on each floor: at ground-floor level there are the entrance passage, the guardroom and a store – the latter, in fact, having a door to the adjacent bakehouse, secured by a drawbar. At first-floor level there is a portcullis room above the entrance passage, the lord's hall above the guardroom and the lord's kitchen above the store. The second floor was more private accommodation, including the solar and the lord's camera or private room, with further accommodation in the two upper floors of the

Bolton Castle: a prime example of the northern courtyard type

south-east angle tower. Thus the lord's suite not only isolated him (for whatever reason) from the rest of the occupants, it also enabled him, from the portcullis room above the entrance passage, to observe and control movement in and out of the castle so that he could forestall, or at least delay, any hostile movement either from within or without.

Clifford's Tower, York (SE 606515)
The city of York contains remains of not one but two early castles, both originally built in the earliest days of the Conquest, between 1066 and 1071. They stand on opposite sides of the River Ouse and no doubt part of their function was to control movement thereon, particularly by the Danes who, in 1069, sailed up the river and captured York and its two castles. At this stage both castles were of

Clifford's Tower: the quatrefoil keep

the timber and earth motte-and-bailey type. The castle to the west
of the river, Baile Hill, now consists only of the earthen motte,
although considerable excavations have been carried out on it in
recent years. The castle to the east, Clifford's Tower, likewise
consists of a motte, but in this case surmounted by a considerable
stone structure. The castle apparently takes its name from Roger de
Clifford, one of the rebel barons defeated by Edward II in 1322,
whose body was hung over the ramparts in chains.

The motte beneath Clifford's Tower is a splendid example of the
type and appears to be entirely man-made, giving some indication
of the amount of earth-moving involved in the construction of even
a timber castle. By the middle of the thirteenth century the original
timber work must have been renewed several times, and in 1245
whatever existed on the motte was replaced by the existing stone
tower. This is, in fact, a stone keep, although one of unusual
quatrefoil plan. The only other example of such a plan in Britain is
also in Yorkshire, at Pontefract Castle (p 280), but there are
examples in France (at Étampes, for example) and it was

presumably from there that the idea was derived. Access to the top
of the motte is via a flight of stone steps straight up one side. These
are not original but must replace an original approach which would
not have been much different. They would have been preceded by a
drawbridge across the moat (now filled in) which originally
surrounded the motte and separated it from the bailey. At the head
of the flight is a rectangular tower housing the entrance, with a
chapel above, and a portcullis room on the second floor. The
interior of the keep is now open to the sky; originally it was of two
storeys, although it has been suggested that a third storey was
planned but never built. The walls (c. 9 ft thick) are preserved to
rampart-walk level (c. 32 ft), and although the keep is relatively
low, nevertheless there is a commanding view from the wall head.
The interior space, at least at ground-floor level, was probably
divided by radial walls into four rooms corresponding to the four
lobes of the plan. There are fireplaces and latrines in the northern
and western lobes. There was originally a central pier (the base is
still visible) which helped to support the floor above and the roof,
which at its apex must have risen well above the level of the
rampart. The principal accommodation was probably at first-floor
level, but there is little or no indication of how, if at all, it was
subdivided.

To the south-east of the motte, behind the group of museum
buildings which face it, is part of the bailey wall, built about the
same time as the keep to replace the original timber palisade. It
consists principally of a round angle tower with adjacent stretches of
curtain wall, together with a half-round interval tower and a further
stretch of curtain wall.

Conisbrough Castle (SK 517989)

The circular keep at Conisbrough was built c. 1180, about the same
time as the great square keep at Dover was being completed
(1170–80), and is one of the first circular keeps in Britain. It is also
one of the most unusual, having six massive wedge-shaped
buttresses supporting it. These rise to the full height of the surviving
tower and, together with the great thickness of the walls (c. 15 ft)
and the solidity of the plinth, explain why the Conisbrough keep is

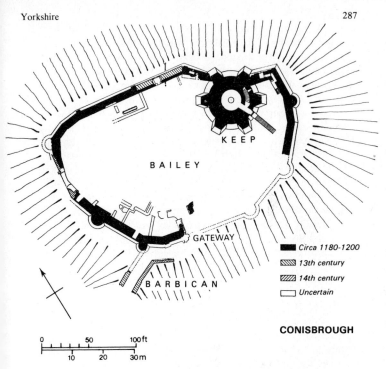

KEEP

BAILEY

GATEWAY

■ Circa 1180-1200
▨ 13th century
▨ 14th century
☐ Uncertain

BARBICAN

CONISBROUGH

0   50   100 ft
10   20   30 m

still standing some 75 ft high today. The castle was built by Hamelin Plantagenet who held the manor from 1163 to 1202. The keep was apparently built first, c. 1180, with the stone-walled bailey following about ten years later, c. 1190; although in the intervening period there was probably a temporary wooden palisade so as not to leave the keep without an outer line of defence. The stone wall which replaced it is notable for its solid half-round towers, one of the earliest uses of round, as opposed to the then almost universal rectangular, towers in Britain.

The chief interest of Conisbrough, however, is the great buttressed keep. It is noticeable that the curtain wall bends inwards

Conisbrough Castle: the circular keep has six buttresses

to leave a portion of the tower outside, providing a possible means of escape should the keep itself be in danger of being taken. Access to the keep is at first-floor level via a flight of stone steps (modern), replacing an original flight either of stone or timber which involved a drawbridge in front of the entrance. Below the entrance level is a vaulted basement, reached only from above and contained within the high sloping plinth on which the upper part of the keep stands. There were originally four storeys above the basement, although all the floors (of timber) and the roof have now gone. Access to the upper parts was (and is) via stone staircases in the thickness of the wall, rising concentrically with curving walls. In the absence of floors a number of curving platforms have been built against the inner walls of the keep to enable some of its features to be seen more clearly. A noticeable feature of the third and fourth storeys (counting the basement as the first) are the fireplaces, and these were quite clearly the two main living-rooms. Each room also had a two-light window and a latrine; and the upper room also had a most interesting chapel, contrived partly in the thickness of the wall and partly in one of the great buttresses, immediately behind it. Above this room is what appears to be the rampart walk, from which visitors can get a panoramic view of the whole castle and its surroundings. In fact, the original rampart walk was one level higher, for Conisbrough had two tiers of battlements. The lower one (the top surviving level) was a circular gallery or passage running around the top of the tower and forming one fighting platform, with a rampart walk (now gone) forming a second platform immediately above. A similar two-tier arrangement exists in the curtain wall at Denbigh Castle (p 245), and there is a three-tier arrangement (two galleries and rampart walk) at Caernarvon. The two-tier arrangement in the circular keep at Pembroke (p 208) consists of two rampart walks, both open to the sky, one inside and higher than the other.

Helmsley Castle (SE 611837)
One of the first features to strike the visitor to Helmsley is the very considerable earthworks which were quite clearly an important part of the castle defences. Equally interesting are the two barbicans

at the north and south entrances, and the keep, preserved on the inner side to its full height, including the turrets. After being in several hands, including those of Robert de Mortain, a half-brother of William the Conqueror, the manor of Helmsley passed into the ownership of Peter de Roos in 1154 and remained in the family, with one short interruption, until 1508. It was the third member of the de Roos family to own Helmsley, Robert de Roos (1186–1227), who built the original Helmsley Castle, probably in the years around 1200. The boldly projecting circular angle towers and straight curtain walls, similar to those at Skenfrith (about 1200, p 230) suggest a similar date for Helmsley.

The area defined by the curtain walls (or rather their foundations, since not much else remains) is trapeze-shaped in plan. Outside it is a deep, wide ditch, partly cut down into the rock. Curtain wall and ditch are a common defensive arrangement but at Helmsley the system is further elaborated. Surrounding the ditch is a very substantial rampart, with a second, outer ditch beyond that. This rampart appears to have been surmounted by a timber palisade, which in effect turned Helmsley into a concentric castle and raises the question of whether the rampart and outer ditch are as early as the rest of the castle. A similar double ditch arrangement with timber palisade at Caerlaverock Castle (Scotland) belongs to the late thirteenth century, and concentric castles generally do not appear until about 1270. It is a possibility, therefore, that the rampart and outer ditch were added to the original castle somewhat later, possibly around the middle of the thirteenth century, when the two barbicans which stand on the rampart at the northern and southern ends were added to the defensive scheme. Beyond the outer ditch at the southern end of the site is a generally rectangular outer bailey, surrounded by a ditch and presumably defended by a timber palisade similar to the one on the rampart around the stone castle.

Whatever the earthwork arrangements were, the original stone castle consisted of a keep, three circular angle towers, a twin-towered gatehouse (half-round towers), a rectangular gatehouse, a rectangular tower (West Tower), and an associated range of buildings, all of these being linked by straight stretches of

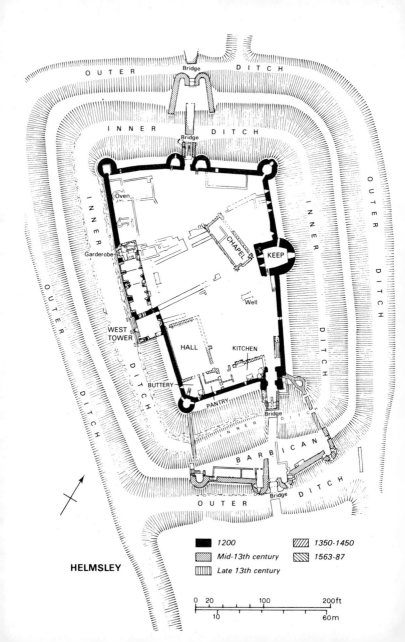

OUTER DITCH

Bridge

INNER DITCH

Bridge

Oven

Garderobe

CHAPEL

KEEP

INNER DITCH

OUTER DITCH

Well

WEST TOWER

HALL

KITCHEN

BUTTERY

PANTRY

Bridge

INNER DITCH

OUTER DITCH

BARBICAN

Bridge

OUTER DITCH

HELMSLEY

1200

Mid-13th century

Late 13th century

1350-1450

1563-87

0 20   100   200ft

10

60m

curtain wall to form a generally trapeze-shaped plan. Of these the
only upstanding portions are the keep, the West Tower and
associated range, and the south barbican. The rest consist of
foundations or very low walls, but there is sufficient to enable the
whole plan to be made out. The keep is semi-circular beyond the
curtain wall and rectangular within, and its somewhat irregular
layout may indicate a change of plan during building. It was
probably planned as a rectangular building at a time (1200) when
circular keeps were coming into fashion (as at Skenfrith, p 230), and
may well have been altered during building to conform, at least in
the part facing a potential enemy, to the new style. Unfortunately,
the semi-circular outer portion was destroyed down to its
foundations after a siege in 1644 during the Civil War. The existing
keep is of four storeys and the rectangular inner portion is
preserved to the top of the two rear angle turrets. In fact as built
c. 1200, the original structure was of two storeys only, the existing
upper half being added around 1300.

On the opposite side of the courtyard is the West Tower with a
range of buildings to the north. This group must have formed the
main domestic suite in the castle after the keep, which at that time
was of two storeys only. Presumably the main part of the range
formed the hall, with the West Tower at the upper (south) end
forming the private family wing and the transverse block at the
north end the service wing, including the kitchen. Although these
buildings have been rebuilt twice (late thirteenth century and
mid-sixteenth century, with windows of the later period), they
belong to the first period of the castle's construction around 1200,
and seem to have remained in use in their original role until the
building of a new domestic range (some time after 1350) in the
south-west angle of the courtyard (below).

The third upstanding section of the castle is the barbican at the
south end of the castle. This was designed to protect the principal
entrance through the square tower at the south-east angle of the
courtyard. This survives only as low walls, but its general plan is
clear. It is approached by a bridge across the inner ditch from the
great encircling rampart and it is on the southern section of this that
the barbican is situated. This was built c. 1250, i.e. about half a

century after the castle itself was built. It consists of a twin-towered entrance with curtain walls on either side running along the outer edge of the rampart, ending in half-round towers, and forms a great screen, c. 220 ft long, blocking any approach from the south. From the towers at either end the timber palisade mentioned earlier would have run around the remainder of the castle. Later in the same century the barbican was further strengthened by wing walls running across the inner ditch from the south-east and south-west angles of the castle to the end towers of the barbican. Remains of these walls are still clearly visible. Their effect was to complete a rectangular stone-walled enclosure which had to be captured before any assault could be made on the inner entrance. The arrangements at the northern end of the castle were somewhat simpler. The inner entrance there, in the middle of the north curtain wall, was protected by flanking D-shaped towers, approached by a bridge across the inner ditch from the rampart in much the same way as the one to the south. On the rampart, the barbican consisted of two half-round towers flanking the entrance, with their outer walls prolonged towards the rear to form a small enclosure which had to be traversed in order to reach the bridge across the inner ditch.

Within the castle courtyard there are foundations, often fragmentary, of a number of buildings. Close to the keep are what remains of the chapel, built in the late thirteenth century, while in the south-west angle are the partial foundations of an L-shaped domestic range built in the mid-fourteenth century, presumably to provide more spacious accommodation than that available in the original West Tower block. A large hall, c 78 by 44 ft, was built against the west curtain, south of the West Tower. South of it, in the angle, were built a buttery and a pantry, while a kitchen and other domestic offices were built along the south curtain as far as the south-east gatehouse. There are other foundations in the northern half of the courtyard, many of them probably belonging to the late period (mid-sixteenth century) when the West Tower and adjacent buildings were extensively remodelled.

In spite of its range of defences, Helmsley had a relatively

Helmsley Castle: the keep

uneventful history. It was not besieged until the Civil War in 1644
when Sir John Crosland held out for three months against Sir
Thomas Fairfax. As a result the castle was slighted, leaving the
outer part of the keep in its present ruinous condition.

Middleham Castle (SE 128877)
Although the structural history of Middleham Castle covers a long
period (twelfth to fifteenth centuries), it must always have been
dominated by the great rectangular keep which rises in the middle
of the surviving remains. This was built c. 1170 and is the earliest
building on this particular site. There is, however, an earlier
Middleham Castle, a motte-and-bailey earthwork about 500 yards
south-west of the present structure, going back to the early days of
the Conquest, probably built around 1086. The stone castle on the
present site was begun about a century later, c. 1170, by Robert
Fitz-Ralph, grandson of the earlier builder. It consisted of the keep
and (presumably) a surrounding curtain wall, although nothing of
the latter now remains. The buildings which now surround the keep
are all of later date, although they may well follow the line of the
original curtain which may indeed be indicated also by the
rectangular ditch which surrounds the castle.

The keep is of the hall type, i.e. it consists basically of two storeys,
a hall and associated apartments above a basement, and is relatively
low as compared with most keeps which have three storeys above a
basement. Entry was at first-floor level via a flight of stone steps
against the east wall, although most of these have now gone. Access
to the basement, divided lengthwise by a cross-wall, was from the
hall-level above via a spiral staircase in the south-east corner, just to
the left of the main entrance. The vaulted basement contained the
kitchen and the storage cellars, and must also have provided
servants' quarters. The large kitchen fireplace is back-to-back with a
similar fireplace in the eastern half of the basement, and this
presumably formed a sort of servants' hall, up the centre of which
were originally five circular columns supporting the barrel-vaulted
ceiling. The floor above was likewise divided lengthwise by the
cross-wall. The hall (its floor now gone) occupied the wider, eastern
half, with wooden screens at the southern end to cut off draughts

from the entrance and to provide the buttery and pantry normally situated at the lower, entrance end of the hall. There is no indication of an original fireplace, so presumably there was an open hearth in the middle of the floor with a louvre in the gabled roof above to allow for the escape of smoke. At the upper end of the hall, in the north-east angle turret, is a small vaulted chapel. The western half of the first floor, beyond the cross-wall, was occupied by the solar or withdrawing-room for the family, alongside the upper end of the hall, with the presence chamber, an apartment for more formal occasions, alongside the lower end. The timber roofs above were gabled, one over each half of the keep on either side of the cross-wall, with the outer walls rising well above them to protect them from attack by fire.

Much of the present outer curtain wall was added between 1250 and 1300, although it has been heightened and added to in later structural developments. As built, it appears to have been a free-standing wall c. 4½ ft thick and 24 ft high, with shallow buttresses (some of which remain) every 23 ft along its outer face. At its south-west angle it had a rounded bastion, the same height as the curtain wall, which now forms the lower part of the later Prince's Tower. At the south-east angle there was a larger rectangular tower which was likewise increased in height later. A new and larger chapel was added around the same time, against the east side of the keep. It was of three storeys, with the chapel (not much of which is preserved) on the top floor, reached from the head of the steps which gave access to the hall. The rooms below probably provided accommodation for the priest.

If there were buildings against the curtain walls at this period they must have been of timber. The existing ranges of stone buildings against the north, south, and west curtain walls are of the fourteenth and fifteenth centuries. In the fourteenth century two-storey ranges were built against the south and west curtains, and rectangular towers were built at the north-west and north-east angles, the latter forming a gatehouse (still the entrance to the remains) with accommodation above. Presumably it was at this time that the original 24 ft curtain wall was increased in height. As in many other castles, the basements of the ranges housed services such as the bakehouse, brewery, storage etc., while the floor above provided residential accommodation of a more private and more comfortable nature than that available in the keep. Bridges (now gone) at this level provided communication between the keep and the courtyard ranges, including, in the middle of the west range, a garderobe tower replacing the ones on the south and west sides of the keep. The north range was added in the fifteenth century, and contains a suite of rooms including a kitchen at ground-floor level and a hall or chamber on the first floor, immediately adjacent to the entrance.

Close to the chapel on the east side of the castle is the base of a tower which was evidently a gate-tower, leading to and from an outer bailey across the ditch to the east of the castle. All trace of this has now gone but it originally contained stables, smithy, slaughterhouse, barn etc., already in ruins as early as 1538 and presumably completely cleared away while the rest of the castle, albeit in ruins, was allowed to remain.

Pickering Castle (SE 800845)

Pickering Castle was certainly in existence in Henry I's time (1100–1135), and may well have been first established as a timber motte-and-bailey castle by William the Conqueror. The castle now consists of the motte and two roughly semi-circular wards completely embracing it, one to the north and one to the south. The original castle seems to have consisted at least of the motte and the ward to the north (Inner Ward); the southern ward (Outer Ward) may be equally early or may have been added later. While the rest of the castle remained timber-built, a stone hall was added in the first half of the twelfth century (1100–1150). This is the oldest stone structure on the site and its remains (foundations only) are in the Inner Ward just north of the New Hall and the chapel. Late in the century, in the 1180s, the timber palisade of the Inner Ward was replaced by a stone wall with a single tower (Coleman Tower) covering the entrance. The existing remains of the shell-keep on top of the motte are of Henry III's time (1216–1272), but they appear to be a rebuilding of an earlier stone shell, so that probably whatever existed originally on the motte (a timber tower?) was rebuilt in stone around the same time as the curtain wall. The

curtain wall of the Outer Ward on the south and east sides of the
castle, together with its three rectangular towers, was not added
until early in the fourteenth century. The Outer Ward itself is
certainly earlier than this and may go back to the earliest days of the
castle or shortly thereafter, retaining its timber defences long after
the rest of the castle was rebuilt in stone.

Entry to the castle is from the south through the ruined
gate-tower of the fourteenth-century defences. Almost directly
across the narrow strip of the Outer Ward is the entrance to the
Inner Ward, with Coleman Tower immediately to the right. This
was quite clearly designed to cover not only the entrance but also
the means of access to the summit of the motte. It was of two storeys
(now much ruined) and entry was at first-floor level; the lower,
ground-floor storey was almost certainly used as a prison and the
tower was referred to as the King's Prison Tower in the fourteenth
century. It was probably built originally under Henry II
(1154–1189), with its upper part probably rebuilt in the fourteenth
century when the outer defences were built. Its first-floor entrance,
on the east side, is reached by a flight of steps along the edge of the

Pickering Castle: the motte and the outer bailey

motte ditch. From the landing at the head of the flight there was (originally) access on the right to the first floor of Coleman Tower and, on the left, to the rampart walk of the inner curtain wall, which from this point crossed the ditch and ran up the west side of the motte to the shell-keep. There was a corresponding wall up the slope of the motte on the north-eastern side, so that the keep stood half inside and half outside the inner curtain wall. Not a great deal remains of the shell-keep, although the original height of the rampart walk can be seen in the highest surviving portion on the north-west side. Originally there would have been lean-to buildings against the walls, leaving a small, open courtyard in the centre. Standing as it does at the centre of the castle, the motte summit provides the best overall view of the whole complex of defences which form Pickering Castle.

The Inner Ward flanks the motte on the north and west. Its oldest feature, the Old Hall, has been mentioned already. To the south are the remains (in the form of low walls) of the New Hall, built in 1314 for Alice, wife of Earl Thomas of Lancaster, son of Edmund, Edward I's younger brother. Although its foundations and lower walls are of stone (and are possibly a rebuilding of an earlier structure) the greater part of the building appears to have been of timber-framed construction. To the south are the fragmentary remains of the domestic services: kitchen, buttery, pantry etc. A corridor or gallery across the north end provided access to the Old Hall (still in use) and to the chapel. The latter has been extensively restored and has a modern roof, but much of the walling belongs to the original building of c. 1226–7, as do the doorway and the two western lancet (narrow, pointed) windows in each of the long walls. At the north-east end of the Inner Ward are the stone foundations of what again appear to have been mainly timber-framed buildings. These were the accommodation for the constable, the man appointed by the king to administer the castle and the associated estates on his behalf. At the south-west end of the ward are further foundations against the curtain wall, including remains of two ovens. This range probably contained the bakery and possibly the brewhouse as well. This accounts for the main features of the Inner Ward.

The later defences of the Outer Ward are much better preserved than those within, and are the work of Edward II in the years 1323–6, as a precaution against further Scottish incursions such as that led by Robert Bruce in the previous year (1322), when the Scots encamped themselves in Malton and raided into the surrounding countryside. Until this time the Outer Ward defences seem to have been of timber and the ward itself seems to have been regarded more as a barbican than anything else, although it seems rather large simply as a protective work for the inner entrance. Edward's work consists of three rectangular towers and a gate-tower linked by a curtain wall, which also linked on to the inner curtain at the south-west and north-east, thus forming a complete curtain wall around the whole of the castle, with the motte more or less in the centre.

Although much of the gate-house has gone the other three towers are well preserved. Rosamund's Tower stands astride the ditch surrounding the Inner Ward and its lowest storey forms a postern gate approached along the ditch bottom. There were two other storeys above this. Because of the tower's position the second storey could be approached only by a passage in the thickness of the curtain wall, reached from a doorway at the edge of the ditch in which the tower stands. The internal floors have now gone, but the third storey was entered from the rampart walk on either side, a passage running through the back of the tower at this point. The Diate Hill Tower is likewise of three storeys, although the bottom storey is at the level of the Outer Ward and is entered directly from there. On either side of its doorway are the remains of the flight of stone steps which formerly gave access to the doorway of the second storey, immediately above the doorway below. The other means of access was from the rampart walk. From the west side a doorway gave access to a spiral staircase in the north-west angle which led downwards to the first floor and upwards to the second. The second floor room provided residential accommodation. It was a well lit room, with a fireplace, a garderobe, and cupboard recesses, and probably formed, with the room below (for a servant?) a small suite for some member of the household. The most substantial of the three towers is at the south-west angle, Mill Tower, probably so-called because it overlooked the mill on the stream below. It was of two storeys, the lower one at ward level probably used as a prison. The upper storey, originally reached by a flight of steps against the west curtain wall, may have provided a gaoler's lodging. Much of the curtain wall linking these towers is preserved to rampart-walk level, with remains of the parapet on its outer edge.

Pickering Castle had a long history and seems to have survived in a reasonable state of repair until, and after, Elizabeth's reign (1558–1603). From the seventeenth century on, however, it seems to have fallen increasingly into decay, until restoration began in the present century with the chapel.

Richmond Castle (NZ 173007)

Like Chepstow (p 222), Richmond was stone-built from the beginning, and was a very early castle, built within the first 20 years of the Conquest. Again like Chepstow, it consisted originally of a hall (rather than a keep) accompanied by a bailey. The keep at Richmond was a later addition although, unlike Chepstow, it was not the hall which was modified for this purpose but the gate-tower. The Saxon owner of the lands of Richmond was Edwin, Earl of Mercia, and he seems to have retained possession until a few years after the Conquest. He died in 1071, and it was probably then that the territory was granted to Alan the Red, son of the Count of Penthièvre. He held it until 1089, and it was probably during the intervening eighteen years that the first Richmond Castle was built.

The site chosen is on the north bank of the River Swale where the river bank provides a high, steep slope which was utilized as the south side of the triangular bailey or Great Court. The stone walls along this side (except for the walls of Scolland's Hall at the east end) are of twelfth- and thirteenth-century date. At this early stage the natural slope was probably surmounted simply by a timber palisade. On the two remaining sides (north-west and north-east) a substantial stone curtain wall was built with a two-storey rectangular gate-tower (now swallowed up in the later keep) at the apex (north), four other towers (one at the south-west angle, the other three along the north-east wall), and a two-storey hall in the south-east angle of the court. If the Cockpit, the walled enclosure on the east side of the latter, formed part of the original castle then it must, like the south curtain, have been originally of timber. The existing walls are of twelfth-century date. Of the four towers on the main curtain wall, the one at the south-west angle is quite small and was presumably intended to strengthen the defences at the point where the stone wall ended and the timber palisade, along the south side, began. On the north-east side, the middle tower of the three is in ruins and not much can be said about it. Robin Hood's Tower, to the north of it, was, as originally built in the eleventh century, of two storeys, both barrel-vaulted. The ground floor was a chapel (St Nicholas), and the room above may well have been for a chaplain. The third storey was added in the fourteenth century. The outer wall of this tower still stands virtually to its full height. The Gold Hole tower, immediately adjacent to Scolland's Hall and so named from a tradition of treasure buried beneath it, originally housed the latrines in two storeys, the lower containing the latrine pits. In the fourteenth century the upper part of the tower was rebuilt and the upper storey was converted into a private room with a fireplace and a garderobe.

Undoubtedly the two main features of interest at Richmond Castle are Scolland's Hall and the keep, which is virtually complete. Scolland's Hall is important in the history of English domestic architecture because, with the hall at Chepstow, it is one of the earliest surviving examples of the stone-built first-floor hall or house, a type introduced to these islands by the Normans and one which was to play an important part in subsequent domestic development. Although the floor and roof of the main, upper storey have gone, the walls are preserved nearly to their full height and the main lines of the original arrangement are fairly clear. The ground floor was relatively low and was used as storage space and probably as a sort of servants' hall. It has two doorways on the courtyard side and was probably divided internally by a cross-wall near the eastern end. This eastern section acted as an entrance lobby at the end of the entrance passage from the Cockpit, from which visitors could then enter the courtyard through the east door of the two mentioned above. Above the basement at first-floor level was the hall proper, the doorway and most of the windows of which are

Richmond Castle: Scolland's Hall seen from the keep

preserved in the surviving north and south walls. The round-headed doorway was approached by a flight of steps leading to a rectangular terrace at threshold level; remains of both of these features can be seen on the ground below the doorway which is now 7 or 8 ft above external ground level. To the left are three of the original two-light windows, with their central dividing shafts now gone. There was originally a fourth, in the position now occupied by the fourteenth-century doorway near the eastern end of the hall. There are four more similar windows in the opposite south wall and there was originally a fifth, at the eastern end, in the position now occupied by the remains of the fourteenth-century three-light window. The solar or withdrawing-room is at the eastern end of the hall, over the arched entrance from the Cockpit mentioned earlier. At the west end there was originally another two-light window, but when the hall block was extended to the west in the twelfth century, this window was made into a doorway and two other doorways were knocked through on either side. The flanking doorways led to the buttery and the pantry, while the central one led into a passage through to the kitchen which was located further west again. This three door arrangement is the standard layout at the lower, service end of a hall.

Undoubtedly the chief glory of Richmond is its keep, a splendidly preserved structure right up to its battlements, from which there is a panoramic view of the castle, of Richmond and of the surrounding countryside. The keep, however, was not an original feature of the castle, but was added about a century later, in the time of, and probably by, Henry II (1154–1189). Originally the site was occupied by a rectangular gatehouse, the main entrance to the castle. This was a two-storey structure about half the height of the existing keep which is 100 ft high. The first floor may have been accommodation for the garrison, while the ground floor contained the entrance passage and, no doubt, guard-chambers. The inner arch of this original gate passage is still intact in the south wall of the keep. It must have been blocked up when the keep was built, but has at some stage been opened up again. The remainder of the gatehouse is now concealed by the keep, which was given thicker walls than the former, and was doubled in height. Access to the new keep was at first-floor level, from the rampart walk on either side, although the west door is now blocked. The east door provides the present entrance to the keep. This leads into a small lobby with a flight of stairs in the thickness of the south wall to the left, and beyond it the entrance to the main room on the first floor. There are small rooms at each end in the thickness of the east and west walls. The central pillar helps to support the floor above and stands directly over one in the ground-floor room, added when the conversion from gatehouse to keep took place; originally such support would have been provided by the walls forming the sides of the entrance passage. The straight flight of steps from the lobby leads up to the third, top storey created when the keep was built up from the original gatehouse summit. The internal arrangement here is generally similar to the one below except that this floor is surmounted by a gabled roof, although not the original one. This roof, as in most keeps, is well below the level of the surrounding keep walls, which were carried up above it to give protection from attack by fire and other missiles. A second flight of steps in the south, and then in the west, wall leads up to the battlements, restored (probably in the eighteenth century), but almost certainly closely following the original lines. The four angle turrets rise one storey higher than the rest of the rampart walk. The line of the original roof can be seen on the walls below the rampart walk.

The original gatehouse had been preceded by a barbican, a walled enclosure with an outer entrance which had to be traversed before the gatehouse proper could be approached. A portion of this remains just to the east of the entrance which replaced the gatehouse when the keep was built over it. The new entrance was immediately alongside the keep to the east and may have been incorporated in a tower, as previously. Neither entrance nor tower is preserved. The existing entrance, although on the site of the original, is modern, as are the buildings accompanying it.

The remaining features at Richmond can be dealt with quite briefly. Along the south side of the Great Court, above the river, the original timber palisade was replaced in the twelfth and thirteenth centuries by a stone wall, and ranges of buildings were built against it, some remnants of which can be seen just west of the large gap in the curtain wall. To the east of the gap are the twelfth-century westward extensions of Scolland's Hall mentioned earlier. In the fourteenth century a range was built against the east curtain, adjacent to the east end of the Scolland's Hall. This contained a Great Chamber and Chapel at first-floor level, and its walls are preserved to about the same height as the hall block. Although it played no very great part in English history, Richmond is a rewarding castle to visit, not least because of its splendidly preserved keep.

Scarborough Castle (TA 048892)

The promontory site of Scarborough has a long history going back to prehistoric times. There was an Iron Age dwelling here, but the earliest visible remnant is that of a late Roman signal station on the east cliff, erected in the fourth century to give early warning of

Scarborough Castle

Saxon raids. The main feature of this was a square stone tower (c. 50 by 50 ft) which must have been several storeys high and in its complete state was probably not fundamentally different from the medieval keep which was built on the promontory some eight centuries later. Before this, however, the promontory was occupied for a while, in the tenth century, by a Viking named Skarthi, who built a stronghold (a *burh*) on it and *Skarthi's burh* gave its name to the later castle and subsequently to the town. Around AD 1000 a small chapel was built on the site of the Roman signal station, and the remains of this, and of two later chapels, can still be seen on the east cliff.

The castle occupies a large (16-acre) diamond-shaped site, with rocky cliffs on the eastern and north-eastern sides and very steep slopes on the west and south-west. The cliffs were never in need of any additional protection, and the earliest, and indeed all later, defence works were concentrated on the west and south-west, the sides facing the visitor approaching along Castle Road from the landward side. The first part of the castle to be encountered is also one of the latest to be built, the barbican housing the outer entrance to the castle, added in the thirteenth century. The barbican is like a small outer fortress, with a double-towered entrance and wall-towers, which had to be overcome before any further progress could be made. The barbican is well preserved and still provides the only means of access to the castle. Beyond it is an elaborate stone bridge which in its original state provided a second formidable obstacle to an attacker. At its centre was a large tower, a substantial portion of it still preserved, which straddled the roadway. The two stone-arched sections, one in front of it and one beyond, were originally occupied by drawbridges. Beyond the bridge two high curtain walls, parallel at first, gradually diverge as they mount the slope until they abut the original curtain wall, forming a great funnel-shaped approach to the original castle. This whole section (barbican, bridge, and funnel) was added, or at least begun, in the thirteenth century, although it may not have been completed until the early fourteenth century.

The castle to which it was added was first built by William Le Gros, Earl of Albermarle, c. 1140. He built the curtain wall along the west and south-west sides, the latter clearly visible to visitors as they approach although the towers strengthening it are a later feature. As first built, the curtain wall was probably fairly plain. Le Gros also built a tower, presumably at this date a keep, but nothing of it now remains unless it is incorporated into the existing keep, the remains of which still dominate the site. This is the work of Henry II (1154–89), to whom the castle was yielded by the Earl in 1155 after the disastrous civil war, known as the Anarchy (1135–1154), over the succession. The keep was built in a small bailey formed on the west and south-west by the existing curtain wall and on the east and north-east by a ditch standing in front of (at first) a timber palisade, later replaced by a stone curtain wall. The bailey walls are in varying states of completion but the section at the wide end of the funnel (above), part of the original curtain, has completely gone.

About half the keep is now missing (except for lower walls), as a result of two sieges during the Civil War, in 1644–5 and 1648.

Because of this the interior is not accessible beyond the threshold, but the removal of one side does provide a very clear view of the internal structure which would be less apparent if the keep were complete. Access was, as usual, at first-floor level, and the flight of steps and remains of the forebuilding are still in place on the south wall. There was probably a chapel on the first floor of the forebuilding. A further short flight of steps within the entrance passage leads up to the first floor of the keep. This consisted of a single rectangular room (c. 32 by 28 ft) with four deep window recesses with two-light windows, and a fireplace. Separate staircases led down to the basement and to the floors above. An arch, now gone, across the middle of the room helped to support the floor above, and there was a similar arch across the next, third storey. This housed the Great Hall and was generally similar to the room below, with a fireplace and four two-light windows. It had mural chambers in the two surviving angle turrets, and possibly originally in all four, although one of the destroyed angle-turrets must have housed a staircase. The fourth storey appears to have been lit in the same way as those below, but does not appear to have had a fireplace. A notable feature of the Scarborough keep, in spite of its partial destruction, are the fine two-light windows, some of them blocked up, which must have made it an exceptionally well-lit keep by the standards of the time.

After Henry's work on the keep King John (1199–1216) is known to have spent some £2,000 on the castle, a very considerable outlay, and this expenditure must include the cost of some, at least, of the half-round towers which were added to the curtain wall in the thirteenth century. This work was probably continued under Henry III (1216–72). The next major structural event was the addition of the bridge and barbican on the west side, already described, and this brought Scarborough Castle more or less to its present shape.

Skipton Castle (SD 995519)

The lands around Skipton were granted to the Norman Robert de Romille beteen 1086 and 1100 and he may have built the first castle on the site. If so, nothing of such an early date now remains. Because of the situation at the head of a steep cliff above the River

Aire, and the underlying geology (rock), a motte-and-bailey castle is unlikely and a stone-walled enclosure backed against the cliff is the more likely solution, generally similar to the early arrangement at Richmond (p 300). This is probably the form of the castle built (or rebuilt) in the twelfth century, of which there is only one remnant the Norman arch in the passage leading to the courtyard of the castle, the Conduit Court. This castle was presumably still in use when it was granted to Robert de Clifford in 1284. It was he who built what was virtually a new castle, before he was killed at Bannockburn in 1314. This building seems to have been damaged in the Scottish wars and was restored, almost certainly on the same lines, by the third Lord Clifford, who succeeded to the title in 1322. The castle has been almost continuously inhabited since then and contains works of many different periods.

Entry to the castle is through the Outer Gatehouse between twin drum towers, with another pair flanking the inner end of the passage. The gatehouse is of fifteenth-century date (possibly 1437) and is presumably the replacement of an earlier outer entrance which the castle must have had. Above the entrance archway are the de Clifford arms, and on the wallhead, in stone letters, the de Clifford motto, *Désormais* (Henceforth). The gate passage leads into what must have been the outer bailey, but little now remains. The existing surrounding walls may be early in parts, but there has been so much rebuilding that it is difficult to make any precise statements, although the area enclosed presumably represents, more or less, the area of the original bailey. The only substantial features of note are the remains of the chapel on the far left from the gatehouse. This was probably built around the same time as the main castle, i.e., c. 1300–1322.

Directly across the Outer Bailey from the gatehouse is the castle proper, built by the de Cliffords in the early fourteenth century. To the right of it is another building of quite clearly different style. Since this is not open to the public and can be viewed only from the outside, and then only at a distance, it is best dealt with here. Now occupied as a self-contained house, it was built as an extension to the castle in the years 1536–7, on the occasion of the marriage of Henry Clifford and Eleanor Brandon, daughter of the Duke of

Skipton Castle: the outer gatehouse

Suffolk and a niece of Henry VIII. One of its principal features was a long gallery at first-floor level, of which the two projecting windows formed part.

The forefront of the castle is occupied by the Watch Tower, one of six original circular towers which form the main structure of Skipton Castle. It should be noted here that all the towers were considerably higher when originally built. Their present state is one of the results of the Civil War, when Skipton was slighted because of its prolonged resistance in the Royalist cause. The castle is D-shaped in plan, with the straight edge on the far (north) side along the cliff above the river. The curved part faces south, and consists of the six towers forming a semi-circle and linked by

straight stretches of curtain wall. Two of these, to the left of the
Watch Tower, formed a gatehouse, although this is now masked by
a later entrance which, in fact, provides the way to the inner section
of the castle. The new entrance at the head of the flight of steps is
the work of Lady Anne Clifford, one of the outstanding
personalities connected with Skipton Castle. She was born there in
1589 and lived to be 86. After the destruction of the Civil War she
restored the castle more or less to its present state in the years
1657–8, and added the new entrance, with a tablet above the
doorway recording her work. This entrance acts as a sort of
vestibule to the original entrance passage on the right which leads
into the inner courtyard. The archway in this passage is the Norman
doorway referred to earlier, the only survival of the twelfth-century
castle.

The inner courtyard at Skipton, the Conduit Court, is one of the
most delightful features of English medieval castle architecture, and
was so called because it was the termination of the water supply
piped from a nearby spring to the castle. The yew tree in the centre
was planted in 1659. The Conduit Court owes much of its character
to the extensive rebuilding carried out by Henry Clifford in the
years around 1500, but the earlier features need to be looked at
first. On the north side of the courtyard (the left as one enters) are
the traditional domestic buildings built when the castle itself was
built, c. 1300. These are at first-floor level and are reached by a
flight of stone steps, leading to the door at the south-west corner of
the hall. The door to the left within the hall leads to the kitchen,
with a serving hatch and hearths for baking and roasting. This is
quite clearly the lower, service end of the hall. A doorway at the
upper end of the hall leads through to another room, the solar or
withdrawing-room, allowing the lord and his family to withdraw
from the general assembly in the hall. The window in this room
provides a view of the castle's situation high above the river to the
north. Beyond the withdrawing-room to the east is the east angle
tower of the D-plan; this is not now accessible but it must have
provided additional private accommodation, including possibly the
lord's bed-chamber. This range, from west to east along the north
side of the courtyard, may well have been the limit of the original

internal buildings. Other accommodation would have been provided by the various floor levels of the six drum towers.

Around 1500 Henry Clifford carried out an extensive rebuilding of the Conduit Court, adding a new range at the east end of the courtyard and rebuilding or recasting the adjacent buildings. The result is the Conduit Court more or less as we see it today, dominated architecturally by the new range at the east end with its central doorway with the de Clifford arms above and its four spacious, symmetrically placed windows, very different from the simple one-light or two-light windows of early castles. The two upper windows were those of a suite of rooms for the lord of the castle, one room (to the left) being his day-room, while the one to the right was his bed-chamber. These rooms can be reached on the circuit of the castle after leaving the solar or withdrawing-room at the upper end of the hall.

There are many other features in Skipton Castle which space does not permit to describe here. Many of the mundane domestic storage and service functions were carried on in the ground-floor rooms around the courtyard. In the Watch Tower and the Muniment (or Library) Tower, both accessible from the lord's suite, the height to which the castle walls were reduced by Cromwell can be clearly seen, as can Lady Anne Clifford's restoration. Although (because of its reduced towers) Skipton does not look particularly military, it is nevertheless rich in both history and architecture, even if the architecture is within rather than without.

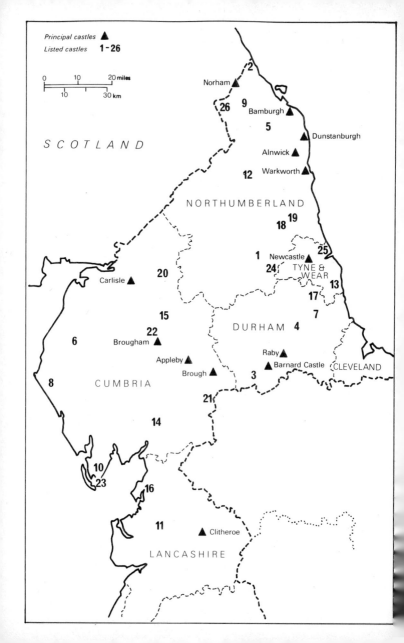

Principal castles ▲
Listed castles 1 - 26

0   10   20 miles
10   30 km

Norham ▲

26   9
Bamburgh ▲
5
▲ Dunstanburgh
Alnwick ▲
12   Warkworth ▲

SCOTLAND

NORTHUMBERLAND

18 19

1   Newcastle ▲   25
24   TYNE &
WEAR
13
17
7

20
Carlisle ▲

15   DURHAM   4

6   22
Brougham ▲
Raby ▲
Appleby ▲   ▲ Barnard Castle   CLEVELAND
8   Brough ▲   3

CUMBRIA   21

14

10
23

16

11   ▲ Clitheroe

LANCASHIRE

The combined north and north-west regions embrace the counties of Cleveland, Cumbria, Durham, Lancashire, Northumberland, and Tyne and Wear. Within this area there are remains of some 40 castles, many of them inevitably in the northern part of the region, adjacent to the Scottish borders, so long fought-over during the medieval period. In the same border area there are also numerous pele towers which are not so much castles as manor houses upended (p 37); for this reason, and because of their sheer numbers, they cannot be dealt with here.

Of the 13 sites in the main inventory no less than eight (Appleby, Brough, Brougham, Carlisle, Clitheroe, Bamburgh, Norham and Newcastle) have rectangular keeps, reflecting the English kings' concern for their northern frontier in the twelfth century. There is a single circular keep, Barnard Castle, and, as originally built in stone, a single shell-keep (Alnwick), much altered in later periods. Of the remaining castles, Dunstanburgh, built early in the fourteenth century, has no keep but boasts a massive gatehouse which must have performed the same function, while Warkworth has a magnificent and unusual tower-house, replacing its original keep which was most probably rectangular. Raby Castle, extensively rebuilt in later centuries, was originally a courtyard catle and the main lines of its original shape can still be seen in the existing buildings.

There are also a number of rectangular keeps (or in some cases remains thereof) among the listed sites. These include Lancaster (where there is also a fine gatehouse), Prudhoe, Bowes, Mitford, Pendragon, Piel, Harbottle, Greenhalgh and (possibly) Gleaston. There is also a polygonal keep at Wark. There is a fine, although much restored, octagonal shell-keep at Durham and another possible (circular) shell-keep at Kendal. The principal feature at Tynemouth Castle is the fine gatehouse with a barbican in front. A number of castles belong to the courtyard class, in addition to Raby mentioned earlier. They include Penrith, Naworth, Lumley, Chillingham, and Ford. Brief details of these and other listed sites are given below:

1. Aydon (Northumberland): a fortified house rather than a true castle.
2. Berwick-on-Tweed (Northumberland): only fragmentary remains.
3. Bowes (Durham): considerable remains of a rectangular keep.
4. Brancepeth (Durham): altered fifteenth-century courtyard castle.
6. Cockermouth (Cumbria): substantial remains of thirteenth and fourteenth-century castle.
7. Durham (Durham): motte-and-bailey with restored octagonal shell-keep and fine buildings in bailey.
8. Egremont (Cumbria): rectangular gate-tower and curtain wall.
9. Ford (Northumberland): part of courtyard castle of 1388.
10. Gleaston (Cumbria): rectangular keep or tower-house.
11. Greenhalgh (Lancashire): fragmentary remains of stone tower.
12. Harbottle (Northumberland): motte-and-bailey, foundations of keep on motte.
13. Hylton (Durham): a tower-house of c. 1400.
14. Kendal (Cumbria): shell or curtain wall on natural hillock.
15. Kirkoswald (Cumbria): late castle, rectangular moat.
16. Lancaster (Lancashire): altered rectangular keep, fine gatehouse (1400).
17. Lumley (Durham): courtyard castle, 1390.
18. Mitford (Northumberland): five-sided keep, inner and outer curtain walls.
19. Morpeth (Tyne and Wear): restored fifteenth-century gatehouse remains.
20. Naworth (Cumbria): courtyard plan, incorporates pele tower.
21. Pendragon (Cumbria): stump of rectangular keep; surrounding ditch.
22. Penrith (Cumbria): remains of courtyard castle, 1400–1480.
23. Piel (Cumbria): remains of rectangular keep on Piel Island.
24. Prudhoe (Northumberland): rectangular keep within later Edwardian work.
25. Tynemouth (Tyne and Wear): fortified monastery, fine gatehouse with barbican.
26. Wark-on-Tweed (Northumberland): motte-and-bailey, remains of polygonal keep.

CUMBRIA

Appleby Castle (NY 685199)

Appleby began as a motte-and-bailey structure, and since there are references to a castle here in 1129–30, it was probably built in the first decade or so of the century. The fine square keep, the principal remnant of the castle, was probably added in the second half of the century, during the reign of Henry II (1154–89), possibly as a result of the capture of the castle by the Scots under William the Lion in 1174. The curtain wall encircling both it and the original bailey could well have been added at the same time. The curtain follows a key-hole plan (although the end and one side of the bailey are now occupied by later buildings), with the keep in the middle of the circular portion which is, in fact, the site of the motte. Beyond the curtain wall are the original earthworks of the Norman motte-and-bailey castle. The curtain wall itself is now flat-topped, probably at the level of the rampart walk. Originally it would have been crowned with a crenellated parapet at its outer edge.

The principal feature of interest at Appleby is the well-preserved keep, even if its present state is due to the same Lady Anne Clifford who restored Skipton Castle (p 307). One of the most noticeable features of the keep is the generous provision of windows, there being two double-light windows in each wall on each of the two main floors (first and second), except where a doorway replaced one window on the east side at first-floor level. Equally noticeable is the fact that these windows are confined to the lower part of the building. The upper part has completely blank walls, and appears to represent an addition to the original keep which was about two-thirds of the present height. This would mean that the keep as built was virtually cube-shaped (c. 50 by 50 by 50 ft not counting the angle turrets), and this is very much the same shape as the keep at Dover (c. 98 by 96 by 95 ft) being built about the same time (1170–80). The addition appears to be of late thirteenth- or early fourteenth-century date and could well have been the work of the de Cliffords, strengthening the castle as a result of the Scottish wars which began in 1296, although why there were no windows is difficult to explain. Perhaps it was intended to make the additional

storey a final refuge in time of danger and windows were omitted in the interests of greater security, although this seems unlikely to be the full explanation. The keep retains its (restored) roof and floors and is completely accessible from basement to battlements, from which there is a fine view of the castle and its surroundings.

Brough Castle (NY 790140)

Brough Castle was built within the surviving earthworks of a Roman auxiliary fort (*Verterae*), the medieval structure standing at the northern end of the rectangular Roman enclosure. The first castle on the site was built in the reign of William Rufus (William II, 1087–1100), but was destroyed by the Scots under William the Lion in 1174. This early castle was stone built with a curtain wall and a tower (presumably a keep) on the site of the present keep. Some of this original curtain wall survives (including a section of herringbone masonry), together with a portion of the foundation of the early tower on the north side of the keep.

After the destruction of 1174 the castle was restored, probably in the last decade or two of the century. The main remnant of this period is the keep, a considerable portion of which has collapsed; although all the floors have gone, it is still possible to reach the battlements and see below, as in a plan, the cobbled courtyard and its surrounding buildings. The keep is now entered by a wooden staircase, at second-storey level; this was the original arrangement, although the approach then was via stone steps, the remains of which still exist in this position. The bottom storey, reached only from above, was used for storage; the existing doorway is probably of seventeenth-century date. The second storey was used as the hall or main living-room. To the right of the entrance a staircase in the thickness of the wall leads up to the level of the third storey, the solar or withdrawing-room for the family. This was the original extent of the keep although later an additional storey was achieved in the original roof space. From the third storey a spiral staircase leads up to the battlements and the panoramic view mentioned earlier.

Appleby Castle: the fine square keep

Brough Castle: the twelfth-century keep

Within the courtyard the most substantial remains are in the
south-east corner (to the right on entering) and include the hall and
the circular Clifford's Tower. This was built c. 1300 by the first Lord
Clifford but in its present state it is largely a restoration by Lady
Anne Clifford some 350 years later. The hall, at first-floor level,
was built in the late fourteenth century and externally still shows
two small, but quite fine, windows (to the right of the gatehouse). It
replaced earlier halls on a different site, against the east curtain
wall. The existing hall has a walled courtyard to the north of it. This
was subdivided into four by Lady Anne Clifford who also built in
one of the sub-divisions a stone staircase to the hall, five steps of
which still remain. Beyond (south of) the courtyard is the vaulted
undercroft of the hall, also subdivided into four. The two western
rooms (at the gatehouse end) were probably used as prisons. The
two eastern rooms were no doubt used for storage, servants and

general domestic purposes, together with the basement of Clifford's Tower. The upper floor of the latter presumably provided additional living accommodation connected with the hall.

In spite of Lady Anne Clifford's efforts in the mid-seventeenth century, the castle was in a poor state by c. 1700, and continued so until the present century. The south-west corner of the keep collapsed as recently as 1920. Three years later it was taken into guardianship by what is now the Department of the Environment and its present state is due to their efforts since then.

Brougham Castle (NY 532290)
Like Brough, Brougham Castle was built on the site of a Roman auxiliary fort, *Brocavum*, the remains of which are situated to the south of the medieval castle. The oldest part of the stone castle is the keep which (apart from its top storey, a later addition) was built in the reign of Henry II (1154–1189). At that time it was surrounded by a timber palisade, presumably on the line of the later stone curtain wall, with timber buildings (hall, stables, chapel, etc) within. As first built, the keep was of three storeys and was entered at first-floor level via a forebuilding housing a staircase, the remains of which can be seen on the east side to the left of the outer gatehouse. Originally the ground floor could be reached only from above via the spiral staircase in the north-east angle, although it is now accessible at ground level via the remains of a passage cut through the forebuilding c. 1300. The spiral staircase now provides access upwards from the ground-floor level. At first-floor level are the remains of the hall, and above is a similar room which was probably the solar or more private room for the lord and his family. The top storey was added late in the thirteenth century, and includes an octagonal main room, a surrounding gallery and a chapel or oratory which can be seen to project externally above the south-east angle of the keep.

As first built the keep was free-standing within the timber-walled courtyard. Over the next century and a half, however, buildings were added to its northern and eastern sides so that eventually it formed part of a large complex occupying the eastern and north-eastern sides of the castle. The earliest addition (c. 1220) was

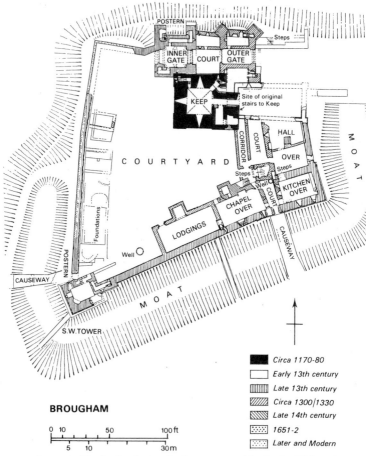

BROUGHAM

Circa 1170-80

Early 13th century

Late 13th century

Circa 1300/1330

Late 14th century

1651-2

Later and Modern

on the east side, in the form of a three-storey block of additional
accommodation for the lord of the castle. Only part of the
foundations of this now remain, on the low grass terrace to the left
of the entrance. Not long after this work began on replacing the

Brougham Castle: the gatehouse (right) and the keep

timber palisade with a stone curtain wall. Within a few years, new ranges of buildings were added against the east and south curtains. Towards the end of the century, possibly c. 1290, the rectangular tower at the south-west angle was built. This was of four storeys, each room equipped with a fireplace, so that presumably it was intended to provide additional living accommodation.

The most important addition of this period however, (c. 1300) was the gatehouse complex. The tall towes (Inner and Outer Gates) are separated by a small courtyard open to the sky, but are linked by a narrow building to the north and by the keep wall to the south. This is, in effect, a barbican and as such is not particularly unusual at this date. What is unusual is the way in which it is associated with the keep to form a powerful keep-gatehouse block. Although the ground floors of both towers were inevitably occupied by entrance passages and guard-chambers, the upper two storeys provided additional accommodation linked to that of the keep. The four windows of the first- and second-floor rooms of the Outer Gatehouse are a prominent part of the façade facing visitors as they approach the castle. This group of three towers (keep, Inner and Outer gate towers), separated by collapse from the rest of the buildings, is now the dominant mass in the castle's profile and correctly indicates where its greatest strength lay.

There were few changes to the castle after c. 1330. Such additions as were made were of a minor character or were straightforward rebuildings or repairs of existing features. Inevitably, it seems, the castle was restored in the seventeenth century by Lady Anne Clifford, who recorded her work, and titles, in an inscription to be seen in the entrance passage in the Outer Gatehouse. Lady Anne lived in Brougham, and died there in 1676, probably in the second floor room of the Inner Gatehouse.

Carlisle Castle (NY 396564)

Carlisle Castle withstood all sieges for five centuries and did not fall until 1644, during the Civil War. The result of this long period of active use is, inevitably, a great deal of rebuilding and adaptation to later military needs, particularly those of artillery. The first castle on the site was built by William II (William Rufus, 1086–1100), but no trace of this now remains. The oldest surviving portion of the existing castle is the keep built in the reign of Henry II (1154–1189). Before entering (or after leaving) the castle it is instructive to walk around the outside where the many building periods involved in the curtain wall are clearly visible. The massive buttresses on the north-eastern side are almost certainly part of the strengthening of the inner bailey walls to support artillery in the sixteenth century, possibly by Henry VIII (1509–47). The same walk will also take visitors round the ends of the wing walls which linked the castle to the city walls. Castle and city walls were linked to form a single unit, with the south side of the castle facing into the city. This side was protected by two ditches, with a clear open space between. Approach to the castle is from the south, across the open space just mentioned. Immediately in front is the inner ditch, while to right and left are remains of the wing walls mentioned above.

Beyond the ditch is the south curtain wall with a rectangular gatehouse at its centre. There must always have been an entrance in this position, but the existing structure was built, or substantially rebuilt, in the years 1378–83.

This gatehouse leads into the outer bailey now lined with nineteenth-century (and later) military buildings, except on the right where a curtain wall and ditch cut off a portion of the main triangle of the castle to form a triangular inner bailey within which stands the keep. Entry is through a square gate tower, in front of which is a half-moon battery for artillery added in the time of Henry VIII. The gate tower is mainly of fourteenth-century date, and was probably built at the same time as the outer gatehouse, although it has been patched up and altered, both externally and internally, on a number of occasions. Immediately to the right on entering the inner bailey is the stepped ramp along the north wall of the keep. This now provides access to the rampart walks, and was probably built when they were thickened to take heavy guns which were almost certainly hauled up by this route. The thickening of the walls was carried out from the inside. One of the results is that the keep, originally free-standing, became hemmed in on two sides when the thickening filled the space between it and the original (and thinner) medieval walls on the south and west. Entry to the keep is now at ground level in the east wall, across the remains of a forebuilding which originally provided access at the first floor; the lower entrance was probably knocked through in the nineteenth century. To the left on entering is a staircase in the thickness of the east wall. Immediately in front, and down a short flight of steps, is a passage with two doors to the left, leading into the three vaulted rooms into which the ground floor is now divided. These probably formed part of the sixteenth-century strengthening of the castle structure for artillery purposes. At the end of the passage is a spiral staircase which was, in fact, the main means of vertical communication in the keep. Ascent, either by this staircase or by the straight one in the east wall, leads up to the main floor of the keep. This, too, is now subdivided but was originally a single large room, with a fireplace in the east wall and a number of chambers in the thickness of the wall, one of them housing the portcullis for the existing entrance

Carlisle Castle: the south curtain wall with the gatehouse and the keep

immediately below. The second floor is reached only via the spiral staircase which now ends here, but which originally continued upwards to the third floor and the roof. The second floor is divided like the first but was originally a single room. Its walls contain a number of mural chambers, those in the east wall being late medieval cells, on the walls of which prisoners' carvings can be seen. The third floor is reached by a modern staircase in the thickness of the west wall. Like the other floors this is now subdivided into two equal parts, with vaulted ceilings supporting the flat roof above. Access to the latter is via a rather steep wooden staircase which leads out on to a flagged platform, surrounded by artillery embrasures, from which there is a fine view of the castle and the surrounding city.

Very little remains of the original internal structures of the inner bailey. The medieval buildings (hall, etc) ran along the north-east side and Elizabeth I added a range along the south, between the keep and the largely destroyed East Gatehouse at the south-east angle. This allowed for movement in and out of the castle beyond the city walls, and was built in the fourteenth century and later. It was largely destroyed in 1825 when this area of the castle was rebuilt. The one surviving feature of the gatehouse is the north-west angle turret which housed the stair. This bears some fine sculptured decoration and is known as Queen Mary's Tower.

DURHAM

Barnard Castle (NZ 049165)

Barnard Castle was built by the Baliol family, famous for providing the founder of Balliol College, Oxford (John Baliol), and a king of Scotland (another John Baliol, son of the above) crowned in 1292. The area in which the castle stands was given by William II to Guy de Baliol, one of his father's companions in the Conquest. It was Guy's son, Bernard, who probably built the first castle, early in the twelfth century, and who gave it his name Bernard's (Barnard) Castle. This first castle was probably a timber-and-earthwork structure. The existing stone castle is largely, if not entirely the work of his son, Bernard II, and his successors, starting in the later decades of the twelfth century. Barnard Castle was the subject of a long dispute between the Baliols (and indeed their successors), and the Bishops of Durham who claimed ownership of the area since it had been ecclesiastical land before the Conquest. The affair dragged on for centuries and claims were still being entered by the Bishops in 1471, again without success. The castle was besieged in 1569 during the Rising of the North in the reign of Queen Elizabeth I (1558–1603), and held out for eleven days under the command of the Queen's steward, Sir George Bowes. By the seventeenth century Barnard Castle was in ruins and was eventually taken into state care in 1952. At the time of writing (1980) the Inner Ward is under excavation and is therefore not accessible, but virtually all parts of the castle can be seen from the accessible Town Ward and keep, and from the exterior. The excavations are visible from the keep.

Barnard Castle: the keep

At its greatest extent the castle consisted of four wards or baileys, although the outer Ward, which formed the southern half of the castle, has completely gone, while the middle Ward was never more than a small space between the other three baileys to the north, east and south. The principal remains are the Town Ward, the Inner Ward, and the keep. The castle takes advantage of a steep cliff on the bank of the Tees. The first structure on the site probably consisted of a bank and ditch, surmounted by timber work, on the north-east and south-east sides, with the cliff providing a natural defence on the two remaining sides. This area, rebuilt in stone, became the Inner Ward which was always the nucleus of the castle and contained the most important buildings, although very little remains above ground apart from the surrounding wall. The Round Tower (the keep) occupies the north angle of the Inner Ward, and was built c. 1250. It stands half within and half outside the curtain wall, a typical arrangement of keep and bailey castles. It is of three storeys, with a still-vaulted basement and a mural staircase at first-floor level leading to the upper floor and the battlements. The part within the ward is squared-off to provide a suitable abutment for the adjacent buildings. The principal range was to the south, against the west curtain wall above the cliff, and included the Great Hall, some of the windows of which can be seen in the surviving curtain wall. This hall was of the fourteenth century, but probably replaced an earlier hall on the same site. The hall was linked to the keep by a two-storey block containing a basement and a Great Chamber above, both of which communicated by doorways with the corresponding floors of the keep. To the south of the hall are the remains of Mortham Tower, probably built (in the thirteenth century) to provide additional accommodation rather than for any military purpose; it was increased to five storeys in the fourteenth century. On the east curtain wall are two polygonal towers, the northernmost of which contained a postern gate.

Present-day access to the castle is via the North Gate in the Town Ward which was probably the bailey to the original timber-built castle. Before entering the gate, much of the castle's exterior can be examined by walking down the slope below the keep and the west curtain wall. To the west of the entrance is a solid half-round tower, and further west again a rectangular tower, on the edge of the Inner Ward ditch. Within the arched entrance are the remains of a two-storey, rectangular gatehouse, with a porter's lodge on one side, opening from the gate passage, and additional accommodation on the other, opening from the main part of the ward. Apart from the curtain wall to the south and east, the other surviving feature of the Town Ward is Brackenbury's Tower on the north-east curtain, so called after a Lieutenant of the Tower of London in Richard III's time, Sir Robert Brackenbury. This is a substantial structure (c. 30 ft square), with a barrel-vaulted basement and (originally) two storeys above, with mural staircases; it is said to have been built, or at least used, as a prison – a function embraced by many castles.

Raby Castle (NZ 130218)

Raby Castle was built, or at least started, by John Neville who
became the fifth Lord of Raby in 1367. The castle was begun in
1381 and was of the rectangular, courtyard type, although it has
been considerably altered and enlarged since then. It is now
essentially a great country house and not much that can be
described as 'castle' remains inside. The outside, however, still has a
fine military appearance, in spite of later alterations, and it is from
the outside that Raby can best be understood in terms of its original
appearance. Additional evidence as to the original shape of the
castle is provided by its plan which shows both thick (presumably
early) and thin (presumably later) walls, and by its rectangular
courtyard which, however altered, almost certainly represents the
original internal space of a courtyard castle. The castle stands on a
broad terrace (originally surrounded by a wet moat, a section of
which remains), so that it is possible to make a complete circuit of
the walls and see the various features referred to below.

Access to the terrace is through a gatehouse at the north-west
corner. Immediately beyond is a large rectangular tower (Clifford's
Tower), now linked to the main mass of the castle, but probably not
originally (below). Apart from Clifford's Tower there are four other
named towers (Bulmer's, Joan's, Watch Tower, and Mount
Raskelf), and these are in positions which would fit in with a
courtyard plan. On the east front, Bulmer's Tower (south-east
angle) is five-sided rather than rectangular and projects boldly
beyond the adjacent walls which were clearly built (or rebuilt) later.
At the north-east angle Mount Raskelf is rectangular and hardly
projects at all, although it rises higher than the adjacent walls.
Between these two towers is the Chapel Gateway, with two slim,
rectangular turrets. However altered and adapted, this arrangement
has the shape and appearance of one front of a courtyard castle of
the Bolton type. Both towers and the gateway have thick walls and
presumably belong, therefore, to the earliest period of building. The
west front tells a broadly similar story. The Watch Tower and Joan's
Tower occupy the north-western and south-western angles
respectively, with a twin-towered gatehouse (the Neville Gateway)
between. Again this is the pattern for one side of a courtyard castle.

Raby Castle

These two fronts (east and west) presumably formed the shorter
sides of an oblong courtyard castle, the longer sides of which are
represented by the existing north and south ranges. The thin walls
of the south range presumably represent later building but thicker
walls in the north range may indicate an intermediate tower made
necessary by the greater length of this side. There would
presumably have been a similar tower in the south range. Although
this does not take account of all the structures at Raby, none the less
all the elements of a thoroughgoing courtyard castle are present and
there seems little doubt that Raby was originally conceived in very
much the same terms as Bolton Castle (p 280) and Bodiam Castle
(p 63).

   If the hypothesis just outlined is correct, Clifford's Tower,
mentioned earlier, must originally have been a free-standing tower
to the north-west of the early castle. As such it must be seen as a
tower-house, possibly a self-contained residence or retreat for the

owner of the castle or his steward. Later building, completely masking the original north front of the castle, has linked the two structures together, but there seems little doubt that, as built, they stood free of each other and were linked only when the need for two independent fortifications had passed.

LANCASHIRE

Clitheroe Castle (SD 742417)

The principal remnant of Clitheroe Castle is the small square keep occupying a natural knoll of rock in what is now a public park overlooking the town of Clitheroe. There are early references to a castle here in 1102 and 1123–4, but these probably do not relate to the surviving stone structures. Presumably the early castle was built of timber or, if of stone, did not include the keep. The stone castle, including the keep, was probably the work of Roger de Lacy, Lord of the Honour of Pontefract in the years 1177–94. The keep is one of the smallest known, with the lower, basement room only 17 ft square and the two floors above slightly larger (19 and 23 ft square), so that there was never a great deal of accommodation within. Entry is at first-floor level in the north-east wall, with a spiral staircase to the upper floor and the battlements in the north angle turret, and a small vaulted chamber in the west angle turret. Alongside the latter is another entrance which communicated with the rampart walk of the surrounding curtain wall. There are some remnants of the surrounding curtain wall, the best portions being close to the keep which it encircles closely on three sides, like a chemise (a wall surrounding the base of a keep or tower). Towards the south the curtain swung away to enclose a triangular bailey, the area of which is now mostly occupied by later buildings.

NORTHUMBERLAND

Alnwick Castle (NU 187137)

Alnwick was one of the major strongholds of the Scottish border

Clitheroe Castle: the keep on a natural knoll of rock

region and began almost certainly as a timber motte-and-bailey
castle, built within a generation or so of the Conquest. It may well
have been the work of Gilbert de Tesson or Tyson, who was
William the Conqueror's standard-bearer at the Battle of Hastings.
Towards the end of the century de Tesson fell from grace and the
castle passed to the de Vescy family; and it was they who translated
the timber castle into one of stone in the following century.
Whatever timberwork was on the motte was replaced by a stone
shell-keep, and stone curtain walls were built around the two baileys
which flank the motte to east and west. Thus already Alnwick was
somewhat more elaborate than the general run of castles, most of
which had a single bailey.

   The de Vescy line died out in 1297 and the castle came to

Anthony Bek, Bishop of Durham; he sold it to Henry de Percy in 1309, and it was he and his successors who transformed the early stone castle into one of the most formidable strongholds on the Scottish border. This was a time of constant warfare in the border region, and no doubt the Percys considered the shell-keep and curtain walls inadequate by the current standards of Edwardian fortification. The shell wall, c. 130 ft in diameter, was strengthened by the addition of seven semi-circular towers. This part of the castle has been heavily rebuilt on two occasions in the post-medieval period, but the plan still reflects the shape imposed upon it at this time. Henry de Percy also built the square inner part of the existing gatehouse to the keep as well as the twin-towered middle gatehouse, with one rectangular and one round-fronted tower, between the two baileys. A number of towers in the baileys are his work, including the Abbots' Tower at the north-west angle of the castle and the Postern and Constable's Towers on the north side of the Middle Bailey.

When Henry de Percy died in 1315 the work or refortification was still not complete and was continued by his son. He strengthened the simple rectangular gate-tower which his father had built for the shell keep by adding twin semi-octagonal towers in front (c. 1350), but his major work was on the great Outer Gatehouse which is one of the most splendid features of Alnwick. The gatehouse proper, flanked by polygonal towers, may be the work of Henry de Percy or his son, but the barbican in front is certainly the son's work. High parallel walls project from the front of the flanking towers across the ditch to the square towers of the outer part of the gatehouse. The roadway between the high walls was originally interrupted by a drawbridge over the deepest part of the ditch. There was another drawbridge across the outer ditch (now gone) in front of the two outer towers. Apart from the two drawbridges, and the outer ditch, the whole structure is substantially intact and is a fine example of a double-towered gate fronted by a barbican.

As thus rebuilt by the Percy family the castle remained more or

Alnwick Castle: the main entrance barbican

less unchanged for several centuries. It was then subjected to not
one but two major rebuildings, although these centred mainly on
the Inner Bailey, i.e. the original shell-keep. Around 1756 the first
Duke of Northumberland, who had married into the Percy family,
began an extensive rebuilding programme. The medieval shell-keep
with its seven towers and double-towered gatehouse was
transformed into a comfortable residence with dining-room,
drawing-room, breakfast-room, library, chapel, bedrooms,
dressing-rooms, etc. Some very distinguished names appear among
the list of people employed by the Duke to carry out the work:
James Paine (building work); Robert Adam (interiors); and
'Capability' Brown (landscape).

About a century later the Inner Bailey was rebuilt again, by the
fourth Duke of Northumberland, and virtually all of the earlier
work was swept away. The Duke employed the famous Victorian
architect Anthony Salvin, who had done a great deal of restoration
work on medieval castles. Once again the interior was rearranged,
some rooms (salon, drawing-room and dining-room) remaining
more or less where they had been (although redesigned internally),
others being switched to new, more convenient, positions. At the
north-west corner the earlier staircase was removed to make way
for the large Prudhoe Tower housing the library, with a new
staircase and vestibule built out into the courtyard.

Quite clearly Alnwick Castle owes much of its present impressive
appearance to Victorian restoration, but in spite of this the castle
still retains enough of its basic medieval shape and feeling to convey
quite forcefully what a formidable castle it must have been in its
heyday in the fourteenth and fifteenth centuries, after the building
work of the Percy family.

Bamburgh Castle (NU 184350)
Bamburgh occupies a long, rocky ridge standing directly above the
seashore on the Northumberland coast. Finds of pottery during
excavation indicate that the site was used (although not necessarily
as a fortress) during the prehistoric and Roman periods. Not long
afterwards, in AD 547, Bamburgh is recorded as the seat of an
Anglo-Saxon king, Ida, and by this time it seems likely that there

was some sort of fortification on the ridge. Thereafter Bamburgh remained a prominent place in early northern history, particularly in the great days of Northumbria under King Edwin in the seventh century.

When the Normans came to build their castle at Bamburgh, there was no question as to where it should be placed, on the great ridge which stands between village and sea. Of the large and complex castle which now occupies the site the keep is the earliest part, although – like the rest of the castle – it has been subjected to a great deal of restoration. The keep was built in the twelfth century and is usually attributed to Henry II (1154–89), although there is no record in his reign of expenditure on Bamburgh sufficient for the building of a keep. It is unlikely to have been built later, so that the probability is that it was built in Stephen's reign (1135–54), Henry's modest expenditure being simply the maintenance of an existing structure. Presumably, like other keeps of the period, it was accompanied by a bailey and it is difficult to see anything other than the present Upper Ward as the original bailey. Presumably at that time it had a plain curtain wall (now incorporated in the later more elaborate curtain), with an entrance at the western end, between an incurving end and the north wall of the keep. The keep as first built was of three storeys, although a fourth was inserted later in the original roof space. It is entered, somewhat unusually for this period, at ground level. Only the ground and first floors are open to the public: the rest is privately occupied. The first-floor room described as the Armoury was originally the chapel, while the two adjacent rooms were probably the hall and solar or withdrawing-room. The rooms below at ground level were probably for storage and servants, and included a well, a great asset in time of siege. Externally the keep stands to its full (albeit restored) height, with four angle turrets, and still dominates the whole complex.

If the keep and bailey are attributed to Henry II (or his predecessor Stephen) then the remainder of the castle is the work of King John and his son Henry III, both of whom are known to have spent considerable sums on Bamburgh. The keep and bailey occupied less than half of the rock plateau, and around the turn of the century (c. 1200) the castle was extended to take in the whole

Bamburgh Castle

summit. There were now three enclosures: the original Inner
Bailey, an Outer Bailey and a West Bailey. The north wall of the
Outer Bailey overlaps that of the Inner Bailey for some 350 ft, the
two walls flanking the roadway that leads in from the East Gate to
the interior. The curtain wall of the Inner Bailey now includes a
series of towers, some rectangular, some semi-circular. The
rectangular towers probably belong to the twelfth century, possibly
additions made by Henry II. The semi-circular towers, which were
coming into fashion c. 1200, are probably the work of King John
(1199–1216), or his son Henry III (1216–72). The double-towered
East Gate, the present entrance to the castle, was probably built by
Henry III. Originally there were a barbican and drawbridge in front
but no trace of these now remains. Beyond the East Gate and
stretching across the roadway mentioned above is the rectangular
Constable's Tower, a second barrier on the route to the interior.

As in most castles of any size, there is a second entrance, and
means of escape in time of danger, represented at Bamburgh by the
remains of St Oswald's Gate at the western extremity of the castle.
This led in and out of the West Bailey, which was more in the nature
of a defended outwork than an integral part of the castle. The main
western defences are on the west side of the Outer Bailey where
there is a high curtain wall linking three towers, with a gatehouse at
the north-west corner.

Internally the main accommodation was in a range of buildings along the south wall of the Inner Bailey. These were mainly the work of Henry III and his son Edward I (1272–1307), although the original buildings have been so altered and restored that very little of the original structure remains. In the north-eastern corner of the Inner Bailey are the remains of the twelfth-century chapel.

Bamburgh must always have been an imposing castle, not least because of its magnificent situation. In spite of extensive restoration in recent times it retains this quality and still conveys much of the effect its impressive appearance would have had in medieval times.

Dunstanburgh Castle (NU 258220)

Dunstanburgh Castle was built by Thomas, second Earl of Lancaster, son of Edward I's brother Edmund, the first Earl. Work began in 1313 and seems to have been completed by about 1316. However, the second Earl did not long enjoy his new castle. Always at odds with his cousin Edward II (1307–27), he was defeated and captured at the battle of Boroughbridge in 1322 and subsequently executed. Dunstanburgh stands on a coastal promontory and its main defences are concentrated along the south side. They consist of a great double-towered gatehouse, two square towers (the Constable's Tower and Egyncleugh Tower), a turret, and a linking curtain wall, spread over a distance of some 450 ft with a rock-cut ditch in front. Of the remaining defences the most prominent feature is another square tower, Lilburn Tower, on the west side above the steep natural slope.

The gatehouse is large by any standards (110 ft wide), and consists of two D-shaped towers, each 50 ft wide and 55 ft deep from back to front. The foundations of an original barbican still survive in front of the entrance passage. The whole structure was three storeys high with the semi-circular front portions of the two towers rising another two storeys, so that the external elevation must have been much more imposing than the inner one; much of the latter is preserved. The ground floors of the towers were used as guardrooms, and the first floor, including a room from which the portcullis was worked, may also have been used for the garrison and for servants. The second floor contained the hall, with service quarters at one end and a great chamber or withdrawing-room at the other. The third and fourth floors in the front part of each tower probably contained smaller private rooms for members of the family and household.

The two rectangular towers on the south curtain are each c. 25 ft square and of two storeys. Attached to the Constable's Tower are the remains of the Constable's House, a rectangular structure some 60 ft square around a small courtyard. The Egyncleugh Tower is, in fact, a secondary entrance, with (originally) a drawbridge across the ditch in front of it. The third tower (Lilburn Tower) on the west curtain wall was probably built for John Lilburn, constable of the castle around 1325. It is 30 ft square and of three storeys and is, in fact, a tower-house, a self-contained residence from which the constable could survey the whole castle and its surroundings.

Dunstanburgh remained as completed for about sixty years. In 1362 John of Gaunt succeeded to the barony and in 1380 altered and strengthened the castle, almost certainly as a result of incessant Scottish raiding in the area. He blocked up the entrance passage of the gatehouse and added a forebuilding, transforming the whole structure, in effect, into a keep. Behind this he built a small Inner Ward (c. 100 by 60 ft) with a rectangular tower at its north-east corner protecting an entrance. Finally he provided a new main entrance to the west of the old gatehouse. This consisted of a long, open-topped passage between the west curtain wall and a new wall (a mantlet), leading into a rectangular barbican in which an attacker could be assailed from all sides. On the right of this was a new gatehouse (John of Gaunt's Gate), leading into the Outer Ward. From here any attacker still had to gain access to the Inner Ward, and if that fell there was still the formidable 'keep' (the former gatehouse) to be overcome. What John of Gaunt's changes had done was to impose a series of obstacles on an attacker, instead of the single major impediment represented by the gatehouse. Once the entrance passage of the latter had been breached the whole castle lay open to the enemy. Under the new arrangement the castle had to be taken section by section.

Norham Castle (NT 907477)

Norham was a possession of the Bishop of Durham and it was one of these, Randulph Flambard, who built the first castle in 1121, almost certainly an earthwork-and-timber structure, the shape of which survives in the present castle with its two baileys, Inner and Outer. The Inner Bailey, over 200 ft in diameter, is too broad and too low to be described as a motte, and the original castle must have been of the ringwork-and-bailey type. The castle was twice captured and once destroyed by the Scots in the first half of the twelfth century. In the second half of the century the first stone castle, including the rectangular keep, was built by Bishop Hugh Purset between 1157 and 1174, in which year it was surrendered to the king, Henry II, because of Hugh's suspected disloyalty. Over the centuries the castle has been subjected to a great deal of rebuilding and much of the visible structure is of early sixteenth-century date when there was a serious threat of invasion from Scotland. The one substantial remnant of the original stone castle is, inevitably, the keep. As first built, Norham consisted of this keep standing in one corner of an oval bailey surrounded by a plain curtain wall, with a square gate tower. There were natural defences around the northern half of the bailey and a ditch around the southern half, separating it from the Outer Bailey. This was likewise defended by a plain curtain wall with a square gate tower and an outer ditch. The outer curtain wall ran across the inner ditch and abutted the Inner Bailey wall to prevent infiltration along the ditch. Although much of this early castle has been rebuilt, its shape survives in the latter structures, the curtain walls of which follow the same lines as the walls they replaced.

The keep still stands some 90 ft high although virtually all of the north wall has gone, together with the roof and all the floors. Like the rest of the castle, it has a history of rebuilding. The original keep was of three storeys. Early in the fifteenth century an additional storey was contrived by changing the original high-pitched roof to a much lower pitch and using the space thus gained. At the same time the whole western side of the keep (the side facing visitors as they enter the Inner Bailey) was refaced. About a century later, in 1513, the castle was besieged by James IV of Scotland and the keep was so

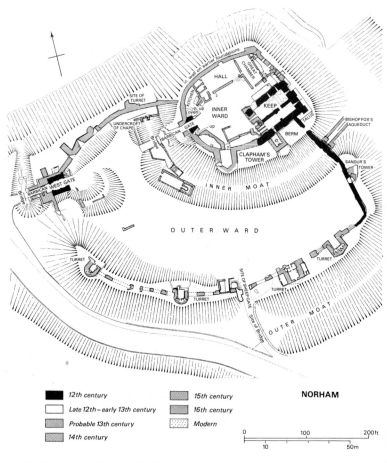

12th century (solid black)

Late 12th – early 13th century (white)

Probable 13th century (vertical hatch)

14th century (diagonal hatch)

15th century (diagonal hatch)

16th century (grey)

Modern (dotted)

NORHAM

0   100   200ft

0   10   50m

Labels on map: SITE OF TURRET; UNDERCROFT OF CHAPEL; IC wall on earlier foundations; KITCHEN; UP (oven); HALL; GREAT CHAMBER; KEEP; TALUS; BISHOP FOX'S AQUEDUCT; INNER WARD; up; BARBICAN GATE; up; BERM; CLAPHAM'S TOWER; SANDUR'S TOWER; BARBICAN WEST GATE; INNER MOAT; OUTER WARD; TURRET; TURRET; TURRET; SITE OF SHEEP GATE; Site of Bridge; TURRET; OUTER MOAT

badly damaged that only the southern half, south of the cross-wall, was re-roofed and re-used. Access to the keep was originally at first-floor level, probably via a forebuilding at the west end. However, when the west wall was rebuilt in the early fifteenth century, a new spiral staircase was built at its centre providing access from ground level to all the floors above. The original three-storey arrangement probably involved, as in many other keeps, a basement (for storage etc) at ground level, with a hall above and a solar or more private room on the second floor.

Later changes in the keep may have had something to do with the development of the accommodation in the other parts of the Inner Bailey. This is mainly concentrated against the north bailey wall and consists of the remains of a hall (the Bishop's Hall), with a great chamber at one end and domestic services (buttery, pantry and kitchen) at the other. The existing remains are of the sixteenth century, presumably rebuilt after the Scottish siege of 1513, but they almost certainly occupy the site of earlier ranges, possibly going back to the original Norman period of the castle's foundation. The bailey wall is virtually all of the sixteenth century, as is the outer part of the gate tower (the inner part is twelfth century), and the remains of Clapham's Tower, built to accommodate artillery on the south side of the bailey. The rectangular structure to the east of it, against the south face of the keep, was probably originally a garderobe (latrine) tower.

The defences of the Outer Bailey belong to a number of different periods. At the eastern end the original Norman wall survives, crossing the inner ditch to abut the south wall of the keep. The arched opening in the wall at the bottom of the ditch was presumably a postern gate, although late in the fifteenth century a stone-lined channel (Bishop Fox's aqueduct) was built outside to lead water from a stream into the ditch when required. Immediately above, on the outer edge of the ditch are the remains of Sandur's Tower, originally thirteenth century but rebuilt for artillery in the sixteenth century. Along the south side of the bailey are fragmentary remains of a thirteenth-century curtain wall and a series of D-shaped towers, overlaid by the remains of semi-hexagonal artillery turrets of the sixteenth century. The earlier, defences represent the upgrading of the Norman castle to Edwardian standards in the thirteenth century. The D-shaped towers were in turn replaced by turrets for artillery, possibly in anticipation of the Scottish attack mentioned earlier. At the west

end of the bailey the West Gate has been rebuilt on a number of occasions but its core is still the original square Norman gate tower. Beyond it, on the south-west side of the bailey, the sixteenth-century curtain wall contains three well preserved artillery embrasures. The building of this part of the wall appears to have begun in 1509. Where it crosses the inner ditch are the remains of the castle chapel, built on an undercroft or vaulted basement.

Because of its position on the Scottish border, Norham remained in active use longer than most castles, up to the year 1550, by which time many another castle had been a ruin for a century or more. However, after that date there was peace along the border and its use was at an end; it gradually fell into decay and was eventually taken into state care in 1923.

Warkworth Castle (NU 247058)

A castle at Warkworth is first mentioned in 1158, but there was almost certainly one there some time before that, probably in the first half of the century. At that time the castle was probably timber-built, on the motte-and-bailey base which is still evident in the existing castle, although it is possible that it was stone-built from the beginning. Whatever its earlier form, before the end of the century the motte was surmounted by a stone keep and there was a stone curtain wall around the bailey. During the late twelfth, the thirteenth, and the early fourteenth centuries the defences were progressively strengthened and added to. A fine double-towered gatehouse was built in the middle of the south curtain, together with the semi-octagonal Carrickfergus Tower at the south-west angle and the square Montagu Tower at the south-east. There is another well-preserved semi-octagonal tower (Grey Mare's Tail Tower) along the east curtain, and a smaller rectangular tower housing a postern gate at the north-west angle. Internally the main domestic range is down the west side of the courtyard and consists of the remains of the hall, with domestic services at the northern end, and solar or withdrawing-room, chapel and private rooms at the

The keep at Norham Castle

southern end. The foundations of the large church which separates most of the bailey from the motte were laid down c. 1400 but the building was never completed. It was intended to be a collegiate church (i.e. a monastic-like foundation) but the deaths (in 1455 and 1461) of two of its patrons, the second and third Earls of Northumberland, in the Lancastrian cause, brought the project to an end.

It was some 80 years earlier, however, that the great tower-house for which Warkworth is chiefly renowned was built, in the years 1380–90. This replaced the rectangular stone keep of which there is now little or no trace. The castle was owned by the Percy family and it was the creation of Henry Percy as the first Earl of Northumberland in 1377 which seems to have stimulated the bout of building activity which included not only the tower-house but also a remodelling of the domestic range on the west side of the bailey. The spacious accommodation in the new tower was much more in keeping with Henry Percy's new social status than the old, austere Norman keep. The tower-house is unusual in plan, a main central block (c. 75 ft square) with a wing projecting from the middle of each side. All twelve angles are chamfered, further adding to the unusual appearance of the tower. Another unusual feature is the lantern or light well, which runs through the centre of the building from top to bottom, providing light at the inner ends of many rooms. Because of its spacious plan, many of the important rooms at Warkworth could be placed side by side on the same floor, adding greatly to the comfort and convenience of the occupants. Entry is in the south wing, facing into the bailey, where there is a staircase up to the ante-room on the first floor. The rest of the ground floor is given over to storerooms, guardrooms, a prison and other facilities, contained within a 10-ft thick wall. The residential accommodation was on the two floors above. The ante-room in the south wing leads into what must have been the screens passage, with the Great Hall to the right and the buttery and pantry to the left. Beyond the buttery a doorway to the left leads into the kitchen where the great fireplaces, on which the cooking was done, survive. At the far end of the screens area is a doorway into the Great Chamber, a withdrawing-room from the hall with another room in the north wing opening off it. Between the Great Hall and Great Chamber is a spacious chapel with its sanctuary in the east wing. A generous provision of staircases completed what was virtually a manor house accommodated on a single floor within a tower-house. The Great Hall, the kitchen, and the east end of the chapel rise through two storeys. The rest of the third storey was occupied by additional rooms, presumably providing more private and more personal accommodation. Altogether the Warkworth tower formed a very spacious and comfortable residence by any standards of the time, tower-house or otherwise, and constitutes one of the most unusual additions to any English medieval castle.

TYNE AND WEAR

Newcastle-upon-Tyne (NZ 253639)
The principal remnants of the castle at Newcastle upon Tyne are the keep and the gatehouse (the Blackgate). The first castle on the site was built as early as 1080 by one of the Conqueror's sons, Robert. This was a motte-and-bailey castle with a timber superstructure; all trace of the earthworks have now gone. The castle remained in this form for about a century, until the reign of Henry II (1154–1189) who rebuilt it in stone, centred on the great keep which is still largely intact, although the vaulted roof and battlements are modern; the other surviving feature, the Blackgate, is a later, thirteenth-century addition (below). Work on the keep seems to have been directed by the same Maurice the Engineer who built the great keep at Dover and the two structures have a number of points in common. Both are entered at second floor, rather than first-floor level and both have a large number of rooms contrived in the thickness of the upper walls.

    The Newcastle keep is rectangular in plan with three square and one polygonal angle turrets. Entry is via an elaborate forebuilding occupying the whole of the eastern wall. The ground floor of the forebuilding, beneath the main flight of steps, is occupied by a richly decorated vaulted chapel of three bays. This was originally entered only from the outside, via the small door to the left of the steps up to the forebuilding door. Access from within the keep, from the adjacent basement, was a later provision. The basement itself has a central column supporting an eight-ribbed vault, and three chambers contrived in the thickness of the walls (c. 14 ft thick). There is a central pier on the floor above (first floor), supporting two arches across the middle of the main room. A long narrow room with a fireplace occupies the thickness of the north wall and there is another room, reached by stairs, beneath it. Access to both basement and first floor is from above, via a spiral staircase in the south-east angle turret which leads down from the second floor and up to the gallery and battlements. A straight stair in the thickness of the east wall leads up from the second floor to another spiral staircase in the north-east angle, and this also leads up to the gallery and battlements.

Access to the keep as a whole is at second-floor level via the forebuilding on the east side. At the head of the main flight of steps is a guardroom, and another short flight of steps at right angles to the first leads up to the main entrance, through a finely decorated round-headed doorway. This leads into the principal room of the keep, the Great Hall, a lofty room some 40 feet high, with a gallery in the thickness of the walls 30 feet above floor level. Opening from the hall is the King's Chamber in the thickness of the south wall, and a small kitchen with a well in the north-east angle turret. Passages from the King's Chamber and from the hall lead to latrines in the broad buttress in the middle of the west wall. The keep is accessible right up to the (restored) roof and battlements, and in its state of preservation, and the retention of its floors, is comparable with Dover, which it resembles anyway, both having had the attentions of Maurice the Engineer.

Henry II's keep originally stood within a triangular bailey wall, some portions of which still remain on the south-eastern and north-eastern sides. The original main entrance was in the north-west side and this was added to in the thirteenth century to form the existing Blackgate, about 150 ft north of the keep. Again, there is a resemblance to the Constable's Gate at Dover, completed c. 1227. The Blackgate was begun c. 1247, and still stands to its full height, although rebuilt in its two upper storeys in 1619. The whole

gate structure consists of two parts, an inner gatehouse and an outer
gatehouse, linked by wing walls to form a barbican. The inner,
rectangular gatehouse is presumably the original entrance, built in
the late twelfth century with the rest of the castle; only its lower part
is preserved. In the mid-thirteenth century the existing oval
four-storey tower with conical roof was built in front of the earlier
gatehouse and linked to it with wing walls, leaving a small open
court between, triangular in plan because the new tower was at an
angle to the existing one. The new enlarged gatehouse projected
boldly beyond the curtain wall and commanded the whole west side
of the castle. It also imposed upon an attacker a difficult passage to
the interior. The first obstacle was a drawbridge, followed in the
entrance passage of the outer tower by a portcullis and a two-leaved
door. At the inner end of the passage were the entrances to the
D-shaped guard chambers on either side. An enemy who passed
beyond this point would find himself in the confined space of the
small triangular courtyard, with further progress barred by a deep
pit across the front of the inner gatehouse, and the entrance passage
beyond blocked by the raised drawbridge. The other defences of the
inner gate passage are not known but they would certainly have
included another portcullis and another two-leaved door, and
possibly other obstacles as well.

   Newcastle's two main remnants, the keep and the Blackgate are,
in spite of their somewhat depressing surroundings, of great
technical interest and the keep is one of the most complete surviving
examples of its type.

Short Bibliography

BRAUN, H., *The English Castle* (3rd edition), London, 1948

BROWN, R.A., *English Castles,* London, 1976

FORDE-JOHNSTON, J., *Castles and Fortifications in Britain and Ireland,* London, 1977

— *Great Medieval Castles of Britain,* London, 1979

GASCOIGNE, B. and C., *Castles of Britain,* London, 1975

HOGG, G., *Castles of England,* Newton Abbot, 1970

JOHNSON, P., *National Trust Book of British Castles,* London, 1978

RENN, D.F., *Norman Castles in Britain,* London, 1973

SIMPSON, W.D. *Castles in England and Wales,* London, 1969

SORRELL, A., *British Castles,* London, 1973

TOY, S., *The Castles of Great Britain,* London, 1953

Index